CONSTITUTIONAL

DELIBERATION

IN

CONGRESS

★

D1286901

CONSTITUTIONAL

CONFLICTS

A Series with the Institute

of Bill of Rights Law at the

College of William & Mary

Series Editors: Neal Devins

and Mark Graber

CONSTITUTIONAL

DELIBERATION

IN

CONGRESS

★

The Impact

of Judicial Review

in a Separated

System

★

J. Mitchell Pickerill

Duke University Press

Durham & London

2004

© 2004 Duke University Press

All rights reserved

Printed in the United States of

America on acid-free paper ∞

Designed by Amy Ruth

Buchanan. Typeset in Minion

by Keystone Typesetting, Inc.

Library of Congress Cataloging-

in-Publication Data appear on

the last printed page of

this book.

For Anne

★

CONTENTS

★

★

I have read a number of books recently in which the author prefaces the work with a statement along these lines: "This is not the book I originally intended to write." They have prompted my own query: Did I do what I set out to do with this project? As I look over the finished product and think back to the origins of the idea and the initial research for the book, I am not sure whether this is the book I set out to write or not. Surely it is not the *exact* book I wanted to write, if only because I received a lot of excellent advice and constructive criticism along the way that helped shape the project and made the final product infinitely better than it would have been otherwise. As I think back, I am only sure of two things. First, I wanted to do research that would teach me something new about the Supreme Court, Congress, and the Constitution (especially federalism). And second, I wanted to write a book. In an important sense, then, I suppose this is what I intended to write. However, my own views on the issues raised in this book have been significantly molded and modified since I had the kernel of an idea for a research project sometime in the mid 1990s. Along the way, I received support and suggestions from many different sources, to each of whom I will always be grateful.

I could not have chosen a better department than the Political Science Department at the University of Wisconsin-Madison for my graduate education in politics and public law. During my time in Madison, the faculty in North Hall taught me the meaning and importance of collegiality, intellectual curiosity, and methodological diversity. Indeed, North Hall is a place where the substantive value of the research question is still the most important part of a scholar's work. While I am thankful to have rubbed elbows with nearly everyone there, a few individuals deserve special mention. Most importantly, I am indebted to the members of my dissertation committee, Don Downs (who served as the chair), Chuck Jones, Charles Franklin, and Bert Kritzer, all of whom dedicated much of their valuable time teaching and advising me as I conducted the dissertation research that provided the foundations for this book. Don Downs inspired me to embrace a broad yet principled view of academic freedom and to pursue my intellectual passions. He has been a greater mentor, teacher, and friend than I could have imagined when I first set foot in North Hall. Chuck Jones embodies the very definition of a scholar, and I owe much of my knowledge of the American political system to him. His influence is reflected by my use of his phrase "separated system" in the subtitle of the book. Charles Franklin and Bert Kritzer taught me the necessary methodological tools for conducting social science research, and each pushed me in different ways to consider my research and arguments from multiple perspectives. David Canon and Ken Mayer were also invaluable sources of information on American political institutions and ideas for studying them, and they each provided me with useful comments and ideas in the early stages of the project.

I received invaluable input from Ann Althouse, Victoria Nourse, and Gordon Baldwin at the University of Wisconsin Law School. My research has also benefited immeasurably from my interaction and friendship with Andy Baker, Michele Claibourn, Kevin den Dulk, Evan Gerstmann, Nelson Graf, Jon Graubart, Dan Lipson, Paul Manna, Paul Martin, Mark Richards, Travis Ridout, and Bob Turner. I am also grateful to have been taught by Mark Gibney and Jon Teaford at Purdue University, who are largely responsible for my initial and enduring interest in things constitutional.

I have been very fortunate to have crossed paths with some of the best Court-Congress scholars in the United States, who have graciously given some of their valuable time to provide me with feedback. In particular, I thank Bob Katzmann, Louis Fisher, and Keith Whittington for their insightful comments and suggestions on different portions of the book and at different stages of my research. I am also grateful to the editors of the Constitutional Conflicts series at Duke University Press, Neal Devins and Mark Graber, for their enthusiastic support for publishing this book, and to all the editors with whom I have worked at the press for all their help and patience. My colleagues at Washington State University deserve mention for providing a collegial intellectual environment; thanks especially go to Andrew Appleton, Cornell Clayton, Amy Mazur, Tom Preston, and Ed Weber for their comments and advice as I transformed my research into a manuscript.

I owe a debt of gratitude to the Institute for Humane Studies for the financial support I received as a Humane Studies Fellow and to the Department of Government at Georgetown University, especially Stephen Wayne, for hiring me to teach constitutional law and providing me with office space. Without these two sources, much of the research that I conducted in Washington, D.C., would not have been possible.

There are of course numerous people who helped provide what I believe were necessary distractions, as all work and no play would be, well, all work and no play. Chris Johnson, Tom MacDonald, John "Monkey" Montgomery, and Paula Schmidlin are as reliable as it gets when it comes to distracting— even from miles away. In Madison, the members of the Lonesome Rogues, Rob O'Connell, Thom Byerley, and Katie Powderly, provided me with one of the greatest extracurricular activities I could hope for and were much more than just bandmates. Much appreciation goes to the Cork 'n' Bottle String Band and all the folks at the old Ken's, particularly Mark Meaney and Eva Shiffrin. For listening pleasure while I logged hours in front of the computer, I am much obliged for the sounds of Bill Monroe, Lester Flatt and Earl Scruggs, Ralph Stanley, Neil Young, Tom Petty, the Beatles, Poi Dog Pondering, Uncle Tupelo, Leftover Salmon, and Widespread Panic. Thanks to my mandolin too.

I owe much more than I can express to my family—Dad, Casey, and Kipp, who thought I had lost my mind when I left a lucrative law practice to become a poor grad student, but who nonetheless always supported me in my endeavors. I know they are all relieved now that I have a job. I am especially grateful to my wife, Anne, to whom the book is dedicated, for her love and patience always. Besides emotional support, she helped me navigate different software, rescued me from mysteriously recurring computer glitches, and edited portions of the evolving manuscript, and she continues to encourage me in my scholarly pursuits. She and our daughter Stella are the reasons for the smile on my face at the end of the day when I turn off the computer and head home.

Alfonso Lopez Jr. was a twelfth-grade student at Edison High School in San Antonio, Texas. On March 10, 1992, he was caught with a .38 caliber handgun on school grounds. Although the gun was unloaded, he had five bullets in his possession. According to Lopez, he was being paid to deliver the gun after school to someone else who was planning to use the gun in a "gang war." Lopez was originally charged under Texas law but was later prosecuted for violating a federal law known as the Gun-Free School Zones Act (GFSZA). The GFSZA was passed by a Democratic Congress and signed by George Bush, a Republican president, in 1990. It defined school zones as the "grounds" of any public, private, or parochial school, or as all areas within "a distance of 1000 feet from the grounds of a . . . school." Under the Act it was illegal "for any individual knowingly to possess a firearm at a place that the individual knows, or has reasonable cause to believe, is a school zone." Uncontroversial in all respects, the GFSZA was introduced on the floor of the Senate, incorporated into the Crime Control Act of 1990 by voice vote, easily passed by both houses of Congress, and signed into law by the president. The bill was never formally debated on the floor of either house, and there is no evidence of opposition to it.

Although Lopez was convicted under the GFSZA, his conviction was ultimately overturned—but not because of his innocence or police misconduct. Rather, Lopez challenged the GFSZA as unconstitutional for falling outside Congress's enumerated powers in Article I of the U.S. Constitution. The Federal District Court allowed the conviction to stand, declaring that the GFSZA was constitutional because it concerned an activity that Congress had the power to regulate under the Commerce Clause. However, the Fifth Circuit Court of Appeals reversed the District Court's decision, and ultimately, the Supreme Court affirmed the Fifth Circuit, declaring the GFSZA unconstitutional in *United States v. Lopez* (1995). Nowhere in the public record is there evidence that Congress considered the constitutional issue raised by *Lopez*— the very issue that ended up setting free a teenager who brought a gun to school for a gang war!

Lopez (as well as other recent cases involving federalism) caused a stir among constitutional law and Supreme Court scholars. For the first time in sixty years, the Court had invoked the limits of the commerce power to strike down a federal law. In fact, the Rehnquist Court has actively exercised judicial review to strike down Acts of Congress for violating federalism principles in the Constitution.[1] The Rehnquist Court's decisions have alarmed some commentators, who fear that the Court is trying to return constitutional doctrine and federal power to the status that they had before the New Deal. While Supreme Court and legal scholars pay close attention to the legal implications of the Court's decisions, an aspect of the Court's power of judicial review often ignored is the effect that judicial review might have on Congress and on lawmaking. What, if anything, did the *Lopez* case mean for Congress? Did any members, staff, or other relevant policymakers think about the constitutional issue while drafting and considering the GFSZA? Why does it appear that the constitutional issue was not raised in Congress? And what impact, if any, has *Lopez* had on the lawmaking process?

Important questions about judicial review and lawmaking are thus raised by *Lopez* and the GFSZA. Those questions are not limited to the specific case and statute, however. They raise more general questions involving the role of the Supreme Court, constitutional law, and judicial review in our systems of government and lawmaking. For instance, what happens in Congress when the Court strikes down a federal statute? Does judicial review simply end the lawmaking process by invalidating a federal law, or does the Supreme Court have a broader impact on the legislative process when it exercises its power of judicial review? When the Court invalidates a federal law, how does Congress respond? When, where, and why do members of Congress deliberate (or fail to deliberate) over constitutional issues, and how do Supreme Court decisions affect constitutional deliberation in Congress? And finally, to what extent is lawmaking a reactive process in which laws are revised and refined in response to events like Court decisions and issues like constitutional interpretation?

In addressing these questions, this book argues that each of the two main theories of how Congress and the Court interact over constitutional matters is incomplete when standing alone: the traditional-institutionalism approach of "coordinate construction" (or "the Constitution outside the Court"), and the rational-choice approach. However, there is a lot of truth in each, and by synthesizing the two approaches and carefully considering the motivations behind congressional behavior, we can come to a better understanding of the impact of the Court's exercise of judicial review on constitutional deliberation in Congress. In this book, I seek to show that members of Congress do sometimes engage in constitutional deliberation, but that deliberation is often motivated and shaped by the Court's judicial review decisions. The subject matter of this book fits squarely into ongoing debates over "the Constitution outside the Court," "taking the Constitution away from the Court," "coordinate construction," and "constitutional dialogues" (see, e.g., Burt 1992; Burgess 1992; Fisher 1985; Fisher 1988; Tushnet 1999; Whittington 1999). Scholars such as Bruce Ackerman (1991), Robert Burt (1992), Stephen Griffin (1996), and Wayne Moore (1996) have shown that judicial review and constitutional construction outside the Court can coexist, and much of the recent scholarship on the subject emphasizes the impact that nonjudicial institutions have on constitutional construction (e.g., Burgess 1992; Fisher 1990; Whittington 1999). And although there may be a movement afoot to "take the Constitution away from the Court" (Tushnet 1999), my primary objective is to show that we should not lose sight of how judicial review can play an important role in encouraging constitutional debate and deliberation in Congress and perhaps elsewhere outside the courts.

We should not expect members of Congress to routinely or systematically consider, of their own volition, constitutional issues raised by legislation. As congressional scholars have shown, members of Congress are primarily motivated by the "electoral connection," notions of representation, and the desire to make good public policy, and the institution of Congress is designed to help achieve these goals efficiently (Arnold 1990; Fenno 1977; Garrett and Vermeule 2001; Kingdon 1989; Mayhew 1974; Shepsle and Weingast 1995). However, Congress does not operate in a vacuum, and it may sometimes need to consider the actions of the judiciary, the presidency, or other institutions (see, e.g., Cameron 2000; Eskridge 1993; Jones 1994; Peterson 1990; Shipan 1997). Likewise, the Court's actions may be viewed as having important effects on other institutions of government and on the broader lawmaking process (see Canon and Johnson 1999). I argue that constitutional issues and judicial decisions are likely to have an impact on debate over legislation in Congress, particularly under certain conditions. Constitutional issues must compete with other factors that influence congressional decision making, and to the extent that constitutional deliberation takes place in Congress, it will often be influenced by the Court's judicial review decisions. I view interaction between the Court and Congress over constitutional matters as a natural byproduct of our separated system (see, e.g., Fisher 1988; Jones 1995).

In the chapters that follow, I pose two questions in an attempt to identify and analyze two distinct types of potential effects that the Court's exercise of judicial review may have on constitutional deliberation in Congress. First, what does the exercise of judicial review do to the specific statute involved in a Court decision? After the Court strikes down legislation as unconstitutional, Congress can succumb to the Court's interpretation, or it can respond to the Court. In responding to the Court, Congress may try to override the Court's decisions, or it may revise the statute and make concessions to the Court on constitutional issues in an attempt to preserve the underlying public policy. Second, how do the Court's judicial review decisions affect debate and deliberation in Congress over newly proposed legislation that raises constitutional questions? When judicial review by the Court over a particular constitutional provision or issue is a real threat, members in Congress may be more likely to consider that issue when drafting relevant legislation, and to draft statutory provisions that will satisfy the Court's constitutional doctrine or preferences.

In our system of government and lawmaking, these types of interactions seem perfectly natural. As one constitutional and institutional tool among many in a complex lawmaking process, the Court's exercise of judicial review should not be understood simply as an obstacle to the lawmaking process. Consistent with our constitutional scheme of separation of powers, judicial review is a check on the other branches of government, but the Court is no more powerful than those other branches. In our separated system, "responsibility is not focused, it is diffused" (Jones 1994)—and proper diffusion requires judicial review as well as the ability of Congress to respond to the Court's decisions. Lawmaking in our separated system is continuous, iterative, speculative, sequential, and declarative (Jones 1995), and consequently each institution in our system must necessarily anticipate, interact with, and react to the actions of the other institutions.

The sources of evidence and data analyzed throughout the book vary from chapter to chapter. Much of the analytical framework and research design is rooted in an "analytical narratives" approach (Bates 1998). That is, I begin with a "soft" rational-choice conception of deliberation and decision making in Congress, and posit that lawmakers in Congress will often strategically consider (or ignore) the Constitution and Court decisions in pursuit of specific political and policy objectives. To flesh out more detailed understandings of how Court decisions influence debate and deliberation in Congress, I then develop descriptive narratives of debates and deliberation in Congress in the traditions of Louis Fisher (1988; 1990) and his work on constitutional dialogues and John Kingdon (1984; 1989; 1995) and his research on congressional decision making and agendas.

To understand what happens to the specific statutes after the Court has struck them down, I begin by analyzing quantitative data on the Court decisions and legislation. I analyze data on all the federal legislation struck down by the Supreme Court since the beginning of the Warren Court in 1953 through the 1996–97 term of the Rehnquist Court. I refer to these Court decisions as the "judicial review decisions." This analysis focuses on how Congress responds to the Court's declaration that a specific statute is unconstitutional and addresses the following questions. How often does Congress attempt to fix and repass the law? How often is it successful in repassing the law? How often does it try to amend the Constitution? How often does it not act at all? If the law is repassed, how has judicial review affected the form and substance of the legislation or policy?

Quantitative analysis of congressional responses alone can only tell part of the story. As King, Koehane, and Verba note, "If quantification produces precision, it does not necessarily encourage accuracy, since inventing quantitative indexes that do not relate closely to the concepts or events that we purport to measure can lead to serious measurement error and problems for causal inference" (1994, 44). It is necessary to examine the content and legislative histories of those congressional responses to gain a more detailed and contextual understanding of *how* and *why* Congress modifies judicially invalidated legislation as well as a sense of whether Congress usually complies with Court decisions as opposed to challenging or circumventing them. I examine the legislative histories and language of amended legislation and assess the extent to which congressional responses appear to be overrides of the decisions or modifications that comply with or show deference to Court doctrine.

To understand the impact of judicial review on constitutional debate and deliberation in Congress, I focus on Supreme Court cases and relevant legislation involving federalism. Federalism cases and legislation are appropriate and important to study because (1) federalism has been insufficiently studied in the recent "Constitution outside the Court" scholarship, (2) the current debate among legal scholars over the "political safeguards" versus the "judicial safeguards" of federalism largely ignores the *interaction* between Court and Congress over federalism, and (3) the Court has recently been very active in the federalism area, which provides an excellent, not to mention timely, opportunity to look at the impact of judicial review in the lawmaking process before and after the recent court decisions.[2]

I examine both the Court's and Congress's treatment of federalism as it relates to the Commerce Clause and the Tenth Amendment. This analysis is designed to establish whether there is a relationship between the Court's treatment of the commerce power and the Tenth Amendment, and the extent to which the two issues are deliberated or considered in Congress. I rely on official sources such as the *Congressional Record* and on journalistic and other secondary accounts to develop a description of Congress's consideration of federalism in relevant legislation. I examine the legislative histories of the Child Labor Act of 1916, the Civil Rights Acts of 1964, the GFSZA (1990), and the Brady Bill (1994). I then compare congressional debate over federalism in legislation like the Violence against Women Act (passed immediately before *Lopez*) and the Hate Crimes Bill (considered immediately after *Lopez* and other federalism decisions in the 1990s).

I also draw on interviews that I conducted with current and former members of Congress, congressional staff, and others in Washington from 1997 to 1999.[3] The interviews serve two purposes: first, to gain details and personal insight from people who were involved firsthand in the drafting, consideration, and passage of legislation involving federalism before and after the recent Court cases, and second, to obtain more general information about the types of constitutional issues that get raised in Congress, how and when they get raised, and who raises them. The federalism interviews were designed to determine the extent to which lawmakers, before and after the relevant Court cases, considered federalism and thought strategically about the possibility that the Court might strike down legislation. I assess whether the Court cases had an impact on constitutional deliberation or strategic consideration of constitutional issues. I also conducted interviews in which I asked about constitutional debate in Congress more generally. From these interviews I made inferences about the degree to which lawmakers think about constitutional issues generally, where the issues will be raised, if at all, and what types of issues are the most likely to be raised.

Chapter 1 explores the ongoing debate between judicial supremacy and coordinate construction theories as well as studies of how the Court and Congress interact. I accept the legitimacy, not to mention desirability, of constitutional deliberation and interpretation in Congress, but I suggest that the Court's judicial review decisions help to create conditions under which constitutional deliberation in Congress is more likely, and that the language of the Court's opinions and doctrines is likely to influence the content of legislation and constitutional deliberation in Congress.

Chapter 2 analyzes the specific statutes struck down by the Court and how Congress has responded to the Court in those cases. This chapter demonstrates that there is legislative life after judicial review. The data suggest that

Congress is highly responsive to Supreme Court decisions striking down federal statutes; that is, Congress usually responds formally to the Supreme Court by repassing the statute in modified form, amending the Constitution, or taking other official action. Often, Court decisions forbid Congress to use particular means to achieve policy goals, and the challenge for Congress is to find permissible means to achieve the same or substantially similar goals. The analysis in chapter 2 also helps to establish that these statute-specific responses to judicial review rarely indicate congressional challenges to Court decisions. Instead, Congress is more likely to amend legislation in a manner that reflects deference to or compliance with the Court's interpretations and doctrines.

In chapters 3 and 4, I examine Supreme Court cases and federal legislation that raise federalism issues, using evidence from archival and documentary sources as well as from my in-depth interviews. Chapter 3 is a brief historical view of Supreme Court federalism doctrine and related legislation. Historical examples show how members of Congress once seriously debated these issues when considering pertinent legislation. However, constitutional deliberation in Congress seems to have occurred when the Court has presented a realistic threat that it might strike legislation down on federalism grounds, as it did for much of the twentieth century. The constitutional historian Robert McCloskey describes the period from the end of the nineteenth century until the New Deal as one of "judicial dualism," during which the Court sometimes upheld and sometimes invalidated federal legislation involving federalism (1960). This judicial dualism created uncertainty in Congress as to whether the Court would uphold the constitutionality of new federal legislation, and I contend that this uncertainty helped shape constitutional debates in Congress. For example, the ten-year-long congressional debate over the Child Labor Act of 1916 often focused on the constitutionality of the legislation, and members of Congress as well as presidents framed the issue in terms of recent Supreme Court decisions and doctrine involving the Commerce Clause. Similarly, the debate in Congress over the Civil Rights Act of 1964 often centered around the commerce power and the "substantial effects" test established by the Court in its New Deal decisions.

Chapter 4 focuses on federalism in the 1990s. By the time Congress passed the GFSZA in 1990, the Court had not struck down federal legislation for violating the commerce power in nearly sixty years. Rather than judicial dualism, the Court established a prolonged period of judicial deference toward Congress over federalism matters. Consequently, by 1990 members of Congress did not perceive a threat from the Court. Interviews conducted with congressional staff, lobbyists, and members of Congress involved in drafting the GFSZA establish that when Congress drafted and passed the GFSZA—legislation that involved *possession* of an object on *local* school grounds—lawmakers did not seriously consider whether such legislation was within the power to regulate *interstate commerce*. The chapter also examines the debate over the passage of the Brady Bill in 1994. Portions of the legislation were ultimately struck down by the Court on Tenth Amendment grounds in *Printz v. United States* (1997). A detailed legislative history and interviews with relevant policymakers involved in drafting and passing the Brady Bill show that the Tenth Amendment received virtually no attention during the decade-long debate over the legislation. Members of Congress and others either did not identify the issue or were unconcerned about it, because the Court did not seem to present a serious threat over the matter.

Chapter 4 then presents evidence that attention to and debate over federalism in Congress has increased in the 1990s. In order to describe in more detail how that debate has taken place, and to connect it to the recent decisions of the Rehnquist Court, I analyze deliberation in Congress over the Violence against Women Act of 1994 (VAWA) and the Hate Crimes Prevention Act of 1997 (Hate Crimes Bill)—two statutes that raise similar commerce power issues but were considered in Congress *before* and *after Lopez*. The legislative histories show that minimal attention was paid to the commerce power in debates over VAWA, but substantial debate over the commerce power occurred in the consideration of the Hate Crimes Bill—and that debate took place almost entirely within the doctrinal parameters established in *Lopez*. A brief review of Democrats' use of federalism issues in debates over Republican-sponsored legislation such as the Religious Liberty Protection Act and the Product Liability Reform Act discounts the notion that the increase in federalism debate in the 1990s is purely a result of the Republicans' electoral victories in 1994. The chapter concludes that the Court's exercise of judicial review has a significant effect on the likelihood and substance of constitutional deliberation over federalism, and perhaps other constitutional issues, in Congress.

In chapter 5, I discuss some broader implications of earlier analyses for the Supreme Court, judicial review, Congress, and the lawmaking process. Mindful of the limitations presented by my focus on federalism in the prior two chapters and concerns about generalization, I draw upon further interviews that I conducted on issues other than federalism and make some general observations regarding constitutional deliberation in Congress. I conclude that members of Congress and other lawmakers frequently consider constitutional arguments in an instrumental and strategic manner, the main objective being to pass or sustain popular public policies. This does not mean that those in Congress are hostile to constitutional deliberation, but it does mean that constitutional issues are not generally institutional priorities in Congress. Constitutional debates in Congress are frequently conducted in reaction to and in anticipation of the Court's exercise of judicial review. I conclude that judicial review is a crucial mechanism in the lawmaking process, as important for federalism as for other areas of the Constitution. The last section of the chapter briefly sketches a theory of "judicial primacy," under which the Court has the *primary role in constitutional interpretation*, as opposed to a supreme role or (at the other extreme) an equal role. Under a theory of judicial primacy, the Court's constitutional interpretations will usually shape constitutional deliberation in the other branches of government, and as such the Court will be the primary interpreter of the Constitution.

One of my main objectives in this book is to insert into the "Constitution outside the Courts" debate a reminder of how judicial review fits into our separated system and how it influences constitutional deliberation outside the judiciary. In most respects, I agree with scholars who argue that members of Congress can and should engage in constitutional construction and deliberation. However, this does not mean that we should be prepared to cast judicial review into the deep blue sea. I hope this book will help to demonstrate how the Supreme Court has an important impact in Congress and on lawmaking when it exercises judicial review—and that we should favor judicial review (as well as other processes and mechanisms) when it leads to increased deliberation over constitutional values.

ONE

Constitutional Deliberation in a Separated System

★

In this chapter, I ask two related questions. First, where should we expect to find constitutional deliberation and construction in the American lawmaking system? Second, what is the likely impact of the Supreme Court and judicial review on constitutional deliberation in our separated system? As I explain in more detail later in this chapter, by "deliberation" I mean reflection and debate over the scope of federal powers under the Constitution in the context of legislation. An underlying assumption of this book is that there is substantial value to constitutional deliberation at multiple decision-making points in our lawmaking process.

In addressing the questions raised in the preceding paragraph, this chapter explores an ongoing and engaging debate over the role of the Court and other governmental institutions, specifically Congress, in interpreting the Constitution. I suggest that there is truth to many of these accounts, and that a synthesis of several approaches is necessary to more accurately account for constitutional deliberation in the American system. I acknowledge that members of Congress do sometimes engage in constitutional deliberation, but I argue that the deliberation is often motivated and shaped by the Court's judicial review decisions. In essence, the theoretical approach taken here merges the rich conception of Louis Fisher (1988) of constitutional dialogues with a strategic view of congressional behavior (see, e.g., Arnold 1990; Kingdon 1989; Krehbiel 1998; Mayhew 1974; Shepsle and Weingast 1995). Although much of the current scholarship on the subject emphasizes the impact that nonjudicial institutions have on constitutional construction, my emphasis is on the impact that the Court's decisions have on lawmaking and deliberation in Congress. To reiterate and emphasize a point made in the Introduction: there may be a movement afoot by some scholars to take the Constitution away from the Court, but we should not lose sight of the role that judicial review can play in encouraging and shaping constitutional debate and deliberation outside the courts. This chapter thus explores the current debates over the Constitution outside the Court, advocates a more synthesized framework for understanding constitutional deliberation in the American system, and concludes with a discussion of the nature and importance of constitutional deliberation in our lawmaking system.

Judicial Supremacy, Coordinate Construction, and the Constitution outside the Court

While an important theoretical matter, the underlying legitimacy of judicial review is rarely questioned today, even though it is not expressly provided for in the Constitution. Chief Justice John Marshall first exercised judicial review over an act of Congress in perhaps the most famous Supreme Court case, *Marbury v. Madison* (1803). Some argue that he announced and in effect granted the Court the power of judicial review, and others argue that he merely exercised and first articulated a power existing in the Constitution, even if only implicitly. As Alexander Bickel puts it: "Curiously enough, this power of judicial review, as it is called, does not derive from any explicit constitutional command. . . . This is not to say that the power of judicial review cannot be placed in the Constitution, merely that it cannot be found there" (1962, 1).

There are different views about if and where the power can be "placed" in the Constitution, and whether the Framers intended for the judiciary to have the power at all. The main argument in favor of judicial review is that the Supremacy Clause of Article VI, read together with the "arising under" clause of Section 2 of Article III, implies the power. Since the Constitution is to be the "supreme law of the land" and the judiciary's "Power shall extend to all Cases . . . arising under this Constitution . . . ," the Supreme Court must be charged with interpreting the Constitution and determining whether government actions are consistent with it (see Berger 1969; Bickel 1962; Corwin 1938; Wechsler 1959). Raoul Berger argues further that there is compelling evidence of the Framers' intention to give the judiciary a fairly broad power of judicial review to determine the constitutionality of government action. On the other hand, Judge Learned Hand argues that the power was indeed invented by Chief Justice Marshall, and that it can be found neither in the Constitution nor in a majority of the Framers' intentions. Nonetheless, Hand admitted that while he could not find or "place" judicial review in the Constitution, the power is consistent with the structures of the Constitution, and it is not a "lawless act to import into the Constitution such a grant of power" (Hand 1958, 29).

The upshot of these debates is that at worst, judicial review can be considered consistent with the Constitution, and two hundred years of history have legitimized it; at best, the language of the Constitution supports the device, and it is consistent with original intent. However, accepting its underlying legitimacy does not end the inquiry into the nature of judicial review. Far from it, for it begs many questions regarding the *legitimate exercise* of judicial review. Two centuries after John Marshall and the Supreme Court first exercised judicial review in *Marbury v. Madison*, scholarly debates continue over the proper scope of judicial review, methods of constitutional interpretation, and judicial supremacy over constitutional interpretation. Much of the scholarly literature on judicial review has been spawned by Alexander Bickel's concerns that the Court's exercise of judicial review is undemocratic, or countermajoritarian (1962), although some scholars have questioned the antimajoritarian nature of judicial review (see, e.g., Dahl 1957; Graber 1999). For my purposes, the most important scholarly question is whether the Court's exercise of judicial review amounts to the final, definitive, and only legitimate interpretation of a constitutional provision, or, rather, the other branches of government may also engage in constitutional construction. And where *should* we usually expect to find deliberation over constitutional values in the political and lawmaking processes?

An ongoing and vibrant scholarly debate has been waged in recent years over the roles of the Supreme Court and Congress in interpreting the Constitution. Advocates of "judicial supremacy" argue that the Court should be the final arbiter of the Constitution, and at least by implication, that the Court's pronouncements of constitutional law are the most important declarations of constitutional meaning (e.g., Alexander and Schauer 1997; Bork 1990; Dworkin 1981; Ely 1980). The Court itself has made this pronouncement on more than one occasion. Chief Justice Marshall's language in *Marbury v. Madison* certainly lends itself to an interpretation that the Court has the final say in constitutional disputes; Marshall noted that the Constitution is intended to be the "supreme law of the land," and he declared, "It is emphatically the province and duty of the judicial department to say what the law is" (at 177). Perhaps most famously in modern times, the Court declared its interpretations of the Equal Protection Clause of the Fourteenth Amendment the supreme law of the land in *Cooper v. Aaron* (1958). At issue in *Cooper* was whether states that had not been parties to *Brown v. Board of Education* (1954) were bound by it. In *Brown*, the Court had overruled *Plessy v. Ferguson* (1896) and the "separate but equal" doctrine, and declared that state-sanctioned segregated schools violated the Equal Protection Clause. The *Brown* Court thus ordered the school district in the case to desegregate its schools. In *Cooper*, Governor Orval Faubus of Arkansas opposed the desegregation of Arkansas schools, arguing that his state, which was not a party to *Brown*, did not have to follow the decision because it is the Constitution that is supreme, not the Court's interpretations of it. Needless to say, Faubus and other southern segregationists disagreed with the *Brown* court's interpretation of the Equal Protection Clause. The *Cooper* Court ruled that Arkansas most certainly did have to follow *Brown*. The unanimous Court held that Marshall's opinion in *Marbury v. Madison* "declared the basic principle that the federal judiciary is supreme in the exposition of the law of the Constitution, and that principle has ever since been respected by this Court and the Country as a permanent and indispensable feature of our constitutional system" (at 18).

More recently, a majority of the Supreme Court reaffirmed the view that its decisions are "supreme," in *City of Boerne v. Flores* (1997). That case concerned the Religious Freedom Restoration Act (RFRA) of 1993. Congress passed RFRA in response to another Supreme Court decision, *Employment Division v. Smith* (1990). In *Smith*, the Court determined that Alfred Smith's religious freedom had not been violated when he was fired and refused unemployment benefits by the state of Oregon for using the illegal hallucinogenic drug peyote in Native American religious ceremonies. Congress passed RFRA in an attempt to undo the holding in *Smith* and use statutory means to protect those engaged in religious activities from discrimination. Members of Congress argued that they had the power to pass RFRA pursuant to the enforcement powers granted to Congress in Section 5 of the Fourteenth Amendment. In *City of Boerne*, the Court essentially held that Congress did not have the authority to "undo" or alter the Court's constitutional holding, or interpretation of the Free Exercise Clause, in *Smith*. Justice Kennedy wrote for the majority: "The power to interpret the Constitution in a case or controversy remains in the Judiciary" (524). He concluded: "It is for Congress in the first instance to 'determine whether and what legislation is needed to secure the guarantees of the Fourteenth Amendment,' and its conclusions are entitled to much deference [citations omitted]. Congress' discretion is not unlimited, however, and the courts retain the power, as they have since *Marbury v. Madison*, to determine if Congress has exceeded its authority under the Constitution. Broad as the power of Congress is under the Enforcement Clause of the Fourteenth Amendment, RFRA contradicts vital principles necessary to maintain separation of powers and the federal balance" (536). Kennedy, like other justices before him, essentially interpreted *Marbury* to stand for the proposition of judicial supremacy.

Constitutional scholars have traditionally agreed with the Court's declarations of judicial supremacy, and some have sought to provide deeper theoretical justifications in support of judicial supremacy. The theory of judicial supremacy has been accepted by scholars from across the ideological spectrum and on different sides of debates over interpretivism and noninterpretivism, judicial restraint and judicial activism, including the likes of Robert Bork, Raoul Berger, Richard Epstein, Christopher Wolfe, John Hart Ely, Laurence Tribe, Ronald Dworkin, and Michael Perry. One of the most comprehensive contemporary justifications of judicial supremacy comes from the constitutional scholars Larry Alexander and Frederick Schauer (1997). They make a strong case that a "single authoritative decisionmaker" is needed in order to avoid "interpretive anarchy" (1997, 1379). Alexander and Schauer argue that constitutional law needs to be clear and consistent in order to provide clear guidance to other government actors and individuals in society—in essence, it is important to have one authoritative interpretation of the Constitution at play in order to comply with a principle of legality and the rule of law. Alexander and Schauer, like other judicial supremacists, maintain that the courts are the best institution to serve as this single authoritative decision maker because that is what they are designed to do. This is especially so because of judicial independence and legal training. And because the Supreme Court sits atop the judicial hierarchy, it is best situated to be the single and final authoritative decision maker. The justices on the Supreme Court are only indirectly influenced by the electoral process, and they are trained in methods of legal interpretation. Accordingly, judicial supremacists believe that the justices are the most likely to engage in serious constitutional deliberation and interpretation, and least likely to be influenced by more overtly political and public policy concerns.

The theory of judicial supremacy has not gone unchallenged, however. In the past two decades, an increasing number of scholars have argued that Congress and other government institutions should engage in "coordinate construction" of the Constitution, or "departmentalism" (see, e.g., Burgess 1992; Burt 1992; Dimond 1989; Fisher 1988; Jacobsohn 1986; Levinson 1988; Macedo 1988; Murphy 1986; Nagel 1989), and that various types of "constitutional construction" have historically taken place outside the Court (see, e.g., Ackerman 1991; Agresto 1984; Burt 1992; Fisher 1990; Whittington 1999). At least one scholar has argued for "taking the Constitution away from the Court" and for a "populist constitutionalism" (Tushnet 1999). These scholars all seek to show the importance of understanding "the Constitution outside the Court," and they reject judicial supremacy.

Fueled by historical and American political development studies, these constitutional scholars have shown how the Constitution has structured debates and political conflicts outside the Courts throughout America's relatively short history. For example, Keith Whittington has shown how the Constitution has not always been viewed merely as legal verbiage to be interpreted by lawyers and judges, but over time has helped to structure political debates, decision making, and processes without judicial intervention—as it was intended to do—suggesting that judicial supremacy is incompatible with original conceptions of the Constitution and judicial review in early American government (1999; see also Burt 1992; Graber 1998; Graber 1999). Louis Fisher has demonstrated how Congress and presidents have resolved separation of powers issues under the Constitution through compromise and accommodation, often without judicial intervention (1988; 1990; 1997). Additionally, theories of American constitutionalism advanced by scholars such as Bruce Ackerman (1991) and Stephen Griffin (1996) argue that major shifts in constitutional meaning and values have historically occurred as a result of extrajudicial forces.

Perhaps the culmination of the "Constitution outside the Courts" debate is Mark Tushnet's call for "taking the Constitution away from the Courts" (1999). Tushnet not only refutes the theory of judicial supremacy and notes important examples of constitutional construction outside the judiciary, but advocates a "populist constitutional law" that minimizes, if not eliminates, the role of the Court in much constitutional construction. Tushnet further rejects the notion that the Court's constitutional decisions have "given us a rich vocabulary of practical political philosophy," arguing in the end that there is little value to judicial review (1999, 194). He concludes that democratic processes and institutions are capable of producing adequate and even beneficial interpretations of the Constitution.

The various coordinate construction and Constitution outside the Courts studies show that members of Congress (and other nonjudicial actors) have in fact, at least occasionally, engaged in constitutional debates. Although the different scholars emphasize different theoretical justifications for and benefits of constitutional construction outside the Court, they present a collective case that Congress can, does, and should challenge, ignore, or reject the Court's interpretations when the majority of Congress finds fault with those interpretations. There are also constitutional issues debated in the political branches that do not involve "cases or controversies"; hence, they do not involve the courts at all. The emphasis in much of this scholarship is placed on historical examples of constitutional debates and construction in Congress and elsewhere outside the Courts, and on normative preferences that the Court's interpretations should not go unchallenged. Many of the scholars express concern that if judicial review amounts to judicial supremacy, and if judicial supremacy is widely accepted, little constitutional deliberation will take place outside the Court. While not all Constitution outside the Courts scholars go as far as Tushnet in urging that the Constitution be taken away from the Court altogether, the role of judicial review is often deemphasized. I believe it might be instructive to explore in more detail the role that the Court's exercise of judicial review may play in influencing constitutional deliberation outside the Court.

Inter-Institutional and Interactive Perspectives on the Court and Congress

Some of the scholars cited above who advocate coordinate construction of the Constitution by Congress do accept a role for the Court and judicial review in constitutional interpretation. For instance, Susan Burgess (1992) and Keith Whittington (1999) accept that the Court's legal doctrines sometimes influence the course of constitutional deliberation in Congress, and Robert Burt (1992) argues for a pluralistic and institutionally egalitarian conception of constitutional interpretation. As previously noted, Bruce Ackerman (1991) and Stephen Griffin (1996) argue that American constitutionalism has evolved as a result of both judicial and nonjudicial interpretation. And Terri Jennings Peretti (1999) contends that the Court is, and is designed to be, a political (and "redundant") institution that simply asserts its policy preferences alongside the other political institutions. While these scholars accept a pluralistic view of the Court and Congress, I subscribe to the even more explicitly interinstitutional perspective of scholars who explore *how* the Court and Congress *interact* over constitutional interpretations. Most instructive for my purposes are two approaches that focus on the interactive nature of the Court and Congress over constitutional matters—one more jurisprudential and traditional-institutionalist, the other more new-institutionalist and informed by rational choice.

First, Louis Fisher and Neal Devins argue that the Court and Congress (and other institutions) engage in "constitutional dialogues," alternately adding meaning to constitutional law (e.g., Devins 1996; Fisher 1988; Fisher 1985; Fisher and Devins 2001). Fisher and Devins have argued, together and separately, that the development of constitutional doctrine occurs in all branches of government, state as well as federal. This approach is largely jurisprudential in focus. And while the notion of dialogues accepts the role of the court as a party to those dialogues, the focus of much "constitutional dialogues" research is on how institutions outside the Court influence conceptions and the course of constitutional law. For instance, in his analysis of separation of powers issues, Fisher has shown that the Court's rulings have hardly been the last word; instead, the boundaries of separation of powers under the Constitution are usually more influenced by compromises and accommodations reached between Congress and presidents (1990; 1978; 1997). And Congress appears to have rejected the Court's interpretation that legislative vetoes are unconstitutional and found new ways to continue exercising them (e.g., Fisher 1993). Devins has demonstrated how Congress and state legislatures have pushed the development of constitutional law in the abortion-rights area by passing various types of regulations on abortion (1996). And together, they have published a collection of documents and materials for use in the classroom that helps instruct students how nonjudicial institutions influence the development of constitutional law (Fisher and Devins 2001). There are other examples as well, but the important point is that Congress does not simply accept judicial doctrine and sometimes acts in response to the Court to alter doctrine in an interactive manner.

Second, rational choice and other empirical theories posit that the Court and Congress interact by strategically battling over *a priori* policy preferences. Thus, the Court's decisions can be informative for members of Congress who wish to avoid adverse actions by the Court, and Congress may try to override unpopular court decisions (see, e.g., Eskridge 1993; Eskridge and Ferejohn 1992; Gely and Spiller 1992; Martin 2001; Meernik and Ignagni 1997; Rogers 2001). Rational-choice theories assume that justices make decisions to maximize their policy preferences while minimizing the likelihood that Congress will enact legislation to "override" the judicial decision. Likewise, they assume that members of Congress are goal-oriented, rational actors who have incentives to inform themselves of Supreme Court decisions and tailor the language of statutes so as to minimize the likelihood of adverse Court decisions. Studies of the interaction between Court and Congress have examined both the Supreme Court decision-making and congressional decision-making aspects of the model. The basic argument is that justices may desire to vote their policy preferences, but they must act strategically in light of the constraints they face, both within the Court and with respect to the other institutions in our system of separated powers (Cooter 2000; Epstein and Knight 1998; Epstein and Walker 1995; Eskridge 1991; Segal 1997). The recent interest in how the Court and Congress interact has also spurred research on congressional overrides of the Court's statutory interpretation decisions and congressional circumvention of the Court's constitutional decisions (e.g. Eskridge 1991; Eskridge and Ferejohn 1992; Hausegger and Baum 1999; Meernik and Ignagni 1997; Segal 1997). My intention is not to develop another game or formal model to depict this interaction, but rather to acknowledge that in pursuit of their goals, members in Congress must strategically consider the effects of both internal and external constraints; hence, lawmakers in Congress might be motivated to consider Court decisions when those decisions appear likely to threaten legislative goals.

There are great strengths to both inter-institutional approaches, but unfortunately their proponents seem to be talking past one another. It is worth considering two limitations to the constitutional dialogues approach. First, the evidence that Congress does in fact consider constitutional issues and sometimes challenge the Court's interpretations begs the question: Do members of Congress routinely debate or otherwise consider constitutional aspects of proposed legislation, and what factors motivate constitutional deliberation in Congress? Second, the focus on how Congress and other political institutions contribute to and influence constitutional jurisprudence does not necessarily answer the converse question: What influence does judicial review have on lawmaking and deliberation in Congress? The rational-choice conception of interactions between Court and Congress might help us to understand the theoretical motivations underlying at least some constitutional deliberation in Congress. Perhaps members of Congress address Court decisions in a strategic pursuit of legislative and policy goals. If the rational-choice perspective adds some theoretical rigor to the enterprise, the constitutional dialogues approach adds context to deliberation in nonjudicial institutions, and it embodies an important appreciation of deliberation and jurisprudence that is absent from much of the rational-choice and empirical scholarship on the subject.

Judicial Review, Congress, and Constitutional Deliberation in a Separated System

I suggest that there is a lot of truth in most of the approaches reviewed earlier in this chapter, but that none of them fully captures the relationship of Congress, Supreme Court, judicial review, and constitutional deliberation. In essence, I argue that Fisher's constitutional dialogues approach to coordinate construction can be made more complete by accounting for the strategic motivations underlying much of the constitutional debate that takes place in Congress. Conversely, rational-choice theories and relevant statistical studies are often reductionist and incomplete and fail to account for many of the contextual factors that influence process, debate, and statutory language in Congress. Taken together, these two approaches suggest that lawmakers in Congress are willing to engage in constitutional debates, and that in the pursuit of their policy preferences and other goals, they may have strategic reasons for considering Court decisions, or the threat of judicial review.

The first questions that must be asked are, Why do lawmakers in Congress consider constitutional issues, and do they routinely or systematically consider constitutional dimensions of proposed legislation? In the modern legislative process, it is difficult to believe that members of Congress are motivated to seriously and routinely consider constitutional issues arising in the context of proposed legislation (see, e.g., Devins 2001, 460). As Donald Morgan found in his survey of Congress almost forty years ago, a large number of lawmakers in Congress believe that public policy and constitutional issues are distinct, and that Congress should "pass constitutional questions along to the Court rather than form its own considered judgment on them" (1966, 336). In the 1980s Judge Abner Mikva echoed Morgan, claiming that Congress passes legislation with little consideration of constitutional principles or implications, leaving constitutional review to the judiciary, and that "at best, Congress does an uneven job of considering the constitutionality of the statutes it adopts" (1983, 587). Mikva argued that members of Congress concentrate on getting something, perhaps anything, passed in order to claim they are dealing with issues perceived as problems by constituents, interest groups, and others (see also Bamberger 2000). Mikva concluded that Congress too often ignores constitutional problems with legislation, and he called on members of Congress to increase the degree of constitutional scrutiny during the legislative process (1983, 605–10). And more recently, Elizabeth Garrett and Adrian Vermeule agreed, contending that Congress's "constitutional performance" is lacking because Congress as an institution is designed to achieve legislative goals other than constitutional deliberation, and arguing for specific institutional reforms that could result in more constitutional deliberation in Congress (2001).

In response, Fisher argues that Congress is well equipped to deliberate constitutional issues and "makes significant contributions by participating in that constitutional dialogue" (1985, 708). Like other advocates of coordinate construction, Fisher relies on anecdotal evidence to show that members of Congress address constitutional issues during the legislative process at least some of the time and that various institutions and mechanisms allow the issues to come to the attention of congressmen (1985, 722–31). Fisher concludes that members of Congress can avail themselves of resources for learning about the constitutional issues raised by bills during the legislative process, and that just because the Court eventually uses judicial review to overturn legislation, members of Congress might not, contrary to Mikva's assertion, ignore the constitutional issues altogether (1985, 44–45). While Fisher may identify mechanisms that make constitutional deliberation in Congress possible, it is not clear when the possibility is realized.

Congressional scholars have identified specific variables that systematically influence congressional behavior. From classic studies by David Mayhew (1974) and Richard Fenno (1978; 1973) to more recent studies by Douglass Arnold (1990) and others, theories and observations of legislative behavior suggest that members of Congress act primarily to satisfy their various constituencies for the sake of winning reelection and to make good public policy. According to congressional scholars, "the electoral connection" explains most congressional behavior, in addition to the desire to make good public policy, congressional leadership, party positions, committee structures, institutional procedures, and potential presidential vetoes (e.g., Arnold 1990; Fenno 1978, 1973; Jackson and Kingdon 1992; Kingdon 1989; Mayhew 1974). John Kingdon (1995; 1984) argues that members of Congress are "policy entrepreneurs" who look for "windows of opportunity" to move items onto the legislative agenda.

Within the institution of Congress, the pressures of democracy and party membership along with individual notions of representation and policy preferences affect agenda setting, policy formation, and the drafting of statutes.

Members of Congress are largely interested in being able to "claim credit" for popular legislation and policies and for being on the "right side" of issues in the eyes of their constituencies (Mayhew 1974). Institutional arrangements like committee structures facilitate the decision-making process during which members balance often conflicting or competing preferences of districts, party leadership, and interest groups, and personal preferences (see, e.g., Fenno 1973; Krehbiel 1991; Shepsle 1979; Weingast 1979). Moreover, the constitutional requirements of bicameralism and the executive veto require each house of Congress to satisfy the other *and* the preferences of the president. Consequently, lawmakers work through a very complicated process in which building support and simply getting a policy passed as legislation takes a tremendous amount of time, effort, and resources. Even the drafting of legislation entails a large degree of "creative speculation" over the level of support that the legislation will garner as well as the actual effects of the policy after it is passed and implemented (Jones 1998). And so it is not clear that we should expect members to routinely add constitutional issues to the list of factors routinely considered during the legislative process. Nor is it clear that legislators will routinely consider judicial decisions. According to Robert Katzmann, "Congress is largely oblivious of the well-being of the judiciary as an institution, and the judiciary often seems unaware of the critical nuances of the legislative process. But for occasional exceptions, each branch stands aloof from the other" (1988, 7).

In some circumstances, however, Congress does consider the judiciary. The perception of how the judiciary is likely to act can occasionally help shape legislation. For example, in his study of the history of the Federal Communications Act and related legislation, Charles Shipan observes that Congress has sometimes drafted legislative provisions governing how courts can review administrative actions of communications legislation (1997). Shipan suggests that members of Congress will strategically draft provisions of legislation relating to the judiciary to help maximize their policy preferences when the legislation is implemented and interpreted. For instance, when Congress established the Federal Communications Commission (FCC) in the Communications Act of 1934, interest groups and members of Congress alike were concerned about the new independent agency and drafted "judicial review" provisions as a means of monitoring the FCC (Shipan 1997, 121).[1] Shipan's study is limited in scope, but it provides evidence that Congress sometimes considers the role of the judiciary while considering legislation. In accordance with the rational-choice approach discussed earlier, Shipan shows that members of Congress have incentives to consider the Court and to anticipate how the Court might act in the future as a strategic means of achieving legislative and policy goals.

Thus it may be more likely that a constitutional issue will make it onto the legislative agenda if the issue can be used to advance the policy goals of lawmakers in Congress. And when members of Congress suspect that the Court might use judicial review to invalidate legislation, they may be motivated to consider the relevant constitutional issue alongside the usual factors that influence their decisions. When such a threat exists, a "window of opportunity" may open that allows or even invites a constitutional matter onto the legislative agenda. I am not claiming that this is the only way in which a constitutional issue may be raised and debated in Congress, only that judicial review may create sufficient conditions—an open window—for constitutional deliberation.

To think about how judicial review might open a window of opportunity during the legislative process, it is useful to consider the effects of the presidential veto on Congress. Since both the executive veto and judicial review are constitutional checks on Congress's powers, it may be that Congress responds to them in comparable ways. In the first instance, the veto and judicial review can each be formally overridden: the veto by a supermajority, judicial review by a constitutional amendment. When Congress cannot muster the votes to formally override the president or initiate the process of overriding the Court, it may be able to respond to a veto or judicial review in another way. Perhaps Congress can attempt to revise the law to satisfy the president or the Court. For example, during George H. W. Bush's presidency, Congress attempted to pass civil rights legislation, which President Bush twice vetoed. Although supporters of the legislation did not have the supermajority necessary to override the president's veto, they did not let the legislation die. Rather, Congress revised the bill in response to the president's vetoes until the bill satisfied President Bush, at which time he signed the Civil Rights Act of 1991 into law. As I will discuss in subsequent chapters, Charles Cameron has shown how the threat of the veto as well as the exercise of the veto may lead to bargaining between Congress and the president (2000; see also Groseclose and McCarty 2001; Ingberman and Yao 1991; Sullivan 1990; Woolley 1991). Congress may make concessions to presidents in order to pass legislation, preferring compromise legislation to no legislation. The same may be true with respect to judicial review.

Fisher's conception of constitutional dialogues hints at this type of bargaining between the Court and Congress, but his emphasis is typically on how nonjudicial institutions challenge Court doctrine, or supplant it with their own, thus making independent contributions to constitutional law. Here, I suggest that the threat or exercise of judicial review may compel Congress to make concessions to the Court. Thus, Congress does not face a simple dichotomous choice in addressing the Court's judicial review decisions and constitutional doctrine. The choice for Congress may be more subtle and complicated than whether to accept and comply with the Court's doctrine on the one hand or challenge and override it on the other. Consequently, the Court's exercise of judicial review may help to create favorable, if not optimal, conditions for constitutional deliberation in Congress. When the Court presents a realistic threat that it will exercise judicial review, the constitutional dimension of a bill may compete with the "normal" variables that influence congressional behavior. The Court's constitutional decisions may not be the last word in the judicial supremacy sense, but they have an important and significant role in infusing constitutional debate into the lawmaking process and in shaping the language and scope of legislation.

As I briefly identified in the Introduction, I consider two types of impact that judicial review may have on constitutional debate in Congress. First, Congress might debate what to do with a statute that has been struck down, and second, Congress might debate the threat of judicial review when considering new legislation.

In a general sense, there are two potential consequences for a statute that gets struck down by the Court for violating the Constitution. One is that the Court simply invalidated a specific statute or statutory provision, and that is the end of the matter. The statute is dead and no further action is taken. Another possibility is that although the Court has invalidated a statute or provision, Congress might respond to the Court and try to save the policy. Congress might do so by passing a constitutional amendment (that is successfully ratified) or, more likely, by amending the statute and attempting to find alternative means for pursuing the policy. In the first scenario, the Court is a roadblock to lawmaking, while in the second, it is more of a speed bump or detour. The traditional conception of judicial review, and a frequent objection to it, is that it is an obstacle to lawmaking. I suggest, however, that this is not so, and that Congress is likely to respond to the Court.

For instance, in response to *Lopez*, Congress amended the GFSZA by including findings that guns in schools affect interstate commerce, and by narrowing the law to apply only to guns that have traveled in interstate commerce.[2] It is not clear that this will actually satisfy the demands of the opinion or the preferences of the majority of the Court in *Lopez*, but it does demonstrate that Congress, without having to amend the Constitution, can try to respond to the Court by modifying unconstitutional laws to satisfy the Court. Underlying many theories and studies of judicial review is the notion that the Court's exercise of judicial review is simply the end of the law. The *Lopez* case and the GFSZA, as well as other historical examples, give reason to call this assumption into doubt. On the other hand, the congressional response to *Lopez* was not necessarily an override of or challenge to the Court's decision; instead, the amendment to the GFSZA showed some deference to the Court's constitutional holding, while attempting to revive the public policy expressed in the statute. As I will show later in the book, we should expect substantial variation in the ways Congress responds to the Court with respect to specific "unconstitutional statutes." Congress may comply with the Court decision, ignore the Court decision, subtly circumvent the Court decision, or challenge the Court decision outright.

Turning to the second type of impact that judicial review may have in Congress, lawmakers in Congress may consider existing Court doctrine and precedent when drafting new legislation that raises constitutional issues. In this sense, the Court's judicial review decisions might influence, or even promote, constitutional deliberation in Congress in anticipation of future court challenges. As I will emphasize in later chapters, this type of deliberation is both preemptive and reactive, in that members of Congress may anticipate Court action based on past Court decisions. Of course, Congress may or may not pay attention to the Court's constitutional decisions and doctrines. I suggest here that the Court's exercise of judicial review might influence debate and deliberation in Congress in one of several ways.

The first possibility is that judicial review has no effect whatsoever on debate and deliberation in Congress. Gerald Rosenberg (1991) argues that the Court is "constrained" in its ability to implement its decisions. Therefore, the Court offers a "hollow hope" for those who want it to push social change. By extension, it may be that the Court is also constrained in the sense that it lacks the means to force Congress to abide by its constitutional decisions. Given the influence of the electoral connection and other factors identified by congressional scholars, it is possible that members of Congress simply ignore the Court in favor of other considerations. If this is true, it may be that members of Congress just do not consider constitutional issues at all and vote in accordance with their own policy preferences or those of their constituencies (see Bamberger 2000; Mikva 1983). Conversely, it could be that members of Congress consider constitutional issues on their own irrespective of the Court (see

Fisher 1985). After all, as advocates of coordinate construction argue, members of Congress are sworn to uphold the Constitution, and they have an independent duty to interpret the Constitution. These possibilities suggest that the Court has little or no influence over deliberation in Congress.

On the other hand, it is possible, and I believe probable, that the Court's constitutional decisions do have an impact on debate and deliberation in Congress, and on the form and substance of legislation. Members of Congress may consider the Court's decisions and doctrines for one of two reasons. First, perhaps members raise and deliberate constitutional issues on their own, then turn to Court opinions to help them articulate their position. Members may do so out of convenience and opportunism, or out of institutional deference to the Court. That is, they may latch on to judicial doctrine as a means of justifying their opposition to popular legislation, or they may analyze constitutional issues through a judicial prism because they perceive constitutional issues to be primarily legal matters that are most properly within the province of courts. Second, in pursuit of their political and public policy objectives, members of Congress may think strategically about the potential exercise of judicial review. They may address constitutional issues because it appears likely that the Court might address the same issues. For example, members of Congress may not have deliberated over the Commerce Clause when considering the GFSZA because, at least in part, they perceived no threat that the Court would use the clause to invalidate the legislation. Now that the threat of judicial review is realistic in the wake of recent federalism decisions such as *Lopez*, lawmakers in Congress may be more likely to debate the issue and draft legislation designed to address the Court's current doctrine.

A Note on Constitutional Deliberation

Drawing upon the notion put forth by Cass Sunstein (1993) that the United States is a "republic of reasons," an underlying premise of this book is that constitutional deliberation is desirable and perhaps even crucial in our system. Sunstein reviews how the Framers of the Constitution favored public deliberation and designed institutions with an eye toward encouraging deliberation. Sunstein, like the Framers, believes that reasons for passing new laws ought to be made public by lawmakers. I agree that we should favor mechanisms that inject deliberation over constitutional values into the lawmaking process. Thus, an important objective of this book is to further our understanding of how and why constitutional deliberation takes place in the lawmaking process, and how it influences lawmaking and legislative outcomes. I agree that constitutional deliberation should be viewed as an essential element of our constitutional democracy. However, while Sunstein shares the normative preferences of other coordinate constructivists that nonjudicial institutions and actors engage in constitutional deliberation, I believe it is important to appreciate the role that judicial review plays as an agent of deliberation.

I contend that the Court's exercise of judicial review and its effects on Congress can be good for the lawmaking system and our sense of constitutionalism for three reasons. First, the Court can force Congress to fine-tune bad laws. In the chaos of the legislative process, bills may be hastily and sloppily drafted without an eye toward constitutional issues. A judicial review decision might force Congress to revise statutory language in a more careful and deliberative manner, incorporating constitutional values that were largely ignored during the statute's initial passage. Undoubtedly, Congress will occasionally pass an unconstitutional law on purpose and count on the Court to "bail it out," so to speak. One example might be the Supreme Court's decision in *United States v. Eichman* (1990), concerning the federal "flag burning" statute. Members of Congress passed the statute soon after the Court invalidated a Texas law against burning the American flag (*Texas v. Johnson* [1989]). Arguably, most members of Congress were well aware of the constitutional problems, and many may have been against the statute, but they responded to public opinion and electoral pressures and passed the statute regardless of the constitutional problems with it (see, e.g., Curtis 1993; Goldstein 2000). Members may even have counted on the Court to invalidate the statute. It might be argued, then, that judicial review can protect Congress from having to address constitutional issues in earnest. While the existence of judicial review may occasionally bail Congress out, that is the exception and not the rule. As I show in chapter 2, most of the time the Court's decision forces Congress to more carefully craft the law if the policy is one that a majority in Congress favors.

Second, if the Court presents a real threat to Congress, I believe that Congress is more likely to consider and debate relevant constitutional issues during the legislative process than it would be if the threat did not exist. If the Court does not present a serious threat, there is no immediate need for members of Congress to deliberate over a relevant constitutional issue, and if Congress is not worried about satisfying the Court, policymakers in Congress are more likely to ignore the constitutional issue. Put simply, members of Congress do not have the time or institutional motivation to routinely raise

and debate constitutional issues that arise in the context of popular legislation. However, if the threat of having a law struck down by the Court is real,
the constitutional issue is more likely to be a factor in the legislative process.
Even though members of Congress may be likely to consider constitutional
issues in a somewhat instrumental fashion—primarily to avoid an adverse
court ruling—some constitutional deliberation is better than none. In a constitutional democracy based on the often-conflicting goals of *centralized but
limited powers*, members of Congress should be reminded occasionally that
ours is not a government of *centralized and unlimited powers*. In short, they
should be prompted or pressured to announce reasons for trekking into new
legislative territories or stretching the bounds of their constitutional powers.
Staunch advocates of coordinate construction of the Constitution often ignore the realities of the legislative process. As studies on congressional behavior and decision making have shown, the incentives in a legislative institution such as Congress do not necessarily encourage its members to routinely
debate constitutional limits on their powers. We should not be alarmed at the
frequency with which Congress ignores constitutional issues; doing so is a
byproduct of representative and majoritarian legislative politics. Our separated system, and its constitutional checks and interactive design, ensure that
the Court can temper the effects of democracy, while Congress can temper the
effects of judicial review.

Finally, sometimes Congress will simply try to do things that are (or should
be considered) beyond the scope of its constitutional powers. Like the presidential veto, judicial review is supposed to be a roadblock some of the time.
Where members of Congress cannot provide reasons that persuade a majority
to override or otherwise respond to a Court decision, legislation probably
deserves to die. There are limits in our system to majoritarian preferences as
manifested in Congress. The Court and judicial review can help to remind
Congress of those limits and to establish the boundaries of Congress's constitutional powers, as it has traditionally been perceived to do.

As I stated at the beginning of this chapter, I use "constitutional deliberation" as a broad concept, encompassing interpretation, construction, and
other forms of discourse and reflection over the meaning of constitutional
provisions and powers. I refer to constitutional deliberation in Congress as
reflection and debate over constitutional issues that arise in the context of
specific legislation. I acknowledge that constitutional construction and debate
take place in other contexts, but the focus of this book is on debates over
whether legislation considered and passed by Congress is "constitutional," or

consistent with constitutional values. Constitutional deliberation takes place in many forms; its impact can be merely symbolic, it can raise "constitutional consciousness," or it can lead to more carefully drafted statutory language (see Burgess 1992). And of course, there are different levels of deliberation in which members of Congress might engage.

Susan Burgess (1992) and Keith Whittington (1999) both suggest frameworks for analyzing different levels of constitutional debates and deliberation in Congress. Each accounts for how Congress may try to work within the Court's legalistic interpretations and standards, or challenge the Court, or create new, and perhaps less legalistic, constructions of constitutional meaning. Therefore, the Constitution is much more than a simple statute inasmuch as it also defines basic structures of American government and its institutions, provides guidance for the resolution of (nonlegal) political conflicts, and establishes general principles for understanding the relationship between the individual and the state. The main thrust of these theoretical conceptions is that the Constitution is not merely a legal document for judges to interpret using legal reasoning and canons of legal interpretation.

In large part, I agree with these conceptions. However, I believe that the "average" and predominant type of constitutional deliberation in Congress is likely to be that which is more legalistic and attentive to Court doctrine, or the type that Whittington refers to as constitutional "interpretation" (1999, 3–9). Much of the scholarship on the Constitution outside the Court has emphasized how nonjudicial institutions construct or create constitutional meaning independent from, or even in spite of, the Court's interpretations, and often during extraordinary historical moments. Certainly this "higher lawmaking" occurs and is important, but "constitutional moments" are rare (see Ackerman 1991). In periods between those moments, or what we might consider "routine" times, levels of deliberation in Congress are likely to vary (see Whittington 2001). When considering legislation in a more routine situation, lawmakers in Congress will usually be focused on political and policy matters, and may need motivation from external sources to help bring about and structure constitutional deliberation.

Every proposed statute has a constitutional dimension. It may be clearly constitutional for Congress to appropriate money for the armed forces, and thus there may be no need to debate the constitutionality of the action—but there is a constitutional dimension nonetheless. As an institution, Congress may often be predisposed to believe that it has the authority to act, or to be focused on so many factors other than constitutional matters, that lawmakers do not thoroughly explore the constitutional dimension of the statute. Court decisions or the threat of judicial review may often serve as illuminations of constitutional issues, and provide parameters for justifying legislation in accordance with constitutional values. While this type of deliberation in Congress may not represent deep constitutional construction according to many scholars, such depth may not be called for in Congress. And while the Constitution may not be simply a legal document, it is law, and the legal aspects of constitutional limits on government and other provisions are not unimportant. After all, Article VI of the Constitution does declare it to be the "supreme Law of the Land." This does not mean that the Court, in these routine times, is supreme or obstructive, but rather that it may serve as the initiator of constitutional dialogues, negotiations, and bargains.

If this is true, I am hesitant to accept the argument that it always amounts to "lesser" deliberation. Rather, it seems to fit well within the design of the American system. By design, the United States is a "separated system" of government with multiple institutions, in which accountability and responsibility are diffused throughout those institutions (Jones 1994; Jones 1995). As James Madison stated in *Federalist 51*: "[T]he great security against a gradual concentration of the several powers in the same department consists in giving to those who administer each department the necessary constitutional means and personal motives to resist encroachments of others. The provision for defense must in this, as in all other cases, be made commensurate to the danger of attack. Ambition must be made to counteract ambition. The interest of the Man must be connected to the Constitutional Rights of the place." It is consistent with the design of our separated system that "ambition" within Congress can be counteracted by the Court, and vice versa. However, ambition need not be conceived simply in terms of public policy outcomes where there are winners and losers in a game of some sort. Perhaps we should evaluate constitutional deliberation as more of a collective and interactive phenomenon in which the Court and Congress both articulate reasons for and against legislation, and in which each institution has a specialty with respect to the types of reasons it brings to the table. And when bargaining among institutions slows down the process and results in compromise, the system can truly be depicted as more *deliberate*. This, it seems, is what a republic of reasons demands. In any event, it is important, I believe, to explore in more detail the relationship between judicial review and constitutional deliberation in Congress during routine times, as the rest of this book endeavors to do.

TWO

Judicial Review:

Roadblock, Speed Bump,

or Detour?

★

I have identified two possible effects of judicial review on lawmaking in Congress. First, judicial review might force Congress to revise a statute that has been struck down, and second, Congress might be more likely to strategically anticipate judicial review and debate constitutional issues if there is a realistic threat that the Court is willing to use the issue to invalidate a federal statute. In this chapter, I look for evidence of the first type of impact: What, if anything, does Congress do with statutes that have been rendered constitutionally invalid by the Supreme Court?

Here, I argue that the exercise of judicial review should not be viewed simply as the end of legislation or an obstacle to it; nor should congressional responses to judicial review necessarily be viewed as "overrides" of the Supreme Court's decisions. Congress often modifies legislation to save statutory policy and also accommodate the Court's constitutional preferences. To revisit a metaphor I used earlier, the evidence in this chapter demonstrates that while judicial review can be a roadblock to legislation, it is often more of a speed bump or detour. That is, while the Court's exercise of judicial review can be the end of a statute, much of the time judicial review simply slows down the lawmaking process, encouraging Congress to decelerate or avoid the speed bump by taking a detour to the same basic destination. And the manner in which Congress responds to the Court varies significantly from statute to statute, depending on the political and policy context. Much of this chapter is necessarily descriptive because, as I explain below, relevant studies have not adequately accounted for variations in congressional responses to judicial review. However, in describing the variations among congressional responses, we can glean possible explanations for the different types of legislative responses to judicial review, and I explore some of these possibilities later in the chapter.

Some Perspectives on Congressional Responses
to Supreme Court Decisions

As I discussed briefly in chapter 1, studies of how the Court and Congress interact have helped scholars to conceptualize how decision making in one branch might affect, or be affected by, the other branch. In particular, scholars have sought to show how Congress can and should respond to the Supreme Court's judicial review decisions by challenging or overriding Court decisions, and that empirically, Congress has in fact done so.

Advocates of coordinate construction have provided anecdotal evidence and detailed case studies showing that Congress does challenge Court decisions by passing responsive legislation. One well-known example involves *INS v. Chadha* (1983) and the legislative veto. In that case, the Court invalidated portions of the Immigration and Nationality Act that granted to Congress a one-house legislative veto over decisions by the Immigration and Naturalization Service (INS) regarding the deportation of aliens. The Court held that the legislative veto violated separation of powers provisions, specifically the constitutional requirements of bicameralism and presentment of all laws to the president. As Louis Fisher and others have shown, however, Congress has largely ignored the Court's holding and continues the use of legislative vetoes (Fisher 1990, 1993). As I will discuss in more detail later in this chapter, Congress eventually amended the Immigration and Nationality Act to re-codify legislative vetoes over INS decisions, and as Fisher illustrates, Congress continues to use legislative vetoes in other policy areas and over other administrative agencies. Coordinate constructionists therefore conclude that Congress substituted its own constitutional interpretation for that of the Court, thus overriding the Court's holding in *Chadha*.

Other scholars have shown that legislative responses to *Roe v. Wade* (1973) indicate challenges to the Court's decision establishing abortion rights for women. While Congress did not ignore or successfully override *Roe*, it did, along with state legislatures, pass legislation that made it more difficult for women to obtain abortions, often with the avowed intent of discouraging and reducing the number of abortions (see Burgess 1992; Devins 1996).[1] Congress passed legislation limiting the availability of federal funding for abortions, and state legislatures passed numerous regulations intended to discourage and reduce abortion. While not an instance of an override, coordinate constructionists view the abortion saga as evidence of both legislative authority and the ability to engage in constitutional construction, influence the course of constitutional law, and reject the notion that the Court's exercise of judicial review is the final say in a constitutional matter.

In addition to the anecdotal and case study evidence provided by these and other coordinate construction scholars, political scientists have employed rational-choice theory and more systematic quantitative methodologies in studying congressional responses to Court decisions. Rational-choice theory and separation of powers models have analyzed how the Court and Congress each have the opportunity to influence the meaning of a statute, and how the members of each branch will consider the other during the decision-making process (e.g., Eskridge 1993; Segal 1997). A number of studies have analyzed how and why Congress "overrides" statutory construction decisions of the Court by passing legislation to undo the judicial interpretation (see e.g., Eskridge 1991; Gely and Spiller 1990; Hausegger and Baum 1999; Hettinger and Zorn 1999). As I discussed in chapter 1, the approach taken in these studies assumes that justices on the Supreme Court compete with members of Congress over *a priori* policy preferences, and thus, members of Congress will pass legislation to override a Court decision if a majority of the members disagree with the decision.

While much of the scholarship on "congressional overrides" has focused on court decisions involving statutory construction, at least one study has extended that conceptual framework to analyze congressional responses to judicial review. James Meernik and Joseph Ignagni examine the frequency with which Congress introduces and passes legislation or amendments to legislation in response to the Court's exercise of judicial review (1997; see also Gely and Spiller 1992). Citing coordinate construction scholars and theories, Meernick and Ignagni conclude that Congress engages in coordinate construction when it amends legislation that addresses the Court's judicial review decisions (1997, citing Agresto 1980; Burgess 1992; Choper 1980). They find that members of Congress often modify legislation in response to the Court's judicial review decisions, and engage in coordinate construction of the Constitution by "overriding" the Court's constitutional decisions.

The analytical picture painted by these studies is helpful for understanding how the Court and Congress interact over matters of judicial review and constitutional interpretation, but there are some limitations. The case studies of the traditional institutional approach provide great detail to affirm that Congress does sometimes deliberately defy the Court and reject judicial supremacy by passing legislation to override or otherwise challenge the Court's constitutional interpretations. However, those studies do not provide systematic evidence of when and how often we should expect Congress to do so. Rational-choice theories and the study by Meernik and Ignagni provide more theoretical rigor and systematic evidence on the matter, but they lack detail and context regarding the substantive nature of congressional responses. For instance, Meernik and Ignagni only analyze one category of congressional response and assume that a response amounts to an override, without accounting for substantive variations in legislative responses. In the final analysis, neither approach explores how congressional responses to judicial review may amount to something other than coordinate construction of the Constitution or challenges to the Court's constitutional interpretations.

An Alternative Perspective on Congressional Responses to Supreme Court Decisions

The empirical research on congressional responses seems to satisfy the normative preferences of many coordinate construction advocates that Congress should actively assert its legitimate role in interpreting the Constitution and rejecting judicial supremacy. However, I believe that those studies overestimate the frequency with which Congress overrides or challenges the Court's constitutional interpretations, and they fail to account for important variations in congressional responses to judicial review. For instance, Congress may make concessions to the Court by modifying legislation in ways that do not amount to overrides or challenges, but do alter and preserve the statute in question.

An analogy to the presidential veto can help illustrate that the exercise of judicial review, like the president's exercise of the veto, may not stop Congress from pursuing legislation even if Congress is unable to "override" the veto or judicial review. Members of Congress may prefer modified or compromise legislation to no legislation. Take, for example, the welfare reform legislation considered and passed in Congress during the 104th Congress. After gaining a majority of both houses in Congress in 1994, Republicans were determined to pass welfare reform legislation—as they had pledged to do in their "Contract with America." In 1995 the Republicans passed a version of welfare reform legislation, largely along party lines. President Bill Clinton was not opposed to welfare reform, but he objected to specific aspects of the Republican bill; he vetoed the legislation, claiming that it went too far in its funding cuts and other measures. Although it did not have the votes to override Clinton's veto, the Republican majority did not throw in the towel. Within months, Congress passed another welfare reform bill, which bore a strong resemblance to the first bill but with funding cuts that were less severe. The second bill was designed to satisfy enough of the president's preferences to persuade him to sign it, while still altering welfare policy in a manner desired by most Republican lawmakers. Again, however, President Clinton vetoed the legislation, claiming that too many of the provisions were still too draconian, and again the Republican Congress did not have the votes to override the veto. In his state of the union address in 1996, Clinton signaled his willingness to sign a bipartisan and less extreme welfare reform bill. The third time proved to be the charm, as the Republicans worked with congressional Democrats to pass a welfare reform bill that lessened funding cuts even further and modified eligibility requirements for various government programs. On August 22, 1996, President Clinton signed the welfare reform bill into law as Public Law 104-193. While the Republicans had to modify many provisions, they were able to accommodate the president's preferences and still pass far-reaching, landmark legislation that accomplished many of their original political and policy goals.

The battle over the welfare reform bill is one example of what Charles Cameron refers to as "veto bargaining." According to Cameron, "the president may use actual vetoes not only to block legislation, but to shape it" (2000, 9; see also Groseclose and McCarty 2001). After the president has vetoed a bill, the two branches may end up "haggling" over the content of legislation, which may kill the legislation or push Congress to make concessions to the president to get a modified version of the bill passed and signed. Cameron concludes, "In most cases Congress and the president find their way to an agreement that reflects the preferences of both parties" (2000, 176).

Likewise, legislation may be modified after judicial review to accommodate the Court and reflect the preferences of both institutions. That is, when the Court strikes down legislation as unconstitutional, Congress may choose to make concessions to the Court by modifying legislation to comply with the Court's constitutional interpretation while maintaining the basic statutory policy. Veto-like bargaining between Congress and the Court, or what might be called "judicial review bargaining" or even "constitutional bargaining," will surely be different from that between Congress and presidents. Congress and presidents can negotiate directly, face to face. Communication between the Court and Congress is indirect at best (see, e.g., Rogers 2001), and as Robert Katzmann has shown, Congress is often "oblivious" to courts and unaware of judicial decisions (1997). Thus, if they are to respond to the Court's decisions members of Congress must be aware of them, and the Court's written opinions must serve as a source of information and communication to Congress regarding the Court's preferences (Hausegger and Baum 1999; Rogers 2001). Another difference between veto bargaining and constitutional bargaining is a temporal element—vetoes are exercised shortly after legislation is passed and before it is implemented, whereas judicial review is often exercised many years after legislation has gone into effect and been implemented. Thus, the political and policy climate in Congress is likely to have changed more after judicial review than it would have after a presidential veto.

Further, the Court and Congress are more likely than the president and Congress to operate on different policy dimensions—the Court on a *constitutional policy* dimension, and Congress on a *public policy* dimension (see, e.g., Morgan 1966). Though the Court's judicial review decisions may have implications for the public policy concerned, it is plausible that the justices are usually operating primarily on a "constitutional policy" dimension. When the Court reviews the constitutionality of a statute, it is not interpreting how the statute will be applied in implementing a public policy. Instead, the Court is determining how a constitutional principle or value is to be applied to the statute. While the justices are primarily concerned with the constitutional policy at issue in the case, members of Congress will usually remain primarily concerned about the public policy and its relationship to democratic or electoral politics.[2]

Take for example *United States v. Lopez* and the Gun Free School Zones Act (GFSZA)—the Supreme Court decision and federal statute that I described in the Introduction. Congress passed the GFSZA to enact the public policy of prohibiting firearms on school grounds in the United States. The Supreme Court struck down the GFSZA because it determined that Congress did not have the federal power under the Commerce Clause of Article I of the Constitution to pass the GFSZA. On the public policy dimension, it is fair to assume that a majority of both institutions support a public policy of prohibiting guns in schools. However, while a majority, if not all, of the Justices may be against guns in schools on public policy grounds, the issue facing them is the constitutional issue of the scope of federal power under the Commerce Clause. While the Justices may be against allowing children to bring guns to schools, they may believe that because of federalism principles and the limits of the commerce power, this particular public policy issue is outside the scope of federal power. In contrast, members of Congress are primarily concerned with the public policy; that is, they want to find policy ways to keep guns out of schools, and they want to claim political credit for supporting measures aimed at that end. This is not to say that no members of Congress have any preferences on the constitutional policy dimension—presumably many or most members of Congress favor broad legislative powers under the Constitution. When the Court struck down the GFSZA in *Lopez*, some members of Congress may have disagreed with the Court's interpretation of the commerce power, but the most immediate concern for most members of Congress was that the public policy of gun-free school zones was no longer good law, and hence could no longer be lawfully applied by federal prosecutors and courts. The goal was to get the GFSZA up and running again and to take credit for doing so—not to engage the Court in a deep debate over the ultimate meaning of constitutional values.

With some policies, these two issue dimensions will be fairly distinct (as with the commerce power and gun-free schools), while with other policies they may overlap. For example, regulation of communication or speech on the internet might raise free speech issues under the First Amendment of the Constitution, and consequently, public policy and constitutional policy preferences would be much more closely related. Still, there is some degree of separation between the issues, leaving the Court primarily concerned with the direction of constitutional policy and Congress with the direction of public policy.

As a result, I argue that it is difficult to explain congressional responses to judicial review *solely* as a battle over *a priori* and unidimensional policy preferences where either judicial supremacy reigns and the Court wins, or Congress overrides or challenges Court decisions in an exercise of coordinate construction and Congress wins. In my estimation, members of Congress are most likely to evaluate the consequences of Court decisions based on public policy implementation and political concerns, then evaluate the nature of a specific Court decision, and then chart a responsive course based on that evaluation. In many ways, then, congressional responses to judicial review will depend on what is at stake for members of Congress if Congress does not respond, and what concessions must be made to the Court to revive the statute. In other words, it is unlikely that the first reaction of most members of Congress to a judicial review decision is, "Do we like the Court's constitutional interpretation?" Rather, it is usually something more along the lines of, "Do we care about the statute and the public policy that was being implemented under the statute?" If the answer to the latter question is yes, *then* members of Congress confront the question, "What do we have to do to get the statute up and running again?"

So when the Court strikes down a statute that has little political support, such as an outdated statute or legislation that has outlived its usefulness, we should not expect Congress to try to save the statute. In fact, we may expect Congress to fully comply with the Court and repeal the now invalid legislation. Moreover, if the Court opinion communicates that the legislation is being struck down "as applied" by an administrative agency, there may be no need for Congress to respond at all—the burden is on the agency to change its behavior and make the *application* of an otherwise facially valid statute constitutional. In these cases there will be no political or policy reason for Congress to make concessions to the Court, much less challenge or defy the Court.

On the other hand, when an invalidated statute has political support and the opinion of the Court communicates that the statute has been invalidated on its face so that it cannot lawfully continue to be implemented, we should expect more congressional resolve to resuscitate the unconstitutional legislation. When more is at stake for a majority in Congress, members will be more likely to explore ways to respond to the Court. As some coordinate construction scholars have found, this can entail challenging or defying the court. However, I make the case that we should often expect legislative responses to judicial review to be designed and drafted in an attempt to satisfy the Court's constitutional tests, while retaining or otherwise focusing on the core public policy elements of the original statute. Much will depend on the nature of the Court decision and what information the written opinions convey to Congress. How Congress defies, challenges, accommodates, or complies with the Court is an empirical question that has not been adequately explored by scholars.

Identifying the Judicial Review Decisions and Congressional Responses

To analyze congressional responses to Court decisions, I began by analyzing data based on Court decisions that strike down federal legislation for violating the Constitution. I refer to these as the judicial review decisions. It is appropriate to select decisions on this basis because if the Court upholds a statute as constitutional, it is unnecessary for Congress to respond—the legislation remains valid and can continue to be applied the same as before the Court decision. Thus, the judicial review decisions germane for a congressional response and relevant for the analysis in this chapter are those that strike down legislation.

To compile a list of Supreme Court cases in which federal statutes were struck down as unconstitutional from the 1953–54 through 1996–97 terms, I used Congressional Quarterly's *Guide to the Supreme Court* (2d ed., 1990) and its annual *Supreme Court Yearbook* (1991 through 1997 editions) and *The United States Supreme Court Database* (Spaeth 1997). I also compiled a separate list of the relevant legislation and citations from those sources. The unit of analysis here is a combination of the Court decision and the federal statute that was struck down.[3] Three Supreme Court cases (*Leary v. U.S.* [1969]; *Frontiero v. Richardson* [1973]; *Buckley v. Valeo* [1976]) were coded as two observations each because each struck down two separate and distinct statutory provisions for separate and distinct reasons. Using these standards, I coded for seventy-four observations in the dataset.[4]

In collecting the data for the analysis in this chapter, my first objective was to determine whether Congress amends or otherwise modifies invalidated statutes so as to remedy their constitutional defects and revive the legislation. While the key part of data collection was coding for Congress's response, it was important to collect as much information about each statute as possible because my second objective was to develop a more complete and accurate description and a more detailed understanding of these congressional responses than previously developed by scholars. I collected as much information as possible about the Court decision and the relevant statute(s) from the Court opinion as published in *U.S. Reports*. Supreme Court opinions vary in the amount of information they give regarding the federal law in question. To obtain complete and accurate information, I looked up each statute in the *U.S. Code Service* and *U.S. Code Annotated*. Using the annotations provided in those services, I recorded full citations and dates of all public laws passed by Congress that established, amended, or repealed the provisions of the statute reviewed by the Court. The *U.S. Code Service* and *U.S. Code Annotated* provide a full history of congressional treatment of each statute before and after the Court decision that declared the statute unconstitutional. I then read every legislative action cited in the annotations as having taken place after the relevant Supreme Court decision, and as I describe below, determined whether the action represented a response to the Court, and if so, what sort of response.

Does Congress Respond to Judicial Review?

To determine whether Congress has revised and revived, or otherwise resurrected, legislation after the Court has declared it unconstitutional, I relied on the annotations in the *U.S. Code Service* and *U.S. Code Annotated*, through December 2000. The annotations for the U.S. Code citations include all the

Public Laws passed by Congress from the original passage of the statute and all amendments to it or repeals of it after original passage. Based on those annotations, I coded for five categories: (1) no response, (2) statute or relevant provision repealed and nothing passed to replace it, (3) statute or relevant provision repealed and a new law passed, (4) statute amended to address the constitutional issue at hand, and (5) Constitution amended.

"No response" was recorded if the annotations did not indicate that the statutory provision struck down by the Court had been repealed, amended, or modified. In other words, neither the *U.S. Code Service* nor the *U.S. Code Annotated* reported that Congress had passed any public laws affecting the invalidated statute. "Repealed" was recorded if the annotations explicitly reported "repealed" and the part of the statute struck down by the Court was repealed by public law, but not modified or replaced by a new statute. "Repealed and Passed New Law" was recorded if the annotations indicated that the law had been repealed or moved. Typically, Congress repealed the invalidated statute but passed a new public law, codified in a new part of the U.S Code, that clearly addressed the same policy as the old legislation in a new statutory scheme. "Amended Statute to Address Issue" was recorded if Congress passed legislation that modified the specific language or provisions of a statute explicitly addressed in the Court opinion striking down the statute as unconstitutional. Lastly, "Amended Constitution" was recorded if the annotation indicated that Congress passed, and the states ratified, a constitutional amendment addressing the subject matter of the unconstitutional statute.

If Congress acted and amended the law or replaced it entirely, I compared the new version with the old and identified the differences. I only coded Congress's action as a response if it clearly addressed the specific provision and language identified in the Court's opinion. I inferred a response to the Court's decision if there was a substantial change in the "problematic" language of the statute (as the Court identified it) after the Supreme Court struck the statute down. To further establish that congressional action was in response to the Court decision, I reviewed committee reports and other legislative history where it existed.[5] Frequently, Congress referred to the Supreme Court case as the specific reason for amending the law. Finding specific mention of the Court in the legislative history helped to confirm that certain congressional actions were indeed in response to a Court decision.[6] Table 2.1 lists, according to the category of congressional response, some examples of statutes that were invalidated by the Supreme Court.[7]

From the beginning of the Warren Court in 1953 through the 1996–97 term

TABLE 2.1 Examples of Congressional Responses to Striking Down of Statutes by the Supreme Court

No response	Brady Bill
	Cable TV Consumer Protection Act
	Flag Burning Statute
Repealed	National Gas Policy Act (legislative veto)
	Subversive Activities Control Act
	Aliens & Nationality Code (citizenship revocation)
	Marijuana Tax Act
Amended statute	Gun Free School Zones Act
	Gramm-Rudman-Hollings (budget deficit reduction)
	Public Broadcasting Act
	Social Security Act (survivors' benefits)
Repealed, passed new law	FECA (campaign finance provision)
	Narcotic Drugs Import-Export Act
	Immigration & Nationality Act (legislative veto)
	Bankruptcy Act
Amended Constitution	National voting age

of the Rehnquist Court, I identify seventy-one Court decisions in which seventy-four federal laws were struck down. Table 2.2 shows the frequencies of each of the five categories of congressional response. Congress has only formally overridden the Court by amending the Constitution once, but it has modified the unconstitutional legislation by amending it or passing new legislation to address the constitutional ailment thirty-five times. The first three shaded categories (Amended Constitution, Amended to Address Issue, Repealed and Passed New Law) collectively make up instances in which Congress responded to the Court by trying to save the public policy—and Congress has acted to save unconstitutional statutes 48 percent of the time. In 14 percent of the cases, Congress showed complete deference to the Court by repealing, and thus abandoning, the statute. In 38 percent of the observations, Congress has not responded at all.

The frequency of congressional responses can also be viewed from a historical perspective. In table 2.3, congressional responses are reported based on who was Chief Justice at the time of the Court decision. Fourteen of the twenty-eight cases where Congress did not formally respond are more recent,

TABLE 2.2 Congressional Responses to Judicial Review, 1954–1997

Congressional Response	Frequency	Percentage
Amend Constitution	1	1
Amend legislation	27	36
Repeal, pass new legislation	8	11
Repeal legislation	10	14
No response	28	38
TOTAL	74	100

Shaded categories indicate congressional attempts to save the underlying statutory policy.

from the Rehnquist Court. Congress formally responded to the judicial review decisions of the Warren and Burger Courts much more frequently. Table 2.3 establishes that over time, Congress has frequently responded to judicial review by amending the old legislation or passing new legislation to replace it, and this pattern is particularly true for the statutes struck down by the Warren and Burger Courts. At least part of the reason why Congress has not responded frequently to the Rehnquist Court may be that the Rehnquist Court decisions are more recent than those from the Warren and Burger Courts.

Figure 2.1 shows in a histogram how the amount of time between the passage of federal statutes and their "death" at the hands of the Supreme Court is distributed. The amount of time varies. Occasionally, federal laws have been reviewed and declared unconstitutional within about a year. Overall, the mean amount of time is 144.4 months (about 12 years) and the median 116 months (less than 10 years). There are several outliers that skew the mean pretty significantly. The most extreme case is *Rubin v. Coors Brewing Company* (1995), in which the Court struck down a provision in the Federal Alcohol Administrative Act of 1935 (FAAA) prohibiting the inclusion of alcohol content on malt beverage labels as violating the First Amendment's commercial speech protections. The time in that case is coded as 716 months, or just under 60 years. The Court rarely considers or strikes down federal statutes of such longevity. Because of the outliers on the upper end of the time measure, the median is probably a better measure of central tendency. Table 2.4 separately displays the means and medians for the Warren, Burger, and Rehnquist Courts.

Like the time from enactment to Court decision, the time from Court

TABLE 2.3 Congressional Response, by Chief Justice

Congressional Response	Warren Court (1953–1969)	Burger Court (1969–1986)	Rehnquist Court (1986–1998)
No response	5 (22.7%)	9 (26.5%)	14 (77.8%)
Repealed	8 (36.3%)	2 (5.9%)	0 (0.0%)
Amended to address issue	7 (31.8%)	17 (50.0%)	3 (16.7%)
Repealed, passed new law	2 (9.1%)	5 (14.7%)	1 (5.6%)
Amended Constitution	0 (0.0%)	1 (2.9%)	0 (0.0%)
TOTAL	22	34	18

decision to congressional response can vary. Figure 2.2 presents a histogram with the distribution of the number of months from the time a law was struck down until a new law or amendment went into effect. Overall, Congress has enacted forty-six responses to unconstitutional statutes (including simple repeals of unconstitutional statutes). As table 2.5 indicates, only four of those involved statutes struck down by the Rehnquist Court. The mean response time is 80.5 months (6.7 years) and the median 44 months (3.7 years). Again, outliers on the upper end of response time probably make the median a better measure of central tendency.

There are also other aspects of the Court's decision that might have a bearing on congressional responses to judicial review. As discussed earlier, the Court may strike down legislation for being unconstitutional as applied or unconstitutional on its face—a distinction overlooked in most studies of how the Court and Congress interact. When the Court invalidates legislation as applied, Congress does not need to modify the legislation to make it constitutional, but instead, those who implement the law—usually executive branch or other administrative officials—must alter the manner in which they do so. On the other hand, when the Court invalidates legislation on its face, it is declaring that the legislation as drafted can never be applied constitutionally.

A typical example of an "as applied" decision is *Marshall v. Barlow's, Inc.* (1978). That case concerned a provision of the Occupational Safety & Health Act (OSHA), passed in 1949.[8] The relevant provisions of OSHA allow for general workplace inspections by Occupational Safety & Health Administration (OSHA) officials to ensure that employers meet OSHA safety and health

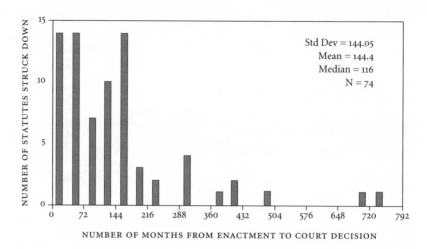

FIGURE 2.1 Time from Enactment of Statute until Court Decision

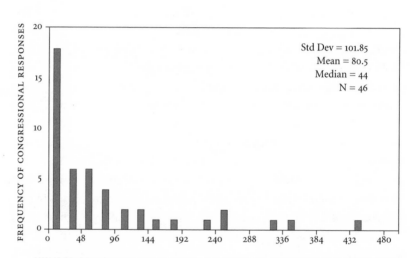

FIGURE 2.2 Time between Supreme Court Decision and Congressional Response

TABLE 2.4 Time between Passage of Federal Statute and Supreme Court Decision (in months)

	All cases (n = 74)	Warren (n = 22)	Burger (n = 34)	Rehnquist (n = 18)
Mean	144.4	140.9	154.4	129.8
Median	116	157.5	113.0	54.5

regulations; the provisions do not make reference to search warrants. The litigation stemmed from an inspection in which OSHA officials did not first obtain a warrant, but claimed authority under OSHA to conduct the inspection. The Court determined that under the Fourth Amendment, administrative agencies need to obtain a warrant for general administrative searches, but that with such a warrant administrative searches of this type are permissible. The Court further established a fairly broad definition of probable cause needed for general administrative search warrants. Congress has not modified these provisions of OSHA since the decision was handed down in 1978. The reason appears clear—the Court clearly stated that if OSHA officials first obtained a warrant in a manner consistent with the Court's opinion, the law could be applied constitutionally. Hence, Congress does not need to modify the law for it to continue to be applied. Today, the same statute remains valid, and it is OSHA's responsibility to apply it in a manner consistent with the Court's opinion.

On the other hand, an example of a law being struck down "on its face" is a provision of the Bankruptcy Act of 1978,[9] struck down by the Supreme Court in *Northern Pipeline Const. Co. v. Marathon Pipeline Co.* (1982). In that statute, Congress attempted to expand the jurisdiction of bankruptcy courts to include civil proceedings arising out of bankruptcy cases. The Court determined that expanding bankruptcy courts' jurisdiction in this way violates judicial power provisions in Article III of the Constitution. Because the explicit expansion of jurisdiction in the statute could never be applied in a manner consistent with Article III, according to the Court, the provisions were unconstitutional on their face. Two years after the Court decision, Congress repealed the invalidated provisions and replaced them with a new jurisdictional scheme for civil proceedings arising out of bankruptcy actions in bankruptcy courts.

TABLE 2.5 Time between Supreme Court Decision and Congressional Response (in months)

	All cases (n = 46)	Warren (n = 17)	Burger (n = 25)	Rehnquist (n = 4)
Mean	80.5	158.9	37.3	17.5
Median	44.0	137.0	25.0	11.5

TABLE 2.6 Congressional Responses and Nature of Supreme Court's Findings of Unconstitutionality

Congressional Response	Unconstitutional as Applied	Unconstitutional on Its Face
Amended Constitution	0 (0.0%)	1 (2.0%)
Amended statute	3 (13.0%)	24 (47.1%)
Repealed, passed new law	3 (13.0%)	5 (9.8%)
Repealed	1 (4.3%)	9 (17.6%)
No response	16 (69.9%)	12 (23.5%)
TOTAL	23	51

Table 2.6 presents the frequencies of congressional responses to court decisions struck down as applied and on their face. Of the seventy-four cases examined here, twenty-three (31 percent) were struck down as applied while fifty-one (69 percent) were struck down on their face. Including repeals, Congress has only responded to seven of the twenty-three "as applied" decisions (30 percent); in contrast, it has responded to thirty-nine of the fifty-one "on its face" decisions (77 percent). Thus, Congress is substantially more likely to respond to the Supreme Court decisions when there is a clear necessity for congressional action just to keep the statutory policy alive. This is one indication that congressional responses tend to be focused less on the Court's constitutional interpretation and more on preserving the statutory policy. It also suggests that the Court's written opinions do serve a communicative and

informational function. Members of Congress appear to be well informed on the need for congressional, as opposed to administrative, action if a statute is to be revived after judicial review.

This analysis affirms that Congress has responded to the Court's exercise of judicial review fairly often. It also shows that although Congress responded more frequently to decisions from the Warren and Burger Courts than it has to decisions from the Rehnquist Court, it is common for years to pass before Congress responds to Court decisions. Thus, the data suggest that in all likelihood Congress will eventually respond to the more recent decisions from the Rehnquist Court. However, the data are limited in terms of what they teach us about the nature of congressional responses; that is, given that Congress appears likely to respond to a majority of judicial review decisions, it is necessary to ask whether congressional responses to judicial review challenge the Court's constitutional interpretations or rather defer to or comply with them. To understand the nature of congressional responses in more depth, it is necessary to examine the language and substance of those responses.

Congressional Responses: Coordinate Construction,
Compliance with the Court or Something Else?

Meernik and Ignagni (1997) confirm the frequency of congressional responses, but their study categorizes all responses as "reversals" of the Court decision, and thus as evidence of coordinate construction of the Constitution. However, a deeper analysis of the congressional responses will demonstrate that this is often an improper characterization of congressional responses to judicial review. Below I explore some examples of responses and show the variable nature of congressional responses to judicial review—particularly the variable nature of congressional action to "save" legislation.

AMENDING THE CONSTITUTION:
OREGON V. MITCHELL AND VOTING RIGHTS
The ultimate congressional challenge to, or "reversal of," a judicial review decision is a constitutional amendment. If Congress wants to assure that the Court's constitutional doctrine is reversed, the clearest, strongest, and most formal method of doing so is to amend the Constitution. However, Congress has only amended the Constitution in response to the Court decisions analyzed in this chapter once, or about 1 percent of the time. The only time Congress amended the Constitution in response to a Court decision striking

down a federal statute was in response to *Oregon v. Mitchell* (1970), in which the Court struck down the Voting Rights Act of 1970. The Voting Rights Act had established a national voting age for state and local elections. Shortly thereafter, in 1971, Congress passed and the states quickly ratified the Twenty-Sixth Amendment to the Constitution establishing a uniform national voting age of eighteen years.

REPEALING LEGISLATION: THE SUBVERSIVE
ACTIVITIES CONTROL ACT AND *ALBERTSON V.*
SUBVERSIVE ACTIVITIES CONTROL BOARD

Whereas a constitutional amendment might be the strongest challenge to judicial review, Congress can also show total deference to the Court by repealing the legislation altogether. Congress repealed legislation in response to ten, or 13.5 percent, of the seventy-four cases examined here. For example, in 1950 Congress passed the Subversive Activities Control Act (SACA) in an attempt to fight communism in America. President Truman vetoed the Act, but Congress voted to override the veto.[10] One provision in the Act required members of the Communist Party to register with the Subversive Activities Control Board. That provision was eventually challenged, and in *Albertson v. Subversive Activities Control Board* (1965) the Supreme Court struck it down on its face for violating individuals' right against self-incrimination, guaranteed by the Fifth Amendment, because the "mere association with the communist party present[ed] a sufficient threat of prosecution . . ." (77). There were two amicus briefs filed against, and none in support of, the constitutionality of the statute. Three years after *Albertson*, Congress voted to repeal the statute and in essence give up on the public policy represented in the statute.[11] Congress may have done so for numerous reasons. The Court's decision was clearly an important factor, as the legislative history of the repealing legislation makes specific reference to *Albertson*.[12] In addition to the original presidential veto, the statute faced opposition by special interest groups during the litigation, with no groups showing support. Opposition to the legislation could hardly have been stronger. Most likely, SACA is an example of a statute that had outlived its usefulness and by 1965 garnered little political support. The country's experience with the fight against communism and McCarthyism probably made the statute so unpopular that many members of Congress viewed a vote to repeal the SACA as being on the "right side" of the issue. Consequently, Congress did not attempt to revive the statutory policy and ended up complying with the Court's constitutional holding by repealing the legislation in question.

MODIFYING LEGISLATION: VARYING DEGREES OF
CONGRESSIONAL DEFERENCE TOWARD THE COURT

The most likely congressional response to judicial review is some sort of mod-ified legislation. As we have seen in this chapter, Congress is likely to even-tually modify legislation in a manner that addresses the holding of a Court decision, regardless of the age of the statute or the decision. Undoubtedly, Congress does sometimes attempt to challenge or override the Court's consti-tutional holdings. For instance, as I briefly noted earlier, in *INS v. Chadha* (1983) the Court invalidated one-house legislative vetoes over administrative agency decisions, holding that such legislative vetoes violated the bicameral-ism and presentment requirements of the Constitution. In 1990 Congress repealed the old Immigration and Nationality Act, which included the legisla-tive veto provisions, and passed new legislation that included another legisla-tive veto provision. In the new statute, Congress claimed authority as "an exercise of the rulemaking power of the Senate," under Article I, Section 5, of the Constitution.[13] Studies have shown how Congress has defied the Court by continuing to use legislative vetoes in various policy areas (see, e.g., Fisher 1993, 1990).

While Congress might challenge the Court in this way, it is in fact rare for it to do so. Instead, congressional responses that amend or modify legislation are usually more deferential to the Court's constitutional interpretation. In fact, in my estimation the legislative veto offers the only example of a con-gressional response that is a clear and direct attempt to override a Court decision (other than the Twenty-Sixth Amendment, considered earlier, passed in response to *Oregon v. Mitchell*). And this may even be a questionable characterization. Congress did not base the new legislation on its considered judgment that separation of powers and lawmaking principles allowed legisla-tive vetoes, but rather rooted the new legislative veto in an alternative consti-tutional provision: Article I, Section 5.[14] This maneuver may indeed represent coordinate construction of the Constitution by Congress while not neces-sarily amounting to an override or reversal of the Court's decision.

It is much more common for Congress to amend legislation in a manner that makes clear concessions to the Court's decision. Sometimes Congress simply narrows the scope of the statute in an attempt to meet the Court's technical legal standards for evaluating a constitutional issue. As an example, I return to *Lopez* and the GFSZA. Recall that Congress initially passed the GFSZA in 1990 to prohibit guns in and around schools. In *United States v. Lopez* (1995), the Supreme Court affirmed a Fifth Circuit decision and struck down the statute for violating the limits on Congress's commerce power. Interestingly, some in Congress were paying attention to the *Lopez* litigation even before the Supreme Court handed down its decision. In 1994—before the Supreme Court decision but after the Court of Appeals decision—the lawmakers in Congress who had initially drafted the GFSZA amended the statute to state explicitly that Congress was acting pursuant to its commerce power; the amendment also provided findings of fact that guns in schools were a national problem with ties to the national economy.[15] The majority opinion in the Supreme Court decision noted the findings of fact but did not consider whether they might save the statute. As part of my research on the GFSZA, I interviewed several members of Congress, congressional staff, and lobbyists involved in drafting the GFSZA and other legislation analyzed in this book.[16] According to counsel for the Senate Judiciary Committee who was primarily responsible for drafting the original GFSZA as well as amendments to it: "In 1994, which was after the circuit court had ruled, the Fifth Circuit ruled against us in *Lopez*, we thought, let's cover ourselves, and let's put in findings of fact—I mean at this point we were a little bit worried, although I still thought we couldn't really lose in the Supreme Court—let's put in findings of fact retroactively. And if you look at the *Lopez* decision, Rehnquist says, 'we don't rule on whether these findings of fact would affect, would make constitutional what we're ruling today is unconstitutional.' So he sort of just ducked the issue" (CS1 interview).

In the first instance, then, Congress tried to save the statute even before the Supreme Court considered the issue, but the Court invalidated the statute anyway. In *Lopez*, the five-member majority of the Court determined that the possession of guns on school grounds did not bear a "substantial relation" to interstate commerce and had little connection to economic activity. In his analysis, Chief Justice Rehnquist wrote for the majority that the GFSZA "contains no jurisdictional element which would ensure, through case-by-case inquiry, that the firearm possession in question affects interstate commerce" (561).

After the Supreme Court decision in 1995, the proponents of the GFSZA decided to further amend the statute in hopes of satisfying the Court. Passed in 1996, the new amendments to the GFSZA explicitly modified the crime; under the new and improved GFSZA, "it shall be unlawful for any individual knowingly to possess a firearm *that has moved in or otherwise affects interstate or foreign commerce* at a place the individual knows or has reason to know is a school zone . . ." (emphasis added).[17] In essence, this amendment created a jurisdictional element: for the federal government to have jurisdiction, the gun would have to be shown to have traveled in interstate commerce—a direct response to the majority opinion in *Lopez*.

According to the counsel for the Senate Judiciary Committee, "As a practical matter, no one was going to bring a case under the Gun Free School Zones Act after *Lopez*, even if it was after [the 1994 amendments]. So we knew we had to go back and, we knew that we had to go back and require that jurisdictional element. We believe that that will—it hasn't been tested yet, but we believe that doing that would assure that the legislation is constitutional" (cs1 interview). Further, the counsel and others involved in the passage of the GFSZA told me that they saw in Justice Kennedy's concurring opinion in *Lopez* a willingness to be more deferential to Congress when legislation included findings of fact and jurisdictional requirements connected to interstate commerce (cs1 and iG1 interviews).

The amendment to the GFSZA cannot properly be characterized as an "override" of the Court's constitutional decision, nor can members of Congress or other relevant lawmakers be described as engaging in serious or independent construction of the Constitution. Instead, lawmakers in Congress drafted amendments to the GFSZA in an effort to satisfy the technical requirements of the Court's legal doctrine, while subtly circumventing the Court. The response to *Lopez* is not an outright challenge to the Court, as was the response to *Oregon v. Mitchell* or even the response to *INS v. Chadha*. The GFSZA amendment showed a small degree of deference in its narrowing of the scope of the regulation in a manner that might satisfy at least some members of the *Lopez* majority. The statute was modified in a fairly minor and some might say technical way and was tailored to accommodate the majority of the Court, or at a minimum Justice Kennedy, who was viewed as the swing vote in the case.

The GFSZA allowed members of Congress to claim credit for addressing the public policy problem of guns in schools, and the "right side" of the public policy issue was clear; a minor alteration of the statute facilitated furtherance of these goals. And when the bill's sponsor, Senator Herb Kohl (D-Wis.), ran for reelection in 2000, his television ads touted his authorship and sponsorship of the bill without mentioning the constitutional issue at all. Thus, members of Congress managed to circumvent the Court's *Lopez* decision with a technical fix to achieve political and policy goals, while paying only minor attention to the underlying constitutional issue. As we will see in the remainder of this chapter, Congress is often even more deferential to the Court's constitutional doctrine.

A good example of a congressional response that showed much more deference to the Court is offered by the Federal Election Campaign Act (FECA) and *Buckley v. Valeo* (1976). In FECA, originally passed by Congress in 1971, Congress attempted to curb campaign abuses in federal elections. Among the many provisions of FECA, the statute created the Federal Elections Commission (FEC) to implement and enforce the statute, and it regulated campaign contributions and expenditures. In *Buckley*, the Court invalidated two parts of FECA. First, it determined that some provisions of FECA that regulated expenditures by candidates for political office, and others in behalf of candidates, unconstitutionally violated the freedoms of speech and association protected by the First Amendment. In essence, a majority of the Court found that campaign spending was a form of political speech protected by the First Amendment. Second, the Court invalidated provisions of FECA that provided the means of selecting the membership of the FEC. The statute called for some members of the FEC to be appointed by the president pro tempore of the Senate and the speaker of the House of Representatives. The Court ruled that because the members of the FEC were "Officers of the United States," this arrangement violated separation of powers principles of the Constitution. The majority opinion relied specifically on the "Appointments Clause" in Article II, which states that Officers of the United States are to be appointed by the president with the "advice and consent of the Senate."

Congress amended FECA within a year in response to *Buckley* by repealing the "unconstitutional" provisions and replacing them with new ones.[18] First, Congress repealed the limits on expenditures in behalf of candidates for federal office, and it passed legislation that nearly codified the Court's First Amendment holding in *Buckley*. The new provisions did not place limits on the types of expenditures that the Court declared were protected under the First Amendment, regulating only those campaign activities that the Court said could be regulated. Similarly, Congress complied with the Court on the issue of composition of the FEC. Under the newly modified FECA, members of the FEC are no longer appointed by members of Congress. In modifying FECA, Congress showed a large degree of deference to the Court. The Court did not prevent Congress from pursuing the public policy of campaign reform entirely, but the constitutional decision in *Buckley v. Valeo* had a clear impact on the means that Congress was able to use to pursue the public policy. In any event, it is clear that the congressional responses to *Buckley* did not challenge the Court's interpretations of the First Amendment or separation of powers.

The congressional responses to *Lopez* and *Buckley* were swift, in large part because the members of Congress and staff who originally drafted the GFSZA and FECA were still in Congress and committed to the public policies furthered by those statutes. However, just as the amount of deference shown to the Court by Congress can vary, so can the time frame for congressional responses to judicial review. As evidence in this chapter has shown, even after long periods have passed, Congress frequently modifies legislation in response to judicial review. For instance, in *Railroad Retirement Board v. Kalina* (1977), the Supreme Court summarily affirmed a lower court that struck down portions of the Railroad Retirement Act of 1937 for violating the equal protection component of the Due Process Clause of the Fifth Amendment. Under the statutory scheme, dependents of deceased railroad employees were entitled to Railroad Retirement Annuity benefits if the survivor was a dependent of the deceased employees. However, while widows were assumed to be dependents, widowers had the burden of proving that half their support had come from their wives. The Court found the scheme to constitute unconstitutional gender discrimination. Congress eventually responded to the Court decision by amending the statute six years later to delete the gender references and require all survivors, regardless of gender, to show that they had depended upon their deceased spouse for half their support.[19] The example of the Railroad Retirement Act and *Kalina* again shows how the Court can force Congress to revise a statute in a fairly narrow yet important way, and it demonstrates a commitment to statutory policy even many years after the legislation was originally passed and years after the Court decision.

That Congress makes concessions to the Court even after much time has passed is telling. When laws have been on the books for a long time and come to be well accepted by political actors and the electorate alike, it is plausible that they enjoy strong public and political support. For example, when the Social Security Act was first passed in 1934, there was considerable opposition to it. However, over time social security can be said to have become part of "permanent government," and it may have become one of the most popular government programs of all time, with high levels of political support. For instance, in *Richardson v. Davis* (1972) the Court struck down provisions of the Social Security Act that made illegitimate children ineligible for survivor's benefits. As in *Kalina*, the Court declared that the scheme violated the equal protection component of the Due Process Clause of the Fifth Amendment. In 1977 Congress passed a law that amended the survivors' benefits provision so that illegitimate children would be eligible for those benefits. The majority in

Congress has long been committed to the underlying policies of social security, and the Court's exercise of judicial review thus spurred Congress to alter the way the law was implemented. By the 1970s it was inconceivable that a majority in Congress would repeal major provisions of the Act. Moreover, a simple modification of the eligibility requirements was all that was needed to satisfy the Court's equal protection doctrine.

Finally, in another example, the Court struck down provisions of the Food Stamp Act of 1964, also for violating the equal protection component of the Due Process Clause of the Fifth Amendment, in *Department of Agriculture v. Murry* (1973). The relevant provisions made a family ineligible for AFDC if someone in the family was declared a dependent on the tax return of someone else (presumably the estranged husband or father). The Court struck the provision down on its face because the means were not rationally related to the ends. According to the Court, the mere fact that a child in a family was claimed on someone else's tax return did not mean that the family was non-needy. The father may have improperly declared a child a dependent, for instance. Congress passed the law in an effort to control abuse of the welfare system, but the AFDC program's purpose was to provide support for needy families. In his concurring opinion, Justice Thurgood Marshall clearly stated that Congress could pursue the policy of barring non-needy families from the AFDC program, but that there must be some "mechanism" or "method" which could achieve the goal in a more narrowly tailored way than the tax dependent provision. He also left it to Congress to figure out the proper mechanism or method for doing so.

In 1977 Congress found new legislative means for carrying out its policy objectives. It delegated power to the Secretary of Agriculture to "establish uniform national standards of eligibility . . . for participation by households in the food stamp program . . . No plan of operation submitted by a state agency shall be approved unless the standards of eligibility meet those established by the Secretary . . ."[20] The amendment then directed the secretary to consider specific factors in determining eligibility, including that of tax dependents "properly declared." The new provisions made clear that being declared a tax dependent on someone else's tax return was not a sufficient criterion for disqualification. In the legislative history of the amendment, the committee report specifically stated that the bill responded to the holding in *Murry*.[21] Here, Congress paid close attention to the language from the written opinions in the Court decision, and crafted a revision that appeared to satisfy the demands of the Court.

NO RESPONSE: THE BRADY BILL AND
PRINTZ V. UNITED STATES

While I have shown how the content of congressional responses can vary in important ways, it is worth considering briefly those judicial review decisions for which there have been no congressional responses. On the one hand, it is difficult to conclude that Congress will never respond to a Court decision simply because it has not responded yet, especially given how long responses can take. There may be decisions in the "no response" category that will eventually result in a congressional response. On the other hand, there might be other explanations for why Congress does not respond, either quickly or at all. For example, I have already discussed the importance of the procedural disposition of the Court's judicial review decisions for understanding the likelihood of a congressional response. When the Court strikes down legislation as applied, rather than on its face, Congress does not need to respond to the Court: the onus is on administrative agencies to change how they apply, or implement, the statute. Table 2.6 confirms this.

"As applied" decisions aside, there may be further reasons why Congress fails to respond to judicial review decisions. One example involves the Brady Handgun Violence Prevention Act ("Brady Bill"), portions of which were struck down in *Printz v. United States* (1997). In chapter 4, I develop the legislative history of the Brady Bill in detail. For our purposes here, what is important is that the Brady Bill established a national waiting period for gun purchases, during which time the statute required local law enforcement officials to conduct background checks of prospective gun owners. The statute did not provide funding for local officials to carry out those background checks. The Supreme Court ruled that under the Tenth Amendment, the federal government could not mandate, or "commandeer," state and local officials to conduct federal policy, and relevant provisions of the Brady Bill were struck down. Although Congress has not yet responded to *Printz*, there is an explanation for the lack of response.

In research that I conducted on the Brady Bill, I interviewed numerous members of Congress, congressional staff, and lobbyists involved in the passage of the legislation in 1993.[22] In addition to asking about the drafting and passage of the Brady Bill, I asked why Congress had not yet passed new legislation to address the Court decision. The reason is twofold. First, under the statute the federal government was to have developed a national computerized system for an "instant check" of prospective gun buyers, and the waiting period and mandatory background checks were to have been phased out after five years under a sunset clause in the statute. The statute was originally passed in 1993, and the *Printz* decision was handed down in 1997. Thus, by the time Congress would have passed a response to the court decision, the relevant statutory provisions were scheduled to expire anyway. Second, it appeared that even after the Court decision, many law enforcement officials around the country continued to conduct background checks voluntarily. According to a lobbyist for a public interest group involved in drafting the Brady Bill, "it became very clear soon after the Supreme Court ruling that the police would continue to do checks. And in fact, even in those jurisdictions . . . which struck down Brady, the police continue to do the checks" (IG1 interview). The reason why most local law enforcement continued doing background checks, according to this lobbyist, was that "most [of] law enforcement realized that probably it would be a career-ending event for someone to buy a handgun in their jurisdiction and shoot someone when a background check could have prevented the sale—and they're responsible for not doing the background check. That is a very powerful political incentive to do the checks" (IG1 interview). Thus, as a political and policy matter, it appeared that the federal law was no longer necessary to implement the public policy of background checks for prospective gun buyers. Hence, the lack of a congressional response to judicial review thus does not always indicate that Congress has given up on the relevant public policy. Instead, there are clearly cases where Congress does not respond to the Court's judicial review decisions because the political and policy goals of those in Congress are simply unaffected by the Court's constitutional interpretations.

The issue of Congress's failure to respond to judicial review decisions brings us back to the Rehnquist Court. Congress has only responded to four of the eighteen Rehnquist Court decisions. Of those eighteen decisions, thirteen struck down legislation on its face, suggesting that some sort of congressional response is needed for most of the legislation if it is to be revived. Earlier, I suggested that the lack of congressional responses to the Rehnquist Court's decisions might be a function of time. Although it is likely that Congress will enact legislation in response to at least some of the Rehnquist Court's decisions, it is also possible that the current Congress will not respond to all or even any of those decisions even with the passage of time. It may be that many of the Rehnquist Court's more conservative decisions do not pose a threat to the political and policy goals of the Republican majority in Congress, especially those decisions that strike down legislation passed by Democratic majorities before the Republicans' electoral victories in 1994. It is certainly possible, however, that over time a Republican Congress might repeal some of the legislation from the Rehnquist Court's decisions; it is also possible that the Republican majority may be forced to revive politically popular legislation or that the Democrats will recapture Congress and pass legislation in response to the Court. Nonetheless, it is doubtful that the lack of response to the Rehnquist Court represents congressional agreement with the Court's constitutional interpretations pursuant to serious independent deliberation in Congress over the meaning of the Constitution. Rather, the lack of response is far more likely to mean that the Rehnquist Court's invalidation of particular legislation has not frustrated the political and public policy goals of recent Congresses—and that not that much time has passed.

CONGRESSIONAL RESPONSES: COORDINATE
CONSTRUCTION, COMPLIANCE, OR SOMETHING ELSE?

The picture of congressional responses that has emerged in this chapter is one in which Congress often remains strongly committed to legislation after it is struck down by the Supreme Court, even if many years have passed since the original passage of the statute. On the one hand, when little time has passed, the membership of Congress is virtually the same as that of the enacting Congress, the president is the same, and the popular or salient political issues of the day are the same, it is reasonable to expect Congress to act on the same public policy preferences that led to the original passage of the legislation. On the other hand, when many years have passed, presidents have come and gone, and political issues have faded into obscurity or been replaced by new, "hot button" issues, the systematic record of congressional responses must be the result of some other dynamic. I submit that congressional responses to judicial review are a natural product of lawmaking in our separated system, as are congressional responses to presidential vetoes.

Lawmaking is by nature iterative, or "a progression of alterations" (Jones 1995, 5). After a statute is originally passed, its status as "law" is hardly static. It is implemented by administrative agencies and interpreted by courts, both of which give new and variant meanings to the law. In fact, alterations of existing laws and policies make up a large part of what government does routinely. Much of what Congress does routinely is build on existing law. In analyzing the relationship between Congress and the president in the lawmaking process, Charles O. Jones argues, "For the most part, the agenda of government itself is continuous from one year to the next. . . . Most important legislation is worked on over time and is connected with precursory laws that are familiar to those in permanent government" (1994, 284). The analysis in this chapter suggests that the same holds true for the relationship between the Court and Congress. Because a substantial part of a legislative agenda is based on existing laws, Congress is poised to revisit statutes over time, particularly in light of how other institutions such as the Court have influenced the law.

At first glance, the frequency of congressional responses to the Supreme Court calls into question the theory of judicial supremacy and supports a claim of frequent coordinate construction in Congress, as Meernik and Ignagni found. However, as the examples above illustrate, Congress's responses to judicial review are often compliant with or deferential to the Court. When Congress responds to judicial review, it usually defers to the Court's constitutional policy, and adapts the statute so that it might conform to the Court's decision in order that the underlying policy can survive, in one form or another. Congressional choices in how to respond to judicial review decisions appear to depend heavily on the policy and political objectives of those in Congress, and congressional responses rarely represent independent instances of constitutional interpretation or construction in Congress.

Members of Congress appear to pay close attention to the Court's opinions in determining the nature of concessions that are necessary to save legislation. That they do suggests a dynamic relationship between the Court and Congress, in which congressional action on public policy issues affects the Court's constitutional law (see, e.g., Fisher 1988), *and* the Court's constitutional interpretations affect the form and substance of statutes. This relationship is often characterized as the establishment of constitutional parameters by the Court, while Congress works within those parameters to pursue public policy. In many ways, then, the exercise of judicial review brings about a type of bargaining between the Court and Congress bearing some similarities to the bargaining that takes place between the president and Congress. This suggests that while the Court may not be absolutely *supreme*, in the sense advocated by Alexander and Schauer (1997) and other judicial supremacists, the Court does play a special role in illuminating constitutional dimensions and forcing Congress to bargain over the content of legislation.

When Congress responds to judicial review, it must engage in "the speculative imagination in democratic lawmaking" (1998). Legislating and policymaking are speculative endeavors. When passing new legislation, for example, members of Congress speculate as to the likely policy effects of the legislation. And when attempting to revive unconstitutional legislation, members of Congress must speculate whether the revised version satisfies the Court's decisions. In this sense, members of Congress must glean information from the Court's opinions and votes to determine what the Court's demands are. If a public policy has political support, members of Congress must assess what concessions are necessary to accommodate the Court. Thus, congressional responses will vary depending upon the nature of the Court's decision, public support for the policy involved, and the availability of alternative means for implementing the policy.

Judicial review can thus be viewed as a unique tool of deliberation in these cases. By motivating lawmakers in Congress to revisit legislation, the Court's exercise of judicial review can force Congress to be more deliberative on certain issues, or in a sense force Congress to incorporate judicial deliberations into the legislation. After the Court has invalidated legislation on constitutional grounds, members of Congress can be expected to weight the Court's constitutional pronouncement with their own public policy preferences and political goals. The role of judicial review in adding constitutional deliberation to the lawmaking mix needs to be emphasized, but the level of deliberation *in Congress* should not be overstated. As I recalled at the end of chapter 1, Keith Whittington has shown how there are different "levels of deliberation" (1999, 3–9). The congressional responses examined in this chapter rarely result in high levels of constitutional deliberation in Congress, or what Whittington terms the "creation" or "construction" of constitutional values. More often, they seem to result in haggling over the proper application of legal "interpretation" of constitutional language—a lower level of deliberation according to Whittington.

However, three points must be made about this "lower level" of deliberation. First, that members of Congress do not necessarily engage in a deeper deliberation does not mean that Supreme Court justices did not do so. As Alexander Bickel observes, "courts have certain capacities for dealing with matters of principle that legislatures and executives do not possess. Judges have, or should have, the leisure, the training, and the insulation to follow the ways of the scholar in pursuing the ends of government" (1962, 25–26). Presumably, judicial independence, legal training and culture, and the justices' own conceptions of their roles make it more likely that the justices engage in a deeper deliberation than lawmakers in Congress who are concerned with numerous other factors. Thus, the amended statutes may be viewed as having incorporated a deeper deliberation. Second, the "interpretive" level of deliberation engaged in by Congress in congressional responses may be an improvement over the "policymaking" deliberation that led to the initial passage of the law. Even if it is only the "legalistic" view of the Constitution that is being incorporated, the role of the Constitution as a legal document is an important one. Finally, because we are a "republic of reasons," interaction, or bargaining, between Court and Congress over these statutes has resulted, I believe, in a more careful consideration and articulation of the reasons that justify the statutory policy and the content of the legislation. In most of these cases, the Court decision *read together with* the legislation and legislative history provides both public policy and constitutional justifications for the ultimate form of the statute.

For example, consider the statutory provisions discussed earlier, establishing various government benefits and struck down by the Court for violating equal protection. In those and other similar statutes, Congress established a public policy rationale for providing government benefits to needy children, the elderly, the retired, the poor, and other disadvantaged groups. Congress made public policy judgments about the best means for delivering those services. The Court then evaluated the public policy means used in those statutes in light of constitutional values expressed in the text of the Constitution, and it demanded that the statutes incorporate a certain understanding of equality in the implementation of the public policy. In response, Congress conceded to the Court on this view of equality, but maintained the basic public policy rationale for these types of government benefits. In my view, we now have more carefully and thoughtfully drafted legislation that reflects an inter-institutionally collective justification for the legislation, as opposed to having institutional winners and losers in a battle over *a priori* and uni-dimensional policy preferences. When bargaining among multiple institutions results in a more comprehensive justification for law and policy, the normative preference for a republic of reasons has been more fully realized.

Encouraging or compelling Congress to revise specific statutes is an important type of effect that the Supreme Court can have on lawmaking when it exercises judicial review. This chapter has shown that congressional responses to judicial review are highly variable, with Congress often making concessions to the Court. Over time, members of Congress show an impressive commitment to statutory policy, often bargaining or haggling with the Court to satisfy the Court's constitutional preferences and Congress's public policy preferences. However, the Court's exercise of judicial review may have effects beyond the specific statute struck down in a specific decision. It may have a broader effect on debate and deliberation in Congress. Once the Court strikes down a statute for violating a particular constitutional provision, Congress may respond to the Court decision by considering the Court's doctrine when drafting new legislation that raises issues under the same constitutional provision. The potential effect of judicial review on drafting, debate, and deliberation is the subject of the chapters that follow.

THREE

The Shadows

of Uncertain Scrutiny:

Legislating in a Period

of Judicial Dualism

★

I now turn to the second question surrounding the effect of judicial review on Congress: How do the Supreme Court's judicial review decisions and constitutional law doctrines influence congressional deliberation and debate over legislation? In this chapter and the chapter that follows, I will examine the Supreme Court's decisions involving two key federalism provisions in the Constitution: the Commerce Clause of Article I and the Tenth Amendment. The purpose of this chapter is threefold. First, I lay out a framework for thinking about how constitutional issues are raised in Congress and how judicial review may influence constitutional deliberation in Congress. Second, I examine some historical examples of how the threat of judicial review by the Court has influenced deliberation over federalism issues in Congress. Finally, I lay the groundwork for the next chapter by highlighting how the threat of judicial review over these issues changed as judicial scrutiny gave way to judicial deference. This chapter helps to illustrate how Congress debated federalism issues during a period of judicial scrutiny, or what Robert Mc-Closkey (1960) calls "judicial dualism," whereas the next chapter will explore in more detail how Congress ignored federalism under the Constitution during a period of judicial deference—until a renewed state of judicial scrutiny and dualism reinvigorated and shaped federalism debates in Congress.

The historical analysis in this chapter is based on secondary and archival sources, and it is not intended to serve as a comprehensive historical study on the subject. The cases and legislation reviewed here will be quite familiar to some, but for those not familiar with the history of the Court, Congress, and federalism, these examples will illustrate the once highly interactive relationship between the Court and Congress over the meaning of the Commerce

Clause and the Tenth Amendment. My aim is simply to draw attention to the fact that early in the twentieth century, the Court engaged in moderate to high levels of scrutiny over the scope of Congress's commerce power. The examples reviewed in this chapter will illustrate how the uncertainty of whether the Court would uphold pertinent legislation contributed to the likelihood and content of constitutional deliberation in Congress. However, by the 1990s the Court had established a position of complete deference to Congress on the issue of the commerce power. This new deference sets the stage for chapter 4 by asking whether Congress would continue to debate its commerce power in the absence of a threat from the Court, and how the reemergence of judicial scrutiny might influence constitutional deliberation in Congress.

Is There a Connection between Constitutional Deliberation in Congress and Judicial Review?

While members of Congress may not be hostile to constitutional issues, the incentives of the institution and of democratic lawmaking are not favorable for encouraging routine constitutional deliberation, as I showed in chapter 1. However, there are conditions under which we may expect members of Congress to be more likely to engage in constitutional deliberation. As I also discussed in the first chapter, I use the term "constitutional deliberation" broadly to mean constitutional debate among members or other relevant policymakers and lawmakers, committee hearings that focus at some length on constitutional issues, language in a bill or statute that reflects constitutional principles or judicial doctrines, or some other indication that constitutional issues played an important part when the legislation in question was considered. Recall that I am interested in how members of Congress incorporate constitutional issues when considering specific legislation—not in other types of constitutional deliberation that most certainly do take place in Congress. For example, I am interested in how members of Congress gauge whether a specific bill falls within Congress's commerce power, but I do not address how members discuss constitutional standards during the impeachment process or activities other than producing legislation.

It may make sense for members of Congress to consider a potential exercise of judicial review as they draft legislation; after all, Congress is a branch of government equal to the others, and members presumably want the public policy embodied in the legislation to be implemented and effective.[1] However, I argue that members of Congress will frequently ignore, in favor of other considerations, the potential that the Court will exercise judicial review. As I have shown, well-established models of congressional decision making and behavior demonstrate that members of Congress are influenced by a host of factors much more immediate and politically influential, such as their own ideological and policy preferences, as well as the preferences of their constituents, the public at large, interest groups, political parties, the president, and so on. In short, political and public policy issues will usually trump constitutional issues in Congress (see Morgan 1966). Political concerns involve issues internal to Congress like political party positions and coalition building, along with others external to the institution like constituents' preferences and interest group pressure. Public policy concerns primarily involve speculation over the actual policy effects of the legislation.

Political and public policy concerns can overshadow constitutional issues in one of two ways. First, the level of public and congressional support for a policy might be so strong that policy makers are simply unaware of a potential constitutional issue. The goal is to get consensus in Congress, pass the legislation, and satisfy voters. Strong consensus for a public policy, and for relevant legislation, means that supporters simply do not look for potentially damaging aspects of a bill. Second, there may be instances where Congress realizes that the Court is in fact likely to exercise judicial review and strike down the legislation, but members feel pressure to vote for the public policy issues nevertheless. In this situation, the constitutional issues may get raised, and a significant number of legislators may realize that Court doctrine is adverse and that the legislation is likely unconstitutional. However, factors such as constituents' preferences and policy considerations favor voting for the bill, and thus some members do so with a belief, or even hope, that the Court will strike the statute down.

In addition to constituents' preferences and public policy, there is another possible reason why policymakers in Congress are not often compelled to consider constitutional law. The likelihood that a particular statute will actually be reviewed and struck down by the Court is relatively small, and so the perceived threat in Congress that a statute will be invalidated by the Court is likely to be low.[2] Even if some members or their staffs actually do identify and consider a potential constitutional issue in a piece of legislation, debating it may not be worth the time and effort. In reviewing the factors that influence congressional behavior, it is easy to see ample reasons for Congress to be unconcerned about constitutional issues and Supreme Court precedent when drafting, debating, and voting on legislation.

Although constitutional issues and judicial review will not usually be at the forefront of debate over policy and legislation in Congress, there are circumstances under which we might expect members of Congress to be more attentive to constitutional issues. To begin with, the politics of the statute might make it more likely that Congress would raise constitutional issues. This can occur, for example, if there is controversy over the policy. Where a public policy is contentious and support for legislation split, there are usually more opponents to raise arguments against it and more decision points where arguments can be made and compromises forged. On the one hand, those members who favor a public policy with wide support are unlikely to complicate the passage of legislation by introducing potentially problematic constitutional issues. On the other hand, the opponents of a policy might use a relevant constitutional issue as an argument against the legislation and a reason for voting against it.[3] A constitutional reason might provide a principled argument against legislation, or political "cover" for a member of Congress to vote against legislation that appears popular with the public—or both. Additionally, the nature of opposition to a bill can affect how the debate unfolds. The opposition may be based simply on partisan politics, or it may involve interest groups. Constitutional issues may be more likely to arise when there is a well-organized and mobilized opposition with significant resources. Established interest groups often have the means, expertise, and incentives to identify relevant constitutional issues, fashion persuasive legal arguments, and mobilize public opinion. Evidence shows that groups have been particularly influential in the areas of civil liberties and civil rights (see, e.g., den Dulk and Pickerill 2003; Epp 1999; Walker 1994).

Constitutional issues may also be more likely to surface in Congress when the Supreme Court has acted recently or frequently on the particular issue. Recent or frequent Court decisions indicate a willingness by the Court to invalidate federal statutes and can create a real or perceived threat to other legislation addressing similar issues. In this sense, a threat of judicial review can force Congress to incorporate the Court's preferences into legislation, just as the threat of a veto can force Congress to incorporate the president's preferences into legislation. As I have discussed earlier, Charles Cameron has shown how presidents may use the threat of a veto (in addition to the actual use of the veto) to incorporate at least some of their preferences into legislation and force members of Congress to negotiate with them (2000). Because the Justices on the Court do not communicate directly with lawmakers in Congress as the president does, the only means of communication are votes in

TABLE 3.1 Conditions Influencing Constitutional Deliberation in Congress

	Constitutional Deliberation Less Likely	Constitutional Deliberation More Likely
Politics and public policy involved	Low controversy, low salience, few opponents, low intensity	High controversy, high salience, many opponents, high intensity, involvement of interest groups
Supreme Court cases on the issue	Obscure, old, few	Well established, recent, many

past Court decisions and doctrine as expressed in the Court's opinions. If the threat that the Court will strike a statute down appears real, the bill's proponents in Congress may feel compelled to draft the bill in a manner that reflects recent Court opinions on the matter or to confront the constitutional issue in another manner. Well-known Supreme Court cases or caselaw may make it more likely that participants in the legislative process will spot a constitutional issue and bring it into the debate. The prominence or notoriety of caselaw can create a better awareness or consciousness of a particular constitutional issue. For instance, *Roe v. Wade* (1973) and its progeny are well known and likely to be quickly invoked whenever abortion regulations are proposed, whereas a single, old, obscure Court decision that might be relevant but that few have heard of is less likely to motivate constitutional debate. In this sense, Supreme Court caselaw or doctrine can create a "constitutional context" for debate and deliberation over proposed legislation.

In sum, constitutional issues are not an automatic item on the legislator's checklist when drafting and considering bills in Congress. Constitutional issues are most likely to get raised and debated if they are connected to political problems for the passage of legislation. They are most likely to be raised when controversial legislation incites strong opposition to a bill, and when the threat of judicial review looms. We can thus conceptualize the likelihood of serious constitutional deliberation in Congress over a statute as a function of the conditions in table 3.1. My purpose here is not simply to determine the likelihood of constitutional deliberation in Congress, especially in any precise quantitative sense. Rather, I want to demonstrate that a realistic threat of judicial review, as manifested in past exercises of it by the Court, is an important form of communication with Congress analogous to veto threats communicated to Congress by presidents (Cameron 2000). The threat of judicial review can bring bargaining over constitutional values into the legislative process. I also want to understand the factors that shape the content and weight of that deliberation. Examples in this chapter help to suggest how these conditions have historically affected constitutional deliberation over the commerce power in Congress.

The Supreme Court, Congress, and Federalism: A Brief Historical Perspective

A description of the Supreme Court decisions and federal legislation involving the commerce power and Tenth Amendment over time can help to illustrate how the court's doctrine and congressional deliberation have changed over time. Figure 3.1 is a timeline of major or otherwise relevant legislation and Supreme Court decisions involving the commerce power and the Tenth Amendment. I seek to establish if lawmakers in Congress considered the constitutional federalism issues, and if so, to what extent previous Court decisions, Court doctrine, and the threat of a future exercise of judicial review influenced that debate and deliberation.

The substantive area of federalism provides an excellent opportunity to study the effects of the Court's exercise of judicial review for three reasons. First, federalism is an inherently important constitutional area involving Court-Congress interaction, and the effects of the Court's recent federalism decisions in Congress have not been adequately studied. Studies of how the Constitution is construed outside the Court have addressed legislative debates over abortion rights (e.g., Burgess 1992; Devins 1996), war powers (e.g., Burgess 1992; Fisher 1978), the legislative veto (e.g., Fisher 1990; Fisher 1993), impeachment (e.g., Whittington 1999), the nullification crisis (e.g., Whittington 1999), and religious freedom (e.g., den Dulk and Pickerill 2003), among other topics. Certainly, scholars who study the Constitution outside the Court have not entirely ignored federalism, but the focus has often been on the New Deal period and the "switch in time that saved nine." Generally, studies of the Court in the period leading up to the New Deal characterize the Court as obstructionist, denying Congress its will (cf. McCloskey 1960). Bruce Ackerman's view that the New Deal represented a "constitutional moment" and a shift in constitutional politics that more or less relegated the Court to a spectator in federalism matters in a new "constitutional regime" has been highly influential (1991). In line with this perspective, scholars seem to hold the view that while there may have been interaction between the Court and Congress at the time of the New Deal, the battle was over constitutional visions and the Court lost (cf. Cushman 1998). In light of the recent federalism decisions and the current debate over the Constitution outside the Court, it is important to examine if and how members of Congress have addressed federalism and what the effects of the Rehnquist Court's decisions might be.

Second, an in-depth analysis of constitutional deliberation over federalism offers an opportunity to evaluate the arguments of the Rehnquist Court's critics and recent debates over the "correctness" of the Court's decisions. To the extent that legal scholars address the recent federalism rulings, they do so largely as part of a debate over the "political safeguards" versus "judicial safeguards" of federalism. The political safeguards approach builds on an argument initially made by Herbert Wechsler (1954) and later elaborated on by Jesse Choper (1980), Mark Tushnet (1999), Larry Kramer (2000), and others (e.g., Nagel 2001). In essence these scholars argue that federalism is a political construct, and that Congress and the states can and should determine proper federalism boundaries without judicial interference. Ruth Colker and James Brudney have gone so far as to say that the Rehnquist Court has "dissed Congress" and that the Court's judicial activism is designed purely to deny Congress its will (2001). On the other hand, the judicial safeguards approach, advocated by scholars such as John Yoo (1997), Steven Calabresi (2001; 1995), and Marci Hamilton (2001), suggests that Congress cannot be trusted to find limitations to its own powers and that therefore the Court must rein in a federal government that has usurped powers reserved to the states under the Constitution (see also Greve 1999). These scholars argue that Congress simply does not consider federalism and that the Court is a necessary evil to help prevent a federal government of unlimited powers. Each of these arguments, that based on political safeguards as well as that based on judicial safeguards, is built on a Bickelian view that judicial review impedes the legislative process and is an obstacle to lawmaking (see Bickel 1962). Only a few scholars have emphasized how the Court and Congress may interact over federalism, or how the Court's exercise of judicial review may influence deliberation over federalism in Congress, as I seek to do here (see Althouse 2001; Whittington 2001).

A final reason why federalism is appropriate for this study is an empirical one. The Court's recent activity in the federalism area provides an excellent, not to mention timely, opportunity to look at three stages of the judicial review and lawmaking sequence from a longitudinal perspective. First, we can

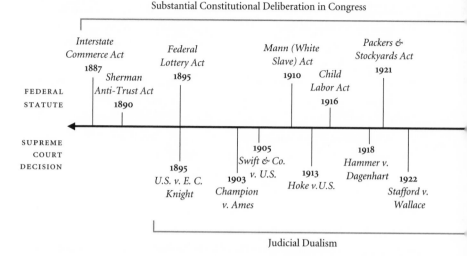

FIGURE 3.1 Commerce Clause–Tenth Amendment Time Line

ask how Congress debated federalism *before* the Rehnquist Court's newfound attention to it. Next, we can look at the Court's recent decisions and assess the nature of the new threat posed by the Court and judicial review. Finally, we can look at how Congress responded *after* the Court's decisions. The recent shift in doctrine and threat of judicial review in the area of federalism allows us to look for relationships and correlations between the threat of judicial review and the nature of constitutional deliberation in Congress.

Before turning to the recent Rehnquist Court decisions in the next chapter, I will examine a few historical examples of how the Court and Congress interacted over federalism and the commerce power. My purpose in doing so is not to present a new view on the cases and statutes discussed, but rather to sketch examples in history where the Court and Congress have interacted to incorporate constitutional deliberation into legislative and policy debates. I wish to be able to place the recent Rehnquist Court decisions and legislative debates in a historical perspective in which the Court influences, as opposed to merely obstructs, debate and deliberation in Congress over federalism.

CONGRESS'S POWER TO REGULATE INTERSTATE COMMERCE BEFORE THE NEW DEAL

In many respects, the power to regulate interstate commerce was one of the most important new powers granted to the federal government in the Constitution. One of the worst failures of the Articles of Confederation was the lack

Substantial Constitutional Deliberation in Congress

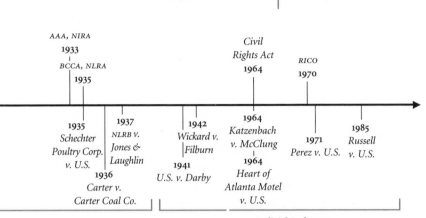

AAA, NIRA
1933
BCCA, NLRA
1935

Civil
Rights Act
1964

RICO
1970

1935
Schechter
Poultry Corp.
v. U.S.

1937
NLRB v.
Jones &
Laughlin

1936
Carter v.
Carter Coal Co.

1942
Wickard v.
Filburn

1941
U.S. v. Darby

1964
Katzenbach
v. McClung

1964
Heart of
Atlanta Motel
v. U.S.

1971
Perez v. U.S.

1985
Russell
v. U.S.

Judicial Deference

of power granted to the federal government to prevent state governments from interfering with free trade. Before ratification of the Constitution, states imposed tariffs and duties on foreign goods and goods from other states, as well as interfering with interstate commerce in other ways. Under the Articles of Confederation, the federal government was incapable of preventing this type of economic discrimination among the states. Thus, the ability to uniformly regulate commerce and prevent one state from discriminating against another was a key new constitutional power. In The Federalist No. 7, Alexander Hamilton expressed his concerns over commercial competition among the states: "Competitions of commerce would be another fruitful source of contention. The States less favorably circumstanced would be desirous of escaping from the disadvantages of local situation, and of sharing in the advantages of their more fortunate neighbors. Each State, or separate confederacy, would pursue a system of commercial policy peculiar to itself. This would occasion distinctions, preferences, and exclusions, which would beget discontent. . . . The infractions of these regulations, on the one side, the efforts to repel them on the other, would naturally lead to outrages, and these to reprisals and wars."

And in Federalist No. 22, Hamilton argued further that to avoid those problems, commerce among the states must be regulated by the national government: "The interfering and unneighborly regulations of some States, contrary to the true spirit of the Union, have, in different instances, given just cause of umbrage and complaint to others, and it is to be feared that examples of this nature, if not restrained by a national control, would be multiplied and extended till they become not less serious sources of animosity and discord than injurious impediments to the intercourse between the different parts of the Confederacy." Given Hamilton's statements and the historical context of the Constitution and the Commerce Clause, it is fair to say that the purpose of a national commerce power was largely to restrain the states from discriminating against one another in commercial matters, and to empower the federal government to assure that commerce was regulated uniformly across all states. The power to regulate commerce was part of the broader attempt by the Framers to strengthen the national government by granting it plenary power over a limited number of specifically defined areas.

Congress's power under the Commerce Clause began its judicial development in the famous case of *Gibbons v. Ogden* (1824). Writing for the Court, Chief Justice John Marshall found that a federal statute regulating the navigation of waters between New York and New Jersey was a valid exercise of the commerce power, and that the federal statute trumped a New York statute regulating navigation in New York waters. Marshall defined interstate commerce as all commercial "intercourse" between or among the states, which the Constitution gave Congress the power to regulate. But Marshall went even further in defining the scope of the commerce power: "It is the power to regulate; that is, to prescribe the rule by which commerce is to be governed. This power, like all others vested in Congress, is complete in itself, may be exercised to its utmost extent, and acknowledges no limitations, other than those prescribed in the constitution" (196). Marshall's opinion in *Gibbons* is important because it still serves as a jurisprudential basis for judicial interpretations of Congress's commerce power—especially the broader interpretations of that power (cf. Epstein 1987). However, it was not until later in the nineteenth century that the Court had to further interpret the scope of Congress's power to regulate interstate commerce.

Toward the end of the nineteenth century and the beginning of the twentieth, as the industrial revolution blossomed and the national economy changed, Congress began passing new types of federal economic legislation such as the Interstate Commerce Act of 1887 and the Sherman Anti-Trust Act of 1890. Some of the new regulations collided with traditional and laissez-faire notions of "interstate commerce," and the Court was called on to determine the scope of Congress's commerce power in the context of the shifting economy and new federal legislation. As figure 3.1 indicates, after 1897 Congress passed and the Court reviewed an increasing number of statutes under the commerce power. What is important for my purposes here is that the Court sometimes upheld and sometimes struck down legislation under the Commerce Clause and the Tenth Amendment. The constitutional historian Robert McCloskey describes this period leading up to the New Deal as one of "judicial dualism," in which the Court sometimes interpreted the Commerce Clause and other constitutional provisions formally and narrowly, and sometimes was more flexible and deferential to Congress (1960, 136–38). While new legislation was being considered during changing political, social, and economic conditions, it was also being debated in the shadow of uncertain judicial scrutiny. Consequently, the threat that the Court might use judicial review to invalidate economic legislation was real, and members of Congress could not be certain that the Court would uphold any particular new economic regulation.

For instance, in *United States v. E.C. Knight Co.* (1895) the Court ruled that the federal government could not regulate a monopoly of sugar refineries under the Sherman Anti-Trust Act. In an 8–1 decision, the Court made a distinction between "manufacturing" and "commerce," and determined that sugar refineries were engaged in manufacturing alone. Thus, even if the sugar refineries in question constituted a monopoly, they were not a "monopoly of commerce" and could not be regulated by Congress as interstate commerce, because the power over activities like manufacturing and mining was reserved to the states by the Tenth Amendment. On the other hand, in *Champion v. Ames* ("Lottery Case") (1903), the Court upheld the Federal Lottery Act of 1895, which prohibited the importing, mailing, or other interstate transportation of lottery tickets. Although the Act was primarily "moral legislation" intended to prohibit lotteries, the Court held that the power to "regulate" items in interstate commerce included the power to "prohibit" them, and since the Court found that lottery tickets were items in interstate commerce, Congress could prohibit their interstate shipment. Thus, the statute was within the commerce power.

One year after the *Lottery Case*, the Court handed down *Swift & Co. v. United States* (1905), in which it upheld an application of the Sherman Anti-Trust Act to price fixing in the meat industry, even though the meat dealers could be characterized as being involved in local or intrastate activity. Justice Holmes wrote, "When cattle are sent for sale from a place in one State, with expectation that they will end their transit, after purchase, in another, and when in effect they do so, with only the interruption necessary to find a purchaser at the stockyard, and when this is a typical, constantly recurring course, the current thus existing is a *current of commerce* among the States, and the purchase of the cattle is a part and incident of such commerce" (398–99) (emphasis added). As this excerpt from Justices Holmes's opinion indicates, the "current of commerce" test meant that if the activity being regulated by Congress was at any point part of the broader flow of commercial activity, regulation of it would be a permissible exercise of the commerce power. The *Lottery Case* and *Swift* seemed to give Congress more room to expand its power over economic matters, but the analysis in each case suggested that the Court would scrutinize the activity being regulated to assure that it was in the current of commerce.[4] And *E.C. Knight* was fairly recent and still good law.

Facing the uncertainty of judicial review and of how the Court might apply its recent precedent to new economic legislation, members of Congress made clear efforts to satisfy the Court's recent decisions. For example, when Congress passed the Packers and Stockyards Act of 1921, setting forth broad regulations of the meat packing industry, it explicitly incorporated into the statute the precise language used by Justice Holmes in *Swift*. The meat industry organized and fought attempts by Congress to regulate it. In describing what activities or items would be regulated, the Packers and Stockyards Act stated that a "transaction in respect to any article shall be considered to be in commerce if such article is part of that *current of commerce* usual in the livestock and meat packing industries . . ." (emphasis added).[5] The statute was no doubt drafted to reflect the Court's most recent and most relevant precedent. While Congress was attempting to enhance its commerce power, it was also mindful of Supreme Court rulings and drafted statutory language to try to satisfy the Court's test. As Barry Cushman (1998; 1992) chronicles, the House Agriculture Committee debated the commerce power at length in committee hearings and in its committee report defended the legislation's constitutionality based on *Swift*; in addition, *Swift* was used to support the constitutionality of the legislation in floor debates over the legislation.[6] The Court applied the "current of commerce" standard to the Packers and Stockyards Act in *Stafford v. Wallace* (1922), upholding the Act as a constitutional exercise of the commerce power. The sequence outlined here—from *Swift* to the Packers and Stockyards Act to *Stafford*—is significant because it is an early example of how the two branches can interact: the Supreme Court established an explicit standard for scrutinizing Congress's commerce power, Congress then adopted statutory language to reflect that standard, and then the Court upheld the new statute. Thus, the final version of the statute included both the public policy preferences of Congress and the constitutional policy preferences of the Court.

Another early attempt to build on the commerce power involved legislative proposals to regulate child labor.[7] It is worth looking at the legislative history of the Child Labor Act in some detail. Although first introduced in 1906, it was not until 1916 that the Child Labor Act was passed by Congress. In 1906 Senator Albert Beveridge (R-Ind.) introduced a bill that would have banned from interstate commerce "the product of any factory or mine that employs children under the age of fourteen years."[8] The bill was carefully drafted to reflect the language used by the Court in the *Lottery Case*, by prohibiting "the carriers of interstate commerce" from transporting items produced by children. The idea had mixed support. Many businesses opposed the bill, but manufacturers subject to state child labor laws supported a national law to take away the advantage of competitors in states without such laws. National labor groups remained somewhat uncommitted, having to make strategic decisions on which labor policies to pursue. Organized labor had many other priorities. And groups like the National Child Labor Committee (NCLC), formed in 1906 to fight the evils of child labor, were not sure what the best course was for eliminating child labor in the United States, and they were split on the wisdom and constitutionality of Beveridge's bill. President Theodore Roosevelt supported the idea but did not push for passage of the bill because "organized labor was lukewarm; the leaders of the child labor movement were divided; [Roosevelt] himself had doubts about the bill's constitutionality; and he knew the opposition the bill would face in Congress" (Braeman 1964, 23).

The constitutionality of the bill was a contentious issue from the time it was introduced in 1906 until it was eventually passed in 1916. Table 3.2 summarizes the timeline of key developments in the decade-long debate over the Child Labor Act. During that period the opponents of child labor laws argued forcefully that such a law would be unconstitutional because labor was a local activity, similar to manufacturing or mining. While that argument could be supported by *E.C. Knight*, Senator Beveridge continued to argue that his bill was constitutional under the *Lottery Case*. In numerous communications with President Roosevelt, on the floor of Congress, in public speeches, and in a lengthy brief, Beveridge argued that under the *Lottery Case* it was "absolutely settled" that Congress had broad power to prohibit goods from entering interstate commerce (see Braeman 1964). Over three days in January 1907 Beveridge made a passionate plea for the necessity and the constitutionality of the bill on the Senate floor (see Fuller 1923, 237; Wood 1968, 13–14).[9]

TABLE 3.2 Legislative Timeline of the Child Labor Act of 1916

Year	Legislative Action or Event
1903	*Lottery Case*
1904–5	National Child Labor Committee (NCLC) formed, publishes annual report on child labor
1906	Beveridge Bill introduced in 59th Congress
1907	Senator Beveridge delivers three-day speech on child labor and constitutionality of his bill
	Beveridge Bill gains little support in 59th Congress
	NCLC withdraws support for Beveridge Bill
	Beveridge Bill is voted down in House Judiciary Committee and does not come to vote on Senate floor
1908–14	Beveridge Bill (or its equivalent) introduced in every Congress with no success
1910	U.S. Census shows increase in the number of child workers
1912	Woodrow Wilson elected; progressive politics revitalized, indicating possible support for child labor legislation
1913	Supreme Court upholds Mann Act in *Hoke v. United States*
	President Wilson calls special session of 63d Congress
	Five child labor laws introduced in special session
	Palmer-Owen Bill drafted by constitutional lawyers to satisfy Supreme Court doctrine from the *Lottery Case* and *Hoke*
1914	National Child Committee on Labor endorses federal child labor legislation in its tenth annual report
	Hearings held in February and March on Palmer-Owen, with focus on constitutional issues
	Southern textile industry mobilizes against Palmer-Owen
1915	House Labor Committee issues unanimous report on February 13 in support of Palmer-Owen
	House votes on February 15 in favor of Palmer-Owen, 233–43
	Senate Committee on Interstate Commerce reports favorably on Palmer-Owen on March 1

TABLE 3.2 Continued

Year	Legislative Action or Event
	Unanimous consent bill to bring bill to vote in Senate fails on March 1
	63d Congress adjourns without enacting Palmer-Owen
1916	Keating-Owen Bill introduced in January
	House Labor Committee on January 17 reports favorably on Keating-Owen
	Keating-Owen passes House, 337–46
	Senate Committee on Interstate Commerce holds hearings February 15–21, again focusing on constitutional issues
	Keating-Owen reported favorably
	Unanimous consent motion on Senate floor fails on June 3, vote on Keating-Owen delayed; Congress recesses for national party conventions
	President (and presidential candidate) Wilson supports Keating-Owen and directs Democratic Steering Committee to support it
	Senate on August 8 passes Keating-Owen, 52–12
	President Wilson signs bill on September 1
	President Wilson reelected in November
1918	Supreme Court strikes down Child Labor Act in *Hammer v. Dagenhart*

Beveridge's biographer Claude Bowers summarizes the senator's spirited speech: "Three days of the scathing indictment of a savage system in the interest of greed had passed, and the infamy of child labor was now conceded; and Senators threw up the Constitution as a barricade, with [Senators] proclaiming the unconstitutionality of a national law. The remainder of the speech, with interruptions and counter-contentions, was a brilliant forensic exhibition. Beveridge insisted that, under the power to regulate interstate commerce, there was a constitutional right to forbid interstate commerce in goods made by the labor of childhood. He closed with a fervent peroration that brought applause from the galleries" (1932, 254).

Beveridge's bill did not come to a vote in the Senate, and on the House side the Judiciary Committee voted the measure down, reporting that it was an unconstitutional exercise of power reserved for the states.[10] Although strongly supported by Senator Beveridge and other progressives in Congress, the bill lacked the support of the president and of the most influential child labor interest group, the NCLC, and it failed to pass the 59th Congress. According to Stephen B. Wood,

> The Beveridge bill . . . provoked strong and persistent opposition. Hostile senators, whether uncompromising defenders of the fundamental principles of laissez faire or progressive legislators who were unable to discern how Congress could regulate the conditions of production, repeatedly interrupted Beveridge's presentation, challenging his interpretation of the commerce power. Federal legislation, according to the opponents' argument, would go beyond constitutional limitations and invade the legitimate powers that were reserved to the states. . . . Most of the opponents were convinced that state legislation afforded an adequate regulatory, and the only constitutionally allowable, remedy. (1968, 17)

Nonetheless, the proponents of child labor legislation in Congress did not give up on the cause, despite persistent questions about the bill's constitutionality. Beveridge's bill (or its equivalent after Beveridge left office) was introduced in every Congress from 1906 to 1914, and slightly different versions were introduced from 1915 to 1916 (Fuller 1923, 236–38). The opponents of the child labor legislation continued their fight against the bill, grounding their opposition in constitutional arguments. During this time, the NCLC continued to serve as the primary advocate for child labor issues in the United States, but it made the strategic choice to focus its resources on the battle against child labor in state legislatures. The NCLC refused to support federal legislation in part because its members viewed the fight for federal legislation as futile, in light of Supreme Court doctrine and strong opposition at the national level. In addition, William Howard Taft won the election of 1908, and Taft was generally on the side of business and industrial interests that opposed government regulation of the economy. And even though Woodrow Wilson won the election of 1912, he did not immediately give support to child labor legislation. Political conditions simply did not favor the passage of a federal child labor statute for many years after Senator Beveridge initially introduced his bill.

By 1914, however, the conditions surrounding proposed child labor legislation were beginning to change. The year before, the Supreme Court upheld the Mann Act, or the "White Slave" Act, in *Hoke v. United States* (1913). Congress had passed the Act in 1910, the express purpose being to "Further

Regulate Interstate and Foreign Commerce by Prohibiting the Transportation Therein for Immoral Purposes of Women and Girls, and for Other Purposes."[11] In *Hoke*, the Supreme Court held that Congress could prohibit the interstate transportation of women for the purpose of prostitution. Justice McKenna summarized the Court's decisions and doctrine regarding Congress's commerce power this way:

> Our dual form of government has its perplexities, state and nation having different spheres of jurisdiction, as we have said; but it must be kept in mind that we are one people; and the powers reserved to the states and those conferred on the nation are adapted to be exercised, whether independently or concurrently, to promote the general welfare, material and moral. This is the effect of the decisions; and surely, if the facility of interstate transportation can be taken away from the demoralization of lotteries, the debasement of obscene literature, the contagion of diseased cattle or persons, the impurity of food and drugs, the like facility can be taken away from the systematic enticement to and the enslavement in prostitution and debauchery of women, and, more insistently, of girls. . . . The principle established by the cases is the simple one, when rid of confusing and distracting considerations, that Congress has power over transportation "among the several states;" that the power is complete in itself, and that Congress, as an incident to it, may adopt not only means necessary but convenient to its exercise, and the means may have the quality of police regulations (227 U.S. 308, 322–23).

The decision in *Hoke* appeared to affirm the broad reading given to the commerce power in the *Lottery Case*. In response to *Hoke*, and frustrated by a lack of success in some states, the NCLC changed its position and its members voted to endorse federal legislation; the group announced its new position in the 1914 edition of its *Child Labor Bulletin*. During the next two years support grew and the various organized groups in addition to the NCLC, such as organized labor and the American Medical Association, came to back a federal child labor statute. As many as six child labor bills were introduced into Congress in 1914 and 1915.

The child labor bill that gained the most momentum was the Keating-Owen bill, named after its sponsors Edward Keating (D-Col.) and Robert Owen (D-Okla.). Explicitly drafted to meet the standards of the *Lottery Case* and *Hoke*, the bill banned the interstate transportation of products made in factories that employed children under the age of fourteen, or children between the ages of fourteen and sixteen who had worked improper hours. The bill ultimately became part of the election-year politics of 1916, but the constitutional issue was still considered in Congress. A report of the House Labor Committee stated:

> In considering . . . the bill, the committee has been strongly impressed by what may properly be termed the broadening view of the powers of Congress under the interstate commerce clause, a view emphasized in a number of recent cases decided by the Supreme Court of the United States, particularly those cases bearing on the lottery act, the food and drugs act, and the white-slave act.
>
> * * *
>
> The question of the constitutionality of the bill was ably argued before the committee. Ex-Gov. W. W. Kitchin, of North Carolina, representing the southern cotton manufacturers, and Mr. J. A. Emory, representing the board of directors of the National Association of Manufacturers, argued against the constitutionality of the bill, and Professor Thomas I. Parkinson, director of the legislative drafting research department of Columbia University, New York City, argued for the constitutionality of the bill.[12]

The House Labor Committee went on to explicitly accept the view that the Child Labor Act fell within the scope of the Commerce Clause because the Supreme Court had "held that the power to regulate commerce included the power to regulate it in the interest of the public safety, the public health, the public morals and the public welfare." The Senate Committee on Interstate Commerce held similar hearings and reached similar conclusions. The Keating-Owen bill was reported favorably out of the House Labor Committee on January 17, 1916, and it passed the House by a vote of 337–46 on February 2, 1916. The Senate Committee on Interstate Commerce held hearings from February 15 to 21, and in the next month reported the bill favorably with amendments. When the bill was brought to the floor of the Senate on June 3, however, a unanimous consent motion failed, delaying a Senate vote on the bill. Congress then recessed for national political party conventions.

During the congressional recess and in the midst of an election season that included national party conventions and the drafting of party platforms, President Woodrow Wilson finally endorsed the Child Labor Act, and on July 18 he implored congressional leaders of his own party to support Keating-Owen (Wood 1968, 66).[13] With support from the president and the NCLC, the full Senate began debating the bill on August 3. At the center of the floor debate again was the constitutional issue. Some Senators claimed to have changed their position on the bill because they had been persuaded that the legislation was constitutional. For example, Senator Jacob H. Gallinger (R-N.H.) described why he changed his mind: "I have since had occasion to consult some of those same Senators and they have told me that they have changed their views, as the President of the United States has changed his views, and that they now believe the legislation to be constitutional. For that reason, having a strong inclination to support this kind of legislation, I have no hesitance today in voting for the bill, assuming that it will go to the Supreme Court of the United States for interpretation and decision."[14] According to Wood, "Among the bill's supporters [in the Senate], some . . . said they had few or no doubts about its constitutionality; others admitted to fairly substantial doubts; but none professed sufficient uncertainty to condemn the bill" (Wood 1968, 71). The Keating-Owen bill passed the full Senate on August 8, by a vote of 52–12. On September 1, 1916, President Wilson signed the Child Labor Act into law, and two months later he was reelected.

While the Child Labor Act was passed in part as a result of election-year politics, proponents argued, as Senator Beveridge had ten years earlier, that the Act was a logical extension of the *Lottery Case* and other precedent (see Braeman 1964, 34–35). Nevertheless, in *Hammer v. Dagenhart* ("Child Labor Case") (1918), the Supreme Court struck down the Child Labor Act for exceeding Congress's commerce power. The Court differentiated the Act from others that it had upheld by arguing that the products regulated by the Child Labor Act were not inherently harmful, unlike lottery tickets and "impure foods and drugs."[15] According to the 5–4 majority, the Child Labor Act "in its effect does not regulate transportation among the states, but aims to standardize the ages at which children may be employed in mining and manufacturing within the states. The goods shipped are of themselves harmless" (*Dagenhart*, 271–72). Because the Court viewed labor as purely local in character, it drew a line allowing Congress to regulate the actual item of interstate commerce, but not the labor that produced the item. As always with an enumerated power, the Tenth Amendment was in the background: "if Congress can thus regulate matters entrusted to local authority by prohibition of the movement of commodities in interstate commerce, all freedom of commerce will be at an end, and the power of the States over local matters may be eliminated, and thus our system of government practically destroyed" (276). With *Dagenhart*, the Court again found limits to Congress's commerce power, leaving Congress with a significant degree of uncertainty over what activities may or may not be regulated by the federal government vis-à-vis the states.[16]

While the Court's jurisprudence during this period might be described as "judicial dualism," the period also witnessed significant incidents of interaction between the Court and Congress. Fisher (1988) describes such interaction as "constitutional dialogues," emphasizing the extent to which Congress passes statutes that push the Court's constitutional doctrine. Additionally, we have seen that the Court's activity and decisions can influence statute making in Congress. The sequence briefly described above—*Swift*, the Packers & Stockyards Act, *Stafford*—demonstrates a type of negotiation between the Court and Congress. In effect the court said to Congress, "If you can show that an activity is in the current of interstate commerce, we will uphold the legislation." When Congress drafted the Packers & Stockyard Act, it explicitly adopted the Court's standards and satisfied the Court's constitutional preferences. And although the Court ended up invalidating the Child Labor Act of 1916, members of Congress did engage in constitutional deliberation over the Act, and that deliberation was motivated and shaped in large part by Supreme Court caselaw. Clearly, these statutes were considered in the unique political context of the progressive movement on one side and a strongly pro-business, laissez-faire lobby on the other, but they were also considered in the constitutional context established by the Court's judicial dualism.

The Court and the Commerce Power after the New Deal

With the election of President Franklin D. Roosevelt and the passage of New Deal legislation, a new relationship between the Court and Congress developed. For my purposes, the "showdown" between FDR and the Supreme Court over the constitutionality of New Deal legislation need not be chronicled in detail. It has been the subject of numerous historical and political studies, and lends itself to various interpretations (see e.g. Ackerman 1991; Cushman 1998; McCloskey 1960; Rauch 1944). What is most important for the project at hand is that the period described by McCloskey as "judicial dualism" had come to an end, and in the area of the commerce power and the Tenth Amendment, the Court became much more deferential toward Congress.

Initially, the Supreme Court engaged in formalistic scrutiny of New Deal legislation. For instance, in *Schechter Poultry Corp. v. United States* ("Sick Chicken Case") (1935), the Court held that the National Industrial Recovery Act, arguably the centerpiece of the first round of New Deal legislation, was invalid for exceeding Congress's commerce power.[17] And the Supreme Court declared the Bituminous Coal Conservation Act of 1935 unconstitutional in *Carter v. Carter Coal Co.* (1936). There is still debate among scholars as to why exactly the Court changed direction and began upholding the constitutionality of the social and economic legislation of the New Deal. Perhaps the Court feared FDR's "court-packing" plan; perhaps Congress drafted the newer legislation more carefully; or perhaps members of the Court simply believed that constitutional doctrine should change to reflect the times (see, e.g., Ackerman 1991; Cushman 1998; McCloskey 1960). The important point for my purposes is that the Court's approach to analyzing the commerce power and the Tenth Amendment shifted. In three Court decisions, *National Labor Relations Board v. Jones & Laughlin Steel Corp.* (1937), *United States v. Darby* (1941), and *Wickard v. Filburn* (1942), the Court not only upheld the constitutionality of the New Deal regulations, but also established the modern, more deferential judicial standards for evaluating the scope of the Commerce Clause and the Tenth Amendment.

In *National Labor Relations Board v. Jones & Laughlin Steel Corp.* (1937), the Court upheld the National Labor Relations Act of 1935, enacted by Congress to regulate manufacturers. The Court declared: "Although activities may be intrastate in character when separately considered, if they have such a close and substantial relation to interstate commerce that their control is essential or appropriate to protect that commerce from burdens and obstructions, Congress cannot be denied the power to exercise that control" (37). The Court thus broadened the test for analyzing Congress's Commerce Power to include those things with a "substantial relation to interstate commerce."

In *United States v. Darby* (1941), the Court dealt with the Tenth Amendment. The Court allowed Congress to prohibit the sale of products manufactured for interstate commerce by employers who violated minimum wage and maximum hours laws. It was in *Darby* that the Court "reconciled" a possible conflict between a broad federal commerce power and powers reserved to the states under the Tenth Amendment. The Court declared that the Tenth Amendment did not affect its analysis because it "states but a truism that all is retained which has not been surrendered" (124). Finally, in *Wickard v. Filburn* (1942), the Court found that Congress, under its power to regulate commerce, could prohibit a farmer from growing wheat for his own consumption. The Court reasoned that Congress could regulate such an admittedly local activity because it "exerts a substantial economic effect on interstate commerce . . ." (124). The determining factor was thus whether the "cumulative effect" of having individuals engage in the same type of economic activity might substantially affect interstate commerce. The Court concluded that many local farmers growing wheat for themselves might cumulatively "exert a substantial economic effect on interstate commerce," which Congress must be allowed to regulate under the Commerce Clause. Together, *Jones & Laughlin*, *Darby*, and *Wickard* established a more deferential attitude by the Court toward the breadth of Congress's commerce power. But how would the new, more deferential standard play in Congress?

With the Supreme Court's decisions upholding New Deal legislation, it was clear that Congress could regulate a fairly broad array of commercial and economic activities that could be characterized as being in the stream of commerce or as having substantial effects on interstate commerce. Congress faced the issue head-on when it undertook legislation to regulate civil rights in the early 1960s. The passage of the Civil Rights Act of 1964 resulted in the first significant set of Court decisions on Congress's commerce power since the New Deal decisions. Although the history of the civil rights movement leading up to the legislation is well documented, as is the legislative history of the Civil Rights Act of 1964 itself, it is important to highlight relevant portions here because the history of the Act provides a stark illustration of how the Court's constitutional doctrine and even a modest threat of judicial review can influence the debate over legislation.

The civil rights movement gained momentum in the 1950s, and various anti-discrimination bills were introduced in Congress. In the early 1960s President John F. Kennedy joined in the debate and supported a broad civil rights act that would penalize discrimination in various ways. After Kennedy's assassination, President Lyndon B. Johnson made the Civil Rights Act a priority and urged Congress to pass it promptly. The bill had the support of civil rights organizations, congressional leaders, and the president, and the president's party controlled both houses of Congress. Conditions appeared favorable for the legislation.

One of the key provisions of the proposed legislation, Title II, would ban discrimination in places of "public accommodation." Title II was designed to prohibit both government and private enterprises that provide services such as lodging or dining from refusing service to or otherwise discriminating against persons based on "race, color, religion, or national origin." Congress had tried to prevent such discrimination once before. In the wake of the Civil War, Congress passed the Federal Civil Rights Act of 1875, to provide to all citizens, regardless of race, the "full and equal enjoyment of the accommodations" of inns and other establishments such as theaters. Congress passed the statute using its power under the Fourteenth Amendment to assure "equal protection" to former slaves. However, the Supreme Court found the Act unconstitutional, declaring that Congress's power under the Fourteenth Amendment extended only to government discrimination and that it could not regulate private actors, including privately owned inns and other establishments that served the public.

So in 1963, as Congress took up the newest Civil Rights Act, it faced a dilemma. It could again claim that the public accommodations provisions were within its power to enforce the Fourteenth Amendment, and challenge the Court to modify its doctrine; it could base the Act on a novel constitutional argument; or it could fail to pass the legislation. Given the broader commerce power standards in place after the New Deal decisions, supporters of the Civil Rights Act argued that the public accommodations portion of the bill was indeed within Congress's power to regulate interstate commerce. That is, the activities of local hotels, restaurants, and other public accommodations had "substantial" or "cumulative" effects on interstate commerce. In its report on S. 1732, the Senate Judiciary Committee summarized the bill: "The purpose of S. 1732 is to achieve a peaceful and voluntary settlement of the persistent problem of racial and religious discrimination or segregation by establishments doing business with the general public, and by labor unions and trade associations. . . . Motels, hotels, restaurants, places of amusement and retail and service establishments *substantially affecting interstate commerce individually or cumulatively* would be covered by the bill, as would labor unions or business associations *affecting interstate commerce*" (emphasis added).[18] As the language of the Senate Judiciary Committee report indicates, Congress ultimately rested its authority for passing the public accommodations provisions on the Commerce Clause, and it did so by very explicitly drafting the bill to reflect the Supreme Court's doctrine. In fact, the first section of Title II explains in detail how the establishments covered by the Act affect interstate commerce. The authors of the Civil Rights Act thus considered the Supreme Court's doctrine from *Jones & Laughlin*, *Darby*, and *Wickard* and incorporated it into the legislation.

While Title II was ultimately rooted in the commerce power, the connection between discrimination in places of public accommodation and interstate commerce was neither immediately nor unanimously agreed on. Civil rights groups, the president, and many congressional leaders favored the bill, but there was considerable opposition. The opponents used a combination of policy and philosophical and constitutional arguments. For example, in 1963 a group calling itself the Coordinating Committee for Fundamental American Freedoms distributed a pamphlet, "Unmasking the Civil Rights Bill," written by six members of the House Judiciary Committee (Willis et al. 1963). In the pamphlet, the members argued that the bill had been "railroaded" through the House Judiciary Committee without adequate consideration or debate, that it would violate various rights of Americans, that it would result in unwise policy in numerous policy areas, and that Title II was "illustrative of the total disregard of the Constitution by those who drafted the legislation" (Willis et al. 1963).

The opponents of the bill articulated their objections in Congress as well. In 1963, the chair of the House Judiciary Committee, Emanuel Celler (D-N.Y.), and the senior minority member of the committee, William M. McCulloch (R-Ohio), drafted a version of the bill and pushed it through the Judiciary Committee with bipartisan support (H.R. 7152). The committee passed the bill and drafted a committee report.[19] Included with the majority report in support of the bill were a minority report and numerous statements by individual members against the bill. For example, Representative George Meader (R-Mich.) argued in the House Judiciary Committee Report:

> The Federal Government has been ingenious in finding ways, through interpretation of these broad constitutional phrases to encroach, little by little, over the years, and to establish a precedent here and there, with the result that today the vitality, autonomy, and even the viability of State and local governments and the governmental powers of the people are seriously threatened. . . . One such governmental power utilized to aggrandize the National Government's authority at the expense of the States and the people is the power of Congress, stated in article I, section 8, clause 2, "to regulate commerce with foreign nations and among the several States. . . ."

The opponents made their arguments and used various procedural ploys to try to prevent the bill from passing. In response to the opposition, the supporters of the Civil Rights Act overcame certain political and procedural hurdles, and they counterattacked the opposition's arguments. A subcommittee of the House Judiciary Committee held twenty-two days of hearings from May 8 through August 2 of 1963, with 101 witnesses, and the Senate Commerce Committee and Judiciary Committee held extensive hearings from July 1 through August 2 of 1963 with forty witnesses testifying on the Senate version of the bill (S. 1732). The witnesses included federal officials, law professors, governors, and others, who testified as to the existence and pervasiveness of discrimination, its effect on interstate commerce, and the constitutionality of the regulations.[20] For instance, Pete Rozelle, the commissioner of the National Football League, testified on the effects of racial discrimination on professional football players who had to travel interstate to play league games.

Among the most dramatic testimony was that of Robert F. Kennedy, attorney general of the United States, who argued that Title II was constitutional under Supreme Court precedent and explained how discrimination in places of public accommodation could have "substantial effects" on interstate commerce.[21] The following excerpts from his testimony highlight the centrality of the commerce power in the deliberations over Title II of the Civil Rights Act of 1964:

> *Senator Mike Monroney* (D-Okla.): [M]any of us are worried about the use the interstate commerce clause will have on matters which have been for more than 170 years thought to be within the realm of local control under our dual system of State and Federal Government. [Is] the test whether the line of business has a substantial effect on interstate commerce? Lodgings are covered, if they are public, and transients are served. Does that mean that all lodging houses under your theory of the effect on interstate commerce would be under Federal regulation, regardless of whether the transients that were using the lodgings were intrastate or interstate?
>
> *Attorney General Kennedy*: That is correct. If it is a lodging, a motel, that opens its doors to the general public, then it would be [covered by the Civil Rights Act]. . . . The point I would make, Senator, is that we are not going beyond any principle of the use of the commerce clause that has not already been clearly established, which has been passed in this Congress, and which has been ruled on by the courts. . . .
>
> *Senator Monroney*: I am trying to get it straight. I am not trying to misinterpret you. If the court decisions and all the precedents that you have mentioned mean that a business, no matter how intrastate in its nature, comes under the interstate commerce clause, then we can legislate for other businesses in other fields in addition to the discrimination legislation that is asked for here.
>
> *Attorney General Kennedy*: If the establishment is covered by the commerce clause, then you can regulate. . . .
>
> *Senator Warren Magnuson* (D-Wash.): I think we ought to get this in perspective. Congress doesn't determine what is under the interstate commerce clause. The Constitution and court decisions determine that. [We]

are talking about how far you want to go in a particular field with a bill. [Whether] a business is in interstate commerce or not is a question of the interpretation of the Constitution and of the courts' rules. . . .

Senator Strom Thurmond (D-S.C.): [Wasn't] it true that all of the acts of Congress based on the commerce clause which you mentioned were primarily designed to regulate economic affairs of life and that the basic purpose of this bill is to regulate moral and social affairs?

Attorney General Kennedy: Well, Senator, let me say this: I think that the discrimination that is taking place at the present time is having a very adverse effect on our economy. So I think it is quite clear that under the commerce clause even if it was just on that aspect and even if you get away from the moral aspect—I think it is quite clear that this kind of discrimination had an adverse effect on the economy. I think all you have to do is look at some of the southern communities at the present time and the difficult time that they are having.

Senator Thurmond: And you would base this bill on the economic features rather than the social and moral aspect?

Attorney General Kennedy: I think the other is an extremely important aspect of it that we should keep in mind.

Senator Thurmond: Now how could the denial of services to an individual who has no intention of leaving that state be a burden on interstate commerce?

Attorney General Kennedy: Because we are talking about a cumulative situation here, Senator. It is not just an individual. If this was just an individual situation and there was one restaurant or one motel or one hotel, we wouldn't all be sitting here today. What this is is a general practice, and a practice that has existed for many, many, many years. What we are trying to do is to get at that general practice. The cumulative effect of a number of establishments which take in transients, and some of which would be interstate, some of which would be intrastate—the cumulative effect of all these has a major effect on interstate commerce. That is the theory, and it is a theory that has been borne out in a number of decisions. And I suppose the best known is [*Wickard v. Filburn*], where the man just ran his own wheat. . . .[22]

These excerpts are representative of much other testimony during hearings conducted over the bill, as well as the floor debates in both houses of Congress. A reading through the legislative history demonstrates that the constitutional issue of whether discrimination in public accommodations substantially affects interstate commerce dominated much of the debate and deliberation. Members of Congress collected evidence to show that discrimination in places of public accommodation does "substantially affect" interstate commerce, using the Court language to frame the debate.

After all the hearings and debate over the Civil Rights Act, it was passed by the Senate 76–18 and by the House 289–126, and signed into law by President Johnson on July 2, 1964.[23] Although a majority in Congress and the president were content that they had satisfied the Court's "substantial effects" test, a court challenge was inevitable. After the Act was signed into law, test cases were quickly brought and expedited for review by the Supreme Court, which upheld its constitutionality.

The primary cases upholding Title II of the Civil Rights Act of 1964 were *Katzenbach v. McClung* (1964) and *Heart of Atlanta Motel v. United States* (1964). In those decisions, both unanimous, the Court paid close attention to the congressional hearings before enactment of the statute, and it found that discrimination in places of public accommodation had a real effect on interstate commerce. For example, in *Heart of Atlanta*, the Court stated:

> While the Act as adopted carried no congressional findings the record of its passage through each house is replete with evidence of the burdens that discrimination by race or color places upon interstate commerce [numerous citations to Committee Hearings omitted]. . . . This testimony included the fact that our people have become increasingly mobile with millions of people of all races traveling from State to State; that Negroes in particular have been the subject of discrimination in transient accommodations, having to travel great distances to secure the same; that often they have been unable to obtain accommodations and have had to call upon friends to put them up overnight. . . . These exclusionary practices were found to be nationwide, the Under Secretary of Commerce testifying. . . . This testimony indicated a qualitative as well as quantitative effect on interstate travel by Negroes. The former was the obvious impairment of the Negro traveler's pleasure and convenience that resulted when he continually was uncertain of finding lodging. As for the latter, there was evidence that this uncertainty stemming from racial discrimination had the effect of discouraging travel on the part of a substantial portion of the Negro community. . . . This was the conclusion not only of the Under Secretary of Commerce but also of the Administrator of the Federal Avia-

tion Agency who wrote the Chairman of the Senate Commerce Committee that it was his "belief that air commerce is adversely affected by the denial to a substantial segment of the traveling public of adequate and desegregated public accommodations." We shall not burden this opinion with further details since the voluminous testimony presents overwhelming evidence that discrimination by hotels and motels impedes interstate travel (252–53).

Similarly, the Court in *McClung* was persuaded by the legislative history regarding the effects of discrimination in restaurants on interstate commerce:

The record is replete with testimony of the burdens placed on interstate commerce by racial discrimination in restaurants. A comparison of per capita spending by Negroes in restaurants, theaters, and like establishments indicated less spending, after discounting income differences, in areas where discrimination is widely practiced. This condition, which was especially aggravated in the South, was attributed in the testimony of the Under Secretary of Commerce to racial segregation. See Hearings before the Senate Committee on Commerce on S. 1732, 88th Cong., 1st Sess., 695. This diminutive spending springing from a refusal to serve Negroes and their total loss as customers has, regardless of the absence of direct evidence, a close connection to interstate commerce. The fewer customers a restaurant enjoys the less food it sells and consequently the less it buys. S. Rep. No. 872, 88th Cong., 2d Sess., at 19; Senate Commerce Committee Hearings, at 207. In addition, the Attorney General testified that this type of discrimination imposed "an artificial restriction on the market" and interfered with the flow of merchandise. . . . In addition, there were many references to discriminatory situations causing wide unrest and having a depressant effect on general business conditions in the respective communities. See, e.g., Senate Commerce Committee Hearings, at 623–630, 695–700, 1384–1385 (citations in original) (299–300).

The Court held that the many hearings on the Civil Rights Act gave Congress a rational basis to conclude that discrimination in restaurants and motels could have substantial effects on interstate commerce. In part, the Court accepted the reasoning of those in Congress and the administration that tourism had become a significant portion of the modern economy, and that discrimination in public places of accommodation could have adverse effects on tourism—as well as on minority businessmen and others who travel for their livelihood. While the commerce power seemed a stretch to many as a constitutional basis for the Civil Rights Act, its supporters had worked hard to establish the commercial nature of the activity being regulated and fend off the arguments of the bill's opponents. Although the Court was being deferential to Congress in the civil rights cases, its deference appeared to have been based in large part on Congress's successful efforts to satisfy the Court doctrine. The legislative history of the Civil Rights Act and the Supreme Court decisions upholding Title II of that Act illustrate again the significant interaction between the Court and Congress over the commerce power—each branch showed an astute awareness of, and in a sense deference to, the other. And Title II was drafted and debated in a constitutional context created in part by Supreme Court doctrine.

After the civil rights cases, the "substantial effects" test originally adopted in the New Deal cases eventually became a toothless doctrine under which the Court showed complete deference to Congress, as legal scholars would observe (see, e.g., Epstein 1987). To some, the role of the Court over federalism was simply and properly diminished in a new "constitutional regime" that represented a fundamental shift in constitutional values (see Ackerman 1991; Choper 1980; Nagel 2001). Regardless, the interaction and negotiation between Court and Congress was over time transformed into complete judicial deference to Congress over the matter.

For example, in *Perez v. United States* (1971) the Supreme Court upheld as a legitimate exercise of the commerce power a provision in the federal Consumer Credit Protection Act making "extortionate extension of credit," or loansharking, a federal crime.[24] The statute allowed for federal prosecution of loansharking that was purely local in character. In *Perez*, a loanshark with no connections to interstate commerce was prosecuted for violating the federal law. The Court reasoned that the "loanshark racket provides organized crime with its second most lucrative source of revenue, exacts millions from the pockets of people, coerces its victims into the commission of crimes against properties, and causes the takeover by racketeers of legitimate businesses" (156). Since racketeering was a national problem, and loansharking was an important component of racketeering, loansharking could be regulated under the Commerce Clause. "Where a class of activities is regulated and that class is within the reach of federal power, the courts have no power 'to excise, as trivial, individual instances' of the class" (154). In essence, the Court showed deference to the judgment of Congress that the commerce power extended to purely local activities if they are within a broader class of activities related to interstate commerce. *Perez* helped to solidify the trend, evident since the New Deal, of judicial deference toward Congress and the commerce power.[25]

From Judicial Scrutiny to Deference: Legislating in a Constitutional Context

These historical examples of interaction between the Court and Congress over the meaning of Congress's commerce power and the Tenth Amendment offer important insights into the nature of judicial review in the lawmaking process as well as the evolution of our system of federalism. The process seems to have been a dynamic one in which each institution both reacted to and challenged the other. Congress explored and expanded its commerce power over time, with the Court sometimes allowing and sometimes denying broader exercises of power. For the most part, Congress made real efforts to satisfy the Court by deliberating over constitutional issues and adapting the language of statutes to accommodate the Court's doctrines. Constitutional questions and the threat of judicial review helped to delay passage of the Child Labor Act of 1916 for ten years, and support for federal legislation grew after the Court in 1914 handed down the *Hoke* decision that appeared to support constitutional arguments in favor of the Act. The long road to final passage of the Child Labor Act was paved with substantial constitutional deliberation. Later, even though the Court after the New Deal appeared willing to defer to Congress, lawmakers continued to engage in constitutional deliberation. The lengthy committee hearings, floor debates, and language of Title II of the Civil Rights Act of 1965 illustrate that Congress paid close attention to the constitutional issues involved. Opponents raised constitutional issues, and supporters responded by collecting testimony and other evidence and developing persuasive arguments in favor of constitutionality.

These historical examples help to illustrate how political factors and the threat of judicial review have shaped constitutional debates in Congress over federalism. Table 3.3 summarizes the various conditions that might have influenced the constitutional deliberations examined in this chapter. My summaries of the politics and influence of judicial review are not intended to be a precise or fixed measurement in any quantitative sense, but instead reflect my relative judgment of the legislative histories considered here. In my estimation, the Child Labor Act, the Packers & Stockyards Act, and the Civil Rights Act were all highly salient, invoked a good deal of controversy, and faced substantial opposition—based on partisan preferences as well as influence by

TABLE 3.3 Legislation and Constitutional Deliberation over the Commerce Power

Legislation	Politics of the Legislation	Prospects for Judicial Review	Nature of Constitutional Deliberation
Child Labor Act (1916)	Highly controversial, intense and organized opposition	Uncertain	Serious, Court doctrine used
Packers & Stockyards Act (1921)	Controversial, narrowly focused and intense opposition	Uncertain	Serious, Court doctrine used
Civil Rights Act (1964)	Highly controversial, intense and fairly well organized opposition	Uncertain or judicial deference likely	Serious, Court doctrine used

pressure groups and other outside parties. With regard to the commerce power and federalism, the threat that the Court might exercise judicial review and invalidate these statutes was somewhat uncertain. At the time of the Child Labor Act, the Court had wrestled with the commerce power and upheld some exercises of it, such as the "noxious goods" standard in the "Lottery Case," but it had rejected Congress's ability to regulate manufacturing in *E. C. Knight*. By the time Congress considered the Civil Rights Act in 1964, the Court had shifted its doctrinal approach to analyzing the commerce power. The substantial effects test, and the declaration in *Darby* that the Tenth Amendment is merely a truism, signaled more judicial deference to Congress; however, membership on the Court had changed between the original New Deal legislation and 1964, and the extent of judicial deference was anything but certain. Given a perceived threat that the Court might give teeth to the substantial effects test, members of Congress built a legislative history to satisfy the doctrine.

These examples are not dispositive, but they do suggest how the Supreme Court, judicial review, Congress, and constitutional deliberation are related. Lawmakers in Congress face many obstacles in trying to get their bills passed, and raising constitutional issues might only make it more difficult to get the votes necessary to pass a policy. Because of this reality in Congress, a perceived threat of judicial review over the commerce power can help to shape constitutional debate. This suggests that members of Congress are willing to consider constitutional issues, and that the Court's position on constitutional issues can significantly influence deliberations in Congress by creating an indirect type of bargaining, analogous to that which takes place between presidents and Congress in the shadow of veto threats.

The conventional wisdom by the 1980s was that the Court would "never" strike down an act of Congress for violating the Commerce Clause or the Tenth Amendment. Congress began "federalizing" criminal law by passing a plethora of federal crime statutes, many of which were viewed as permissible under the Commerce Clause (Task Force on Federalization of Criminal Law and Section 1998). Constitutional law professors and bar review courses alike taught law students and state bar applicants that under the modern "substantial effects" test, at least as the Court had applied it since the New Deal, the federal government could regulate just about anything under its commerce power.

Should we expect members of Congress to engage in constitutional deliberation over commerce when conditions change? Are some of these conditions more important than others for motivating and shaping constitutional deliberation? I hypothesize that the lack of judicial scrutiny of the commerce power contributed to less constitutional deliberation over the issue in Congress. In the next chapter, I will examine how federalism was deliberated in Congress in the 1990s, before and after renewed scrutiny by the Rehnquist Court.

FOUR

The Missing Constitution:

Legislating in the Darkness

of Judicial Deference

★

We assumed we had broad power under the Commerce Clause and weren't very concerned about it. . . . It probably is about time to revisit the issue.
—A former chair of the House Judiciary Committee, 1998

For much of the last century, the Court's doctrine and attitudes toward the scope of federal power were somewhat uncertain. With the New Deal cases in the 1930s and 1940s and the civil rights cases in 1965, however, the attitude and doctrine of the Court became more certain and consistent than they had been in previous decades. In essence, the "substantial effects" test, devised and adopted in the New Deal cases, became one of abject judicial deference toward Congress, and over time the Court simply did not scrutinize Congress's exercise of the commerce power. The Court again created a threat and added a degree of uncertainty by striking down a federal statute for violating the commerce power for the first time in sixty years in *United States v. Lopez* in 1994, and by handing down other decisions involving federalism, such as *Printz v. United States* in 1997.[1] In this chapter, I explore whether and how constitutional deliberation in Congress may have been affected by the changing nature of the Supreme Court's decisions—from deference to renewed scrutiny.

Because the threat of judicial review became minimal after the New Deal and civil rights cases and then became more likely again after *Lopez* and other recent Court decisions, an excellent opportunity presents itself to analyze constitutional deliberation over the commerce power and Tenth Amendment in Congress before and after these recent Court decisions. In light of the deferential attitude of the Court toward Congress, did members of Congress continue to deliberate over the commerce power as they did with earlier legislation, such as the Child Labor Act of 1916 and the Civil Rights Act of

1965? Or were they more likely to ignore constitutionality in favor of political and policy considerations? Have the recent Court decisions influenced
congressional behavior and decision making? Asked another way, does the
Court's action, as opposed to inaction, have effects on constitutional deliberation in Congress?

Constitutional Deliberation in Congress before and after the Reemergence of Judicial Scrutiny

To explore the relationship between Court action and constitutional deliberation in Congress, I first examine the history of the relevant legislation: the
Gun Free School Zones Act (GFSZA) in *Lopez* and the Brady Handgun Violence Prevention Act ("Brady Bill") in *Printz*. Next, I briefly review the decisions to discern why the Court invalidated the statutes. I then review the
legislative histories of two other pieces of legislation, the Violence against
Women Act (VAWA), passed the same year as *Lopez*, and the Hate Crimes
Prevention Act ("Hate Crimes Bill"), considered in 1997–98.[2] In developing
the legislative histories, my ultimate goal is to determine whether constitutional issues were raised while the bills were under consideration, and if so the
extent and content of constitutional deliberation. To develop detailed histories of these statutes, I draw upon archival materials, public documents, secondary accounts, and in-depth interviews that I conducted. For some of the
legislation, there is an abundance of material available that details the debate
and history in archives and public documents, and in secondary sources such
as newspapers of record, scholarly journals, and books. These sources often
provide detailed information about the public debate over the legislation in
question, and sometimes insight into behind-the-scenes negotiations that led
to the final passage of legislation. However, because my focus is specifically on
the role that constitutionality may have played in the drafting and consideration of relatively recent laws, these sources alone may not be authoritative as
far as constitutional deliberation is concerned.

Therefore, I also conducted in-depth interviews with members of Congress, congressional staff, and lobbyists who were involved in drafting, negotiating, or considering one or more of the four bills analyzed in this chapter.
Nearly all the interviews were conducted in Washington from 1997 to 1999.[3]
For this book as a whole, I interviewed forty-four lawmaking participants and
others; of those, fourteen were current or former members of Congress,
congressional staff, or lobbyists who took part in the drafting and consider-

ation of one or more of the statutes analyzed in this chapter, and one was a journalist who had covered and written on the statutes and the relevant constitutional issues.[4] Of the fourteen, three were members of Congress (one Republican representative, one Democratic representative, and one Democratic senator) who served or had served on a Judiciary Committee. Six were professional staff members for one of the Judiciary Committees (three in the Senate, three in the House), two were personal staff members (one for a Democratic senator and one for a Republican representative), and three were lobbyists or attorneys for interest groups. The members of Congress, committee staff, and lobbyists were all deeply involved with the drafting, negotiations, and debate over at least one of the statutes—two or more statutes in the case of three members of the Judiciary Committee staff.

The analysis of the legislative histories and interview questions were designed to determine whether constitutionality was raised while each statute was being drafted and considered in Congress; if so, *when* it was raised, by whom, and *why*; and *how seriously* and *substantively* it was debated. In interviewing some of the key figures, I tried to determine whether constitutional issues were raised out of public view, and how seriously they were taken. I first asked respondents to tell me "the story of the bill" in open-ended form. Next, I asked what were the most important factors that led to its passage. I used a semi-structured approach so that I had the flexibility to follow up on respondents' answers with more probing and detailed questions. If they failed to identify or discuss constitutionality without prompting, I asked whether they could recall any discussions about the relevant constitutional issues and followed up with questions about when, where, and by whom they were raised, and how substantive the debates or discussions over constitutional issues were.

To preview the evidence in this chapter, the legislative histories and interviews indicate that the commerce power and Tenth Amendment were not much debated during consideration of the GFSZA and the Brady Bill. The commerce power was mentioned in the debate over VAWA, but not discussed at length. However, the debate over the Hate Crimes Bill involved more extensive deliberation of constitutional issues. To the extent possible, I also try to elucidate possible reasons *why* constitutional issues were or were not raised. I argue that the renewed threat of judicial review has had a significant impact on constitutional deliberation in Congress. Figure 4.1, a continuation of the timeline in chapter 3 (figure 3.1), presents a chronology of major legislation and Supreme Court decisions relevant to the analyses in this chapter.

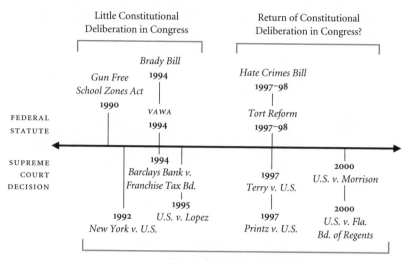

FIGURE 4.1 Commerce Clause–Tenth Amendment Timeline, Continued

Legislating in the Darkness of Judicial Deference:
The Gun Free School Zones Act and the Brady Bill

My goal in this part of the chapter is to identify the conditions that influenced the development of the GFSZA and the Brady Bill, from the initial public policy idea to its consideration and passage. Most importantly, I attempt to establish whether relevant constitutional issues were raised, and if so, the extent to which they affected the debate over the form and substance of the legislation. I submit that potential constitutional problems may have been raised by a few opponents of the legislation, but it is unlikely that they were extensively considered in Congress because, in large part, there was not a realistic threat that the Court would strike down federal legislation for violating the commerce power or the Tenth Amendment.

GUN FREE SCHOOL ZONES ACT

To say that the GFSZA was a noncontroversial bill would be an enormous understatement. There is very little trace of it in public records—no debate on the floor of either house, only one brief hearing, and little coverage by the news media. Almost all the debate, negotiation, and other activity that led to the passage of the GFSZA occurred behind the scenes, in private. Therefore, to build an accurate description of how the GFSZA developed, it is necessary to rely mostly on the interviews I conducted with key staff members, legal counsel, lobbyists, and others who participated in the process when the GFSZA was originally passed in 1990.

A counsel to the Senate Judiciary Committee who played a key role in drafting the GFSZA told me, "It was very uncontroversial. No Senator wanted to stand up *for* guns in schools" (CS1 interview). This statement is representative of those made by respondents regarding the GFSZA. As the counsel's statement helps to illustrate, a vote against the GFSZA could be portrayed as a vote for guns in schools, a position that few, if any, members of Congress would want to be on record for supporting. Consequently, very few objections were raised to the proposed GFSZA, which sailed through the legislative process. According to this legal counsel:

> [W]hen we wrote it, it was just an idea that was partly mine, and partly someone who worked for Senator [Edward] Kennedy [D-Mass.]. . . . And we were just thinking that we wanted to do something in the realm of gun control that we thought could win. And we were sort of kicking around a bunch of ideas, and we thought gee, there was a drug free school zone law, and in Congress we don't generally reinvent the wheel, we just copy good ideas. So why don't we create gun free school zones? So we drafted legislation . . . and got [Representative Ed Feighan (D-Ohio)] to introduce the House version. We introduced the Senate version of the bill—[Senator Herb] Kohl [D-Wis.] did it. . . . So we introduced Gun Free School Zones. Then I believe we stuck it in the 1990 crime bill. And we worked it out on the floor and we made some modifications. I remember that Senator [Phil] Gramm [R-Texas] was holding it up, and we worked it out very late one night. He was holding it up—he was like, I'm not going to let this go through, and we said, "okay fine, go down to the floor and vote against it— we're going to force a vote." And at that point he said, "Well if you make this change and this change we'll accept it." Then, we were not conferees because Kohl at that point was very junior in that 1990 crime bill, but Kennedy was and Democrats controlled both houses, and so we got it into the 1990 crime bill (CS1 interview).

And so the GFSZA was introduced in the House as H.R. 3757 by Representative Feighan on November 20, 1989, and in the Senate as S. 2070 by Senator Kohl on February 5, 1990. Very little action was taken on the bill, however, and by October 1990 it was incorporated into the Crime Control Act of 1990 in the Senate without a recorded vote.[5] The final version of the Act passed in the

Senate by a voice vote, and in the House by a recorded vote of 313–1. The few references to the GFSZA made on the floor of the two chambers indicate that the only topic discussed in any detail was that of public policy. As the Crime Control Act of 1990 was being considered on the floor of the Senate, Senator Kohl spoke in favor of the legislation, in part because it included the GFSZA:

> Mr. President, I rise in support of this consensus anti crime legislation. . . . I am pleased that the conference unanimously accepted S. 2070, my Gun Free School Zones Act of 1990: It responds to a growing problem in America today: The proliferation of firearms in our schools. Indeed, over the past few years we have witnessed a shocking number of attacks against our children as they sat in the classroom and played in the schoolyard.
>
> The National School Safety Center estimates that more than 100,000 students carry guns to school every day, and that more than a quarter of a million students brought a handgun to school at least once in 1987. In New York City alone, school authorities confiscated almost 2,000 weapons from students in 1988. And according to a recent Washington Post article, these incidents are so commonplace that some parents are now dressing their children in bullet-proof vests before sending them off to school. It's a sad and frightening commentary that violence in our schools and on our streets has reached such a level that there's a market for these products.
>
> My home State, Wisconsin, is not immune from this wave of gun violence. Last year, the Milwaukee school system expelled more than a dozen students for weapons violations. And the number of Milwaukee County juveniles charged with handgun possession has doubled over the past 2 years. . . .
>
> To ensure that our school grounds do not become battlegrounds, I introduced the Gun-Free School Zones Act with Edward Feighan of the House Judiciary Committee.
>
> * * *
>
> Mr. President, the widespread support for this proposal underscores its commonsense approach. Already, the National Education Association, the American Association of School Administrators, the National School Boards Association, and the American Academy of Pediatrics have endorsed the legislation. When Congress mandated drug-free school zones in 1984, we declared that our Nation's classrooms deserve special protection. In the same way, this section will help keep the areas around our schools

from becoming sanctuaries for armed criminals and drug gangs. Gun-free school zones are not a panacea, to be sure, but they are an important step toward fighting gun violence and keeping our teachers and children safe.[6]

In Congress, there were only brief statements made in support of the bill on the floor of the two houses of Congress and one brief hearing on the criminal and juvenile justice aspects of the bill in the House Judiciary Committee's Subcommittee on Crime, but there was no testimony or other evidence addressing constitutionality or Congress's power to act. In addition to the public policy at the core of the bill, the legal counsel on the Senate Judiciary Committee claims to have briefly considered adding findings of fact in the original GFSZA stating that the presence of guns in schools has an effect on interstate commerce, and a jurisdiction requirement that the gun be shown to have traveled in interstate commerce:

> The reason we didn't put the jurisdictional requirement in, that is, show that the gun moved in interstate commerce is sort of threefold. One is, we felt that there was enough caselaw and previous congressional gun control statutes that basically made this almost *stare decisis*. That, there was a—essentially that category had been ruled on and you did not need to show it. Two, we thought it was self-evident, because every piece of, every piece of, every gun, virtually every gun moves in interstate commerce in some way shape or form. And parts of the gun are assembled, you know, could be assembled and sort of, the raw materials for the gun come from yet another place, either another state or another country and so we felt like it was sort of self evident, which of course is why of course we think it was a terrible decision by the Supreme Court. The third reason was, and we kicked around the idea of requiring this, we went to Handgun Control and they said, "oh no, no, no, no. We've done so many pieces of legislation where we haven't required this that it would, potentially by putting it in, it might indirectly um suggest that we should have put it in other things. And since it's not necessary anyway, why should you do it?" It was sort of between their argument, which we didn't quite buy, and sort of the sense that it was self-evident.... (CS1 interview)

I pointed out that there was no public record of constitutional deliberation on this score, and I asked why the issue of findings or jurisdictional requirements ever came up in the first place. The Judiciary Committee Counsel responded, "Because we just thought about it as a question of constitutionality—interstate commerce. And we decided that you know, that based on the caselaw, the Supreme Court's interpretation of . . . Supreme Court cases, that we would not lose on this in the Court, and it wasn't even close" (CS1 interview).

As these excerpts illustrate, counsel on the Judiciary Committee and others working on the GFSZA had several discernible reasons for brushing aside concerns over the Commerce Clause. While the issue may have come up in drafting the original bill, it was not taken very seriously because those involved in the legislative process did not believe that the Court would ever strike down a federal statute for violating the commerce power. According to the Judiciary Committee counsel, "you did not need to show it," by which he meant that Congress did not have to explicitly show the connection between the gun regulation and interstate commerce to satisfy the highly deferential Supreme Court doctrine.

Members of Congress and their staffs were not the only participants in the legislative process who were unconcerned about the Court's Commerce Clause jurisprudence. In another interview, the legal counsel from a public interest group based in Washington that advocates stricter gun control laws and works with many members of Congress on gun control legislation put it this way:

See, the problem is, both [the GFSZA and the Brady Bill] became the targets of a new, a rediscovery of states' rights, which was very hard to anticipate jurisprudentially. I mean, there was, there wasn't much of a precursor to *Lopez*, for predicting *Lopez*. Again, the commerce clause, the federal power under the commerce clause was seen to be very, very broad, *Heart of Atlanta*, *Wickard v. Filburn*. I mean, very, very broad. So it would have been very difficult to predict based on the jurisprudence at the time that the statute was passed that it would cause any constitutional controversy at all. I think it's personally understandable why the drafters did not feel it necessary to put findings.

Q. Understandable from a strategic standpoint? In the sense of anticipating Court action?

Well also, there would have been no reason to anticipate constitutional problems. You could ask any constitutional scholar about it they would have said, it's fine. That's another situation in which, when the decision first came down, there was a lot of hand wringing about the possible attack, not only on other gun laws, but federal power generally. (IG1 interview)

Consequently, with bipartisan support for the policy and with little or no reason to be concerned about judicial review of the GFSZA, the bill was passed and signed into law with little debate or deliberation.

The story of the GFSZA shows how a relatively uncontroversial bill was conceived of, drafted, and passed in Congress fairly quickly, without much deliberation over the relevant constitutional issue. The GFSZA did not evoke much debate, and it passed without much objection on any grounds. The legislative process is not always so neat and swift, however. To the contrary, as we have seen in the previous chapter, it is often much more prolonged and inefficient. Thus, it may be that constitutional issues were not much deliberated during consideration of the GFSZA because a threat of judicial review by the Court did not seem imminent. However, there might be another explanation. Perhaps constitutional issues are more likely to be raised with regard to controversial legislation that is considered over a longer period, with more opportunities for opponents of the legislation to raise the issue as a means of defeating it. The story of the Brady Bill provides an opportunity to analyze constitutional deliberation, or a lack of it, under these alternative conditions.

THE BRADY HANDGUN VIOLENCE PREVENTION ACT

The Brady Bill was similar to the GFSZA in that it was also a federal statute concerning gun control and implicating a constitutional issue of federalism that for many decades had not been invoked by the Court to invalidate legislation. In contrast to the GFSZA, however, the Brady Bill was highly controversial, and it was considered over a lengthy period during which the opposition was well organized. These contrasts allow us to compare how the constitutional issues were or were not considered in the drafting of two statutes that involved a similar public policy but different political environments.

To properly analyze the politics behind the Brady Bill and to draw out the contrasts between it and the GFSZA, it is necessary to develop the long history of the bill. The original idea for the Brady Bill arose in the mid-1980s, but the bill did not pass Congress and become a public law until 1993. During those years, opponents of the bill both fought against it and negotiated with supporters to change its form and substance. The history of the Brady Bill will reveal, however, that the Tenth Amendment constitutional issue embedded in the bill was not seriously debated. Table 4.1 summarizes the long legislative timeline for the Brady Bill.

The Brady Bill was conceived in response to the assassination attempt on President Ronald Reagan by John Hinckley Jr. in 1981. The shots from

TABLE 4.1 Legislative Timeline of the Brady Bill

Year	Legislative Action or Event
1981	Assassination attempt on President Ronald Reagan; James Brady permanently disabled
mid-1980s	Sarah Brady and Handgun Control, Inc., mobilize for stricter gun control
1987	Brady Bill introduced in Senate (seven-day waiting period)
1988	House defeats bill, 228–182
1990	James Brady testifies at hearings in both Houses of Congress
	Major law enforcement organizations endorse the bill
	Brady Bill gains 150 sponsors
	House Judiciary Committee passes bill, 27–9
1991	All four living former presidents (Nixon, Ford, Carter, Reagan) endorse the bill
	Key NRA allies in Congress defect and now support the bill
	House Judiciary Committee passes bill, 23–11
	NRA "instant check" alternative introduced in House; defeated, 234–193
	House passes Brady Bill, 239–186
	Senate amends bill (five-day waiting period, development of instant check, mandatory background checks); passes, 67–32
	President George Bush threatens veto
	House passes conference report
	Senate filibusters conference report
1992	President Clinton elected; supports Brady Bill
1993	Public opinion polls show Americans favor Brady Bill and stricter gun control laws
	Brady Bill amended in House (five-day waiting period, instant check, mandatory background checks, sunset provision); Brady Bill passed, 236–198
	Senate filibusters
	Senate finally votes; passes Brady Bill, 63–36
	House passes conference report, 238–187

TABLE 4.1 Continued

Year	Legislative Action or Event
	Senate filibusters conference report
	Senators Mitchell and Dole adopt Brady Bill by unanimous consent in near empty chamber
	President Clinton signs Brady Bill into law, with five-day waiting period, development of instant check system, mandatory checks by CLEOS, sunset provision

Hinckley's handgun also hit Reagan's press secretary, James Brady, and left Brady permanently disabled. James Brady's wife, Sarah Brady, became an active crusader for legislation that would impose a waiting period for gun purchases. She helped to found the public interest group Handgun Control, which began lobbying members of Congress to legislate a waiting period. According to an attorney associated with Handgun Control, "The idea was that a waiting period would give the police the opportunity to do background checks on handgun buyers, and also would serve as a 'cooling off' period" for those wanting to purchase guns in a moment of passion (IG1 interview).

Attempts to regulate guns usually bring out vocal and well-organized groups who either support or oppose gun control. As the newly formed Handgun Control group was working to introduce and gain support for a waiting period, the well-established gun-rights group the National Rifle Association (NRA) was mobilizing to oppose any such legislation. The NRA had traditionally opposed any efforts by Congress toward gun control, citing the "right to bear arms" under the Second Amendment to the Constitution. The Second Amendment has consistently been the NRA's rationale for opposing gun control legislation, even though courts have historically allowed federal regulations of guns that fell short of a ban. By most accounts, the NRA has wielded significant political power over the years, and no major gun control legislation had been passed since the Gun Control Act of 1968. Consequently, even in the wake of the attempted assassination of President Reagan, and the permanent disability that Jim Brady suffered as a result of it, proponents of the Brady Bill faced considerable opposition.

Handgun Control began working with members of Congress who supported its goals. In 1987 Senator Howard Metzenbaum (D-Ohio) introduced the first version of the Brady Bill in the Senate as S. 466. The original Brady Bill would have made anyone wanting to purchase a handgun first wait for seven days. It was during this so-called waiting period that local law enforcement could *voluntarily* do background checks on the prospective gun owner. The Brady Bill gained some support, but the NRA and other opponents of gun control lobbied hard against it. Later in the 100th Congress, the Brady Bill was incorporated into H.R. 5210, the Omnibus Drug Bill, and came up for a vote in the House of Representatives. Representative William McCollum (R-Fla.) introduced an amendment to remove the Brady Bill portions from the Drug Bill. On September 15, 1988, McCollum's amendment passed 228–182; in effect, the Brady Bill had been voted down. Although the vote looked like a victory for gun control opponents, proponents did not give up. In fact, the fight over the Brady Bill would only intensify in the next several years.

By the early 1990s, support for the Brady Bill came from a wide array of organizations and politicians. In 1990 James Brady testified before both houses of Congress in support of the bill that bore his name—a scene made all the more dramatic by his having been brought into the hearings in his wheelchair.[7] As Brady noted in his testimony, most of the major law enforcement organizations in the United States now supported the Brady Bill. From the rank-and-file trade associations like the Fraternal Order of Police to police management groups like the International Association of Chiefs of Police, law enforcement organizations joined to support the Brady Bill along with another bill that would regulate so-called assault weapons. An editorial in the *Washington Post* on September 10, 1990, was entitled "From Police, a Plea to Congress":

> In an open letter advertisement, in petitions carrying more than 40,000 names of supporters and in visits to the Hill for years, representatives of major law enforcement organizations are urging Congress to act now— before adjournment—to stop the spread of deadly assault weapons and to provide a national seven-day cooling-off period for handgun sales. Their plea minces no words.
>
> Noting that far too many officers are being killed, the letter observes that "politicians will rush to the funerals to pay their respects and be photographed with the survivors, but then fail to do anything to prevent the gun violence that threatens all our citizens. . . . The hundreds of thousands of members our organizations represent urge you to enact these

public safety bills now. Yet because of pressure from the gun lobby, there are those among you who are working to defeat or postpone action on these sorely needed measures. . . . Congress now has a clear opportunity to show your constituents that you're serious about winning and serious about standing up for the nation's law enforcement community. Help us stop the domestic arms race. Pass the assault weapon legislation and the Brady bill now (A22).

Police officers at all levels and jurisdictions were urging support for the seven-day waiting period.[8] Their support may have been key to the ultimate success of the Brady Bill. This is the view of the chief counsel to the House Judiciary Committee's Subcommittee on Crime for the five years leading up to the passage of the bill:

Q. What were the most important issues from the conception of it through the passage of it? Who raised them? Why were they important issues?

A. The key to the success of the Brady Bill was the support of law enforcement. That was the turning point in breaking the NRA's stranglehold over that. And for any success of gun control efforts were really back to that day and to the '87, '88, '89 when law enforcement had broke with what until then had been pretty lockstep commonality of interests with the NRA. What broke it was not the Brady Bill itself, but it was cop killer bullets. The NRA was fighting various efforts to regulate, to restrict, ammunition that could pierce body armor. And that caused the break with law enforcement as you can imagine.

Q. Just as a policy disagreement with the NRA?

A. Yea. Yea. Policy-slash-legislative. They tried not to be, there was enacted a cop killer ban, that was called that, that was that, and that's the law now based on how they're made—manufacturing standards. And that fight lasted several years. . . . But it was based over that fight that the cops and the NRA broke ranks, or kind of broke ranks, with the NRA for the first time. And it was that that paved the way for police support of the original Brady Bill. And without that there would not be a Brady Bill. And without police support of ANY gun control effort, it's DOA. So that's one of the reasons why you don't see a whole lot more—you know once the NRA was on the run, why you don't see a whole lot more [gun control] proposals. You know in a Republican Congress you wouldn't get much, but even the

White House and the Democrats have been restrained in proposing things because without the cops with them you're not getting anything, and the cops aren't much beyond Brady and assault weapons. . . . But that, in thinking about that over that over the years, I think that was key. (cs2 interview)

Journalistic accounts as well as reflections from those involved in the making of the Brady Bill indicate a growing broad-based support for the bill (as well as other gun control measures) and a weakening of the forces that had so successfully resisted gun control for many years. In 1990 the Brady Bill gained a total of 150 sponsors, and it passed in the House Judiciary Committee by a vote of 27–9. Moreover, former Presidents Nixon, Ford, and Carter had publicly endorsed the bill, and in 1991 former President Ronald Reagan also came out in support of the bill, calling it "just plain common sense."[9] Nonetheless, the NRA continued to fight passage; the chief lobbyist for the NRA, James Jay Baker, responded to Reagan's endorsement, "The former president doesn't sign bills and he doesn't veto them."[10] Even as the NRA stood firm, the Brady Bill was gaining support from both Democratic and Republican members of Congress who had been long-time opponents of gun control and allies of the NRA. On April 23, 1991, the House Judiciary Committee once again passed the Brady Bill, this time by a vote of 23–11.[11]

As support grew and the House Judiciary Committee again approved the Brady Bill, the NRA and its allies in Congress changed tactics somewhat. The NRA still maintained that the waiting period in the Brady Bill was an unconstitutional infringement of law-abiding citizens' Second Amendment right to bear arms—a consistent argument of gun control opponents for years. However, by 1991 the NRA also argued that it supported the policy objective of keeping guns out of the hands of criminals, but that there were less intrusive policy means of accomplishing that goal. The NRA now argued for a national "instant check" system, and as the Brady Bill was coming to a vote in the House of Representatives, Representative Harley Staggers Jr. (D-W.Va.) introduced an alternative bill that according to the *Washington Post* "would have created a nationwide hotline at gun stores to enable instant checks in the backgrounds of prospective buyers."[12] On May 5, 1991, however, the alternative backed by the NRA failed in the House by a vote of 234–193, and on May 8, 1991, the Brady Bill passed the full House by a vote of 239–186.

As much as the tide seemed to be turning and support for the Brady Bill to be growing, there remained considerable opposition to the simple seven-day waiting period in the Senate. In June 1991 the Senate majority leader, George Mitchell (D-Me.), together with the Senate minority leader Bob Dole (R-Kan.) and Senators Al Gore (D-Tenn.) and Herb Kohl (D-Wis.), drafted a compromise plan, which according to the *Washington Post* "add[ed] to the House-passed bill a mandatory criminal records check that is tied to federal incentives for states to improve their records systems."[13] The compromise "split the difference between the seven-day waiting period approved by the House last month and a computerized instant check plan sought by the National Rifle Assn. as a substitute."[14]

And thus, the waiting period imposed by the Brady Bill was transformed by the Senate into one of five days, during which state and local law enforcement officers would be *required* to do background checks on prospective gun buyers for a temporary period, two to five years, until the attorney general of the United States could develop a national computer system that would do instant checks on the criminal backgrounds of gun buyers. This was a significant development in the evolution of the Brady Bill: not only did it mark the birth of mandatory background checks by state and local officials, but the alternative was supported by many opponents of the original Brady Bill. The compromise version was attached to the Omnibus Crime Bill of 1991 in the Senate, where it passed by a vote of 67–32. The two houses of Congress had to resolve their differences in conference committee. With a presidential veto threatened, the House passed the conference committee version, but Senate Republicans filibustered, objecting to various provisions in the compromise crime bill and preventing a final Senate vote.

The end of 1992 and the 102d Congress brought several more important changes. President Bill Clinton took office at the beginning of 1993, and he made numerous public statements in support of the Brady Bill. Moreover, according to the *Los Angeles Times,* a Harris Poll showed "for the first time a majority of Americans—52%—favor not just the registration requirements contained in the Brady Bill, but 'a federal law banning the ownership of all handguns.'"[15] The opponents of the Brady Bill seemed to be fighting a losing battle.

In the fall of 1993 everything came together for the supporters of the Brady Bill, albeit not exactly as they had foreseen over six years earlier. The bill once again worked its way through the legislative process. On October 29, 1993, by a vote of 10–3, the House Judiciary Committee's Subcommittee on Crime approved H.R. 1025, a version of the bill that included a five-day waiting period and directed the Department of Justice to develop an instant check system that would identify criminals, the mentally ill, and others and prevent them from purchasing handguns, rifles, or shotguns; the waiting period would be phased out when the instant check system was deemed 80 percent effective.[16] On November 11, 1993, the full House debated and voted on H.R. 1025. The full House passed several amendments, modifying H.R. 1025 further. The key modification came in amendment A002, offered by Representative George Gekas (R-Pa.). The Gekas amendment added a "sunset" provision that would automatically eliminate the waiting period after five years, during which the Department of Justice would be required to develop a national instant check system. The amendment passed the House 238–189, and then the newly modified Brady Bill passed 236–198. The bill was then sent to the Senate, where it had faced the strongest opposition and where it had been killed in previous years.

Once again, opponents of the Brady Bill fought back. On November 19, 1993, supporters in the Senate tried to force a vote, but opponents filibustered. According to *The Washington Post*:

> Voting 57 to 41, the Senate fell three votes short of the 60 necessary to force passage of the handgun bill. . . . An earlier attempt to break the impasse also failed by three votes, and after nine hours of arm-twisting by Democratic leaders and Clinton administration officials failed to switch a single vote. * * * [The Senate] rejected, 54–45, a proposal strongly backed by the National Rifle Association to preempt state or local waiting periods, some of them far tougher than the proposed national rules. As threatened, this triggered a filibuster by Republican NRA supporters and a need on the part of the bill's supporters to produce 60 votes for passage. * * * Nine Republicans, mostly moderates, joined all but seven southern and western Democrats in voting to end the stalling tactics and pass the bill.[17]

The negotiations on November 19 failed, but the bill was not dead yet. Negotiations continued into Saturday, November 20. According to newspaper accounts and interviews that I conducted with various people involved in the final passage of the Brady Bill, the pressure to pass some form of bill was "at an all time high"; with the pressure and change in positions, the Senate ended the filibuster on November 20 and passed the newly modified version, 63–36.[18] Sixteen Republicans and forty-seven Democrats voted in favor of the bill, and twenty-eight Republicans and eight Democrats voted against it.

The conference committee agreed on a final version quickly and sent a conference report on H.R. 1025 to the House and Senate the following Monday, November 22. The conference report dropped key modifications made by the Senate. The House moved quickly and approved the conference report 238–187. In the Senate, however, the Republican minority leader, Bob Dole, "angrily blocked a preliminary move to pass the legislation [on Monday, November 22] and served notice that he would stop it again [the following day]. 'What we got was zippo, zero,' he said."[19] Thus, the Republicans led another filibuster to kill the legislation by preventing it from coming to a vote. Once again, it looked as if the opposition had prevailed. Would Brady ever pass?

After a long and dramatic legislative road, the Brady Bill would indeed pass. The final step would be notably less dramatic, however. The *New York Times* described the events of November 24—the Wednesday before Thanksgiving:

> After days of personal animus and futile backroom dealing, Republicans backed down without much to show for their efforts. The bill passed without debate, with only three Senators sitting in a chamber emptied by the Thanksgiving holiday.
>
> As Vice President Al Gore and Mark Hatfield, an Oregon Republican who supported the bill, watched, the two Senate leaders, Bob Dole of Kansas and George J. Mitchell of Maine, pronounced the measure adopted by unanimous consent. That is a parliamentary device allowing the leaders to pass the legislation themselves by voice vote after ascertaining that no senator would object.
>
> "All of us are happy to have this issue put behind us," Mr. Dole said. "After a long, long, hard fight, Jim Brady has won."[20]

The final version of the Brady Bill included the statutory requirement that states must carry out the federal policy of conducting background checks. The Supreme Court, in *Printz v. U.S.* (1997), would ultimately determine that this requirement raised a question of federalism and violated the Tenth Amendment. However, the story of the Brady Bill as it unfolded in public does not indicate that members of Congress considered the relevant constitutional issue. Thus, it is necessary to look deeper into the history of the bill to determine if the Tenth Amendment was raised and debated, and why or why not.

A long-time counsel to the House Judiciary Committee told me that a few staff members who were states' rights proponents may have raised states rights in a general way, but the Tenth Amendment was "not an issue during the drafting of the Brady Bill" (CS3 interview). As the debate on the floors of both houses of Congress indicates, both the supporters and the opponents of the Brady Bill focused on policy arguments. The proponents cited statistics and examples of gun violence in America. The following statement by Senator Edward Kennedy (D-Mass.) on the floor of the Senate is typical:

> We face an epidemic of violence in this country, and it is fueled by the promiscuous availability of firearms. The statistics are shocking: Every year, more than 24,000 Americans are killed with handguns. Over half a million violent crimes are committed each year by individuals armed with handguns. Every 2 minutes, a handgun causes an injury. . . . Behind each statistic is a human tragedy. A young child killed or maimed as a bystander in a schoolyard dispute. A mother shot dead as she drives home from work. A shopkeeper struck down in an armed robbery. Congress' failure to act in the face of this carnage is inexcusable. Perhaps the most horrifying aspect of gun-related violence is its impact on children. Firearms are the second leading cause of death for the young, second only to automobile crashes. Every day in America, 12 children are killed with guns. . . . Firearms kill more teenagers than cancer, heart disease, and all other natural causes combined. Among young people 15 to 24 years old, one in four deaths are by firearms. . . . At the heart of the problem is the ease with which teenagers and young adults can acquire handguns. The Brady bill will reduce handgun violence in two important ways. First, it will stop thousands of illegal handgun purchases by providing law enforcement with a window of opportunity to conduct background checks on would-be purchasers. This step will help keep guns out of the hands of felons, minors, those with a history of mental illness, and others who should not possess these lethal weapons. It will also reduce the number of shootings by providing a cooling off period for potential purchasers who are inclined to commit violent acts in the heat of the moment.[21]

As Senator Kennedy's statement shows, the focus was on the level of gun violence in the United States, the need for Congress to act, and the policy benefits of the Brady Bill.

Although, as I have argued, it might make sense for *supporters* of the bill not to have raised potential constitutional problems, it is more surprising that the problems went unaddressed by opponents, most of whom were sympathetic to the NRA. Instead, they mostly argued that the Brady Bill amounted to "bad" or "unnecessary" policy. The following statement by Representative William McCollum (R-Fla.) is typical:

I am opposed to the Brady bill, the waiting period bill today, for two reasons. One, it is unnecessary; two, it is simply symbolic and a distraction from the real issue we ought to be getting at to address the violent crime crisis in America. The 5-day waiting period in this bill is unnecessary for the simple reason that you can do in 5 minutes, or certainly in 5 hours, in 1 day, the amount of check that you can do with this waiting period to find out if somebody is a felon going to try to purchase a gun from a gun dealer. We have the ability to check the names today through the NCIC system throughout the Nation, through the police systems that are already set up. We do not have to wait for an instant check to find that out. We do need to improve the records. . . . So it is unnecessary. But worst of all, it is symbolic, in the sense that it is conceded by most people not to be the real answer. Too many people on the other side of the aisle in the Democrat Party believe that taking guns off the street is the answer to violent crime. Mr. Chairman, that is not the answer. The answer is to take the violent criminal off the street, lock him up, and throw away the key.[22]

The opponents of the Brady Bill did not rely on the Tenth Amendment to oppose the legislation. That is not to say that the Constitution was ignored altogether. As the NRA and its supporters almost always do in opposition to gun control proposals, some members of Congress argued that the Brady Bill violated the Second Amendment right to bear arms, but even they usually blended the Second Amendment argument with the policy arguments. Representative Bill Sarpalius (D-Texas) did so on the floor of the House:

[T]his amendment has bothered me, the Brady bill, for quite some time because I feel very strongly that it goes against the very belief of the Second Amendment. And I contacted the Archives, and I asked for some research work on the debate that was said at that time when Samuel Adams made the motion for that particular amendment. During that debate it was made clear that every American citizen should have the right to own and bear their own arms, to protect themselves. Now we can pass tough gun control laws. Look at which city has the toughest gun control laws in the country. It is this one, Washington, D.C. But what city has more murders than any other city? It is this one, Washington, D.C. If we are going to pass tough gun control laws to prevent people from killing people, why do we not look at passing laws to outlaw knives, or hammers or other weapons?[23]

The opponents of gun control saw the public policy dimension as intertwined with the Second Amendment. There are indeed multiple views about the constitutionality of gun regulations under the Second Amendment.[24] However, the provisions of the Brady Bill that the Court struck down in *Printz*, those regarding background checks, were not held to be in violation of the Second Amendment.

While the Tenth Amendment was not debated at any detectable length, there was at least one reason why members might have been expected to consider it. Unlike the commerce power involved in the GFSZA, the Tenth Amendment at issue in the Brady Bill was the subject of recent Supreme Court precedent. In *New York v. United States* (1992), the Court invalidated on Tenth Amendment grounds a federal regulatory scheme governing the disposal of nuclear waste by the states. The *New York* decision was handed down one year after mandatory gun checks were originally introduced in Congress, but two years before the Brady Bill was passed. And so with such recent precedent seeming to create problems for the Brady Bill, why does it appear that no one raised it?

According to those I interviewed, the *New York* case was not raised for four reasons. First, the decision seemed minor and narrow. Second, it appeared to be an anomaly, and nobody believed that the Court would become active in Tenth Amendment or other federalism jurisprudence. Third, it had taken years of hard work and compromises to get the votes needed to pass the Brady Bill, and supporters did not want to raise any new obstacles that might cause defections. Finally, the NRA and other opponents of the original Brady Bill were in a precarious position because they were the ones who suggested the mandatory background checks in the first place.

The first two reasons stem from the nature of the Supreme Court decision. A former counsel to the Senate Judiciary Committee who now is a law professor claims that *New York* was seen as a "minor case" at the time, involving a "complicated regulatory scheme that most law school professors did not even bother teaching" (CS4 interview). Most people involved in the consideration of the Brady Bill were either unaware of the *New York* decision or simply did not think it was anything to be concerned about. In the minds of the few who even bothered paying attention to it, the decision was a proverbial "blip on the map." Another staff member for the House Judiciary Committee told me that some "people were aware . . . of *New York*," but that "there was no reason to think that, hey, there hadn't been any Tenth Amendment jurisprudence in two hundred years. Now there's this case, this is just likely to be a blip, you know, an anomaly, as it is a trend in a new line of cases" (CS2 interview).

This leads to the last two reasons why the *New York* decision did not cause members of Congress to raise the Tenth Amendment, reasons that are more political in nature. It had taken such a long time and so many compromises to get to the point where the Brady Bill was on the verge of passing, supporters did not want to jeopardize passage of the bill by raising any new hurdles, and it was not clear how much damage the *New York* precedent might actually cause. An official at Handgun Control contended that the Supreme Court's recent federalism decisions were "very hard to anticipate jurisprudentially," and told me:

> [O]ne of the reasons why we were not all that concerned about this constitutional issue is because we felt that the worse that could happen is that the mandatory check would be struck down, that Brady as a whole would survive. And we would basically be in the position we were when we just had the waiting period bill, which we thought was fine. So there really was—what's the downside risk of . . . ? We debated internally, what are we going to do about this mandatory check? Should we eliminate it then risk all these people who had committed themselves to this bill saying, you took out the most important thing! You took out the background check provision! That's what I wanted in this bill so I can't support it. That was an extreme political risk. Versus, well, what is the ultimate downside if the *New York* case is held to apply to Brady, and the mandatory check provision is unconstitutional. And we did an analysis and determined that the rest of the bill would survive. And that's what happened. The NRA of course, challenged the mandatory check provision on Tenth Amendment grounds hoping to bring the entire bill down, and they failed (IG1 interview).

And in an interview with a senator who originally sponsored the Brady Bill in 1987, I asked whether federalism issues were raised in light of the recent Court decision. He responded, "To the best of my recollection, they were not. We were fighting to get votes. I don't think anybody said, well, we better not put this in because the Supreme Court might not look favorably upon it. I never heard that kind of comment. I think the arguments always were how do we pick up one more or two more votes" (MC1 interview). And so although there was a question of how damaging the *New York* case might be to portions of the Brady Bill, whatever risk the Supreme Court posed was minor when weighed against the difficulty of winning a majority of votes for the bill.

As for the possibility that opponents of Brady would use the *New York* holding as an argument against the bill, the problem for them was that the holding applied most clearly to the mandatory background checks—a provision added to the bill midway through the process by opponents of the original waiting period, and a provision supported by the NRA. And so it would have been difficult for the NRA to now go to its supporters in Congress and ask them to oppose a provision that they had earlier worked to add—especially for what must have seemed to many lawmakers a minor and somewhat technical part of the bill.[25]

Turning on the Light: United States v. Lopez *and* Printz v. United States

Although members of Congress did not expect it, the Supreme Court struck down both the GFSZA and the Brady Bill. In *United States v. Lopez* (1995) the Court declared that the GFSZA exceeded Congress's commerce powers, and in *Printz v. United States* (1997) the Court declared that the mandatory background checks of the Brady Bill violated state sovereignty under the Tenth Amendment. The decisions are noteworthy because they marked a change from the deference the Court had shown to Congress for decades.

UNITED STATES V. LOPEZ

In *Lopez* the Court considered a constitutional challenge to the GFSZA. Recall that the Act defined school zones as the "grounds" of any public, private or parochial school, or as the area within "a distance of 1000 feet from the grounds of a . . . school." Under the Act it was illegal "for any individual knowingly to possess a firearm at a place that the individual knows, or has reasonable cause to believe, is a school zone." The Act was auspiciously passed pursuant to Congress's commerce power. Lopez, who had been convicted under the Act, argued that possessing a gun on school grounds was neither interstate nor commercial and therefore was outside the scope of the commerce power.

Writing for the majority in a 5–4 decision, Chief Justice Rehnquist found that mere possession within a single state cannot be considered interstate commerce. Rehnquist analyzed precedent, and held that under the Commerce Clause, Congress could only do the following:

1. regulate the use of the channels of interstate commerce,
2. regulate and protect the instrumentalities of interstate commerce, or persons or things in interstate commerce, even though the threat may come only from intrastate activities, and
3. regulate those activities having a substantial relation to interstate commerce. (*Lopez*, 1995, 1634)

Rehnquist reasoned that the only category under which the Gun Free School Zones Act could possibly be analyzed was the third—and that therefore the dispositive question was whether the regulated activity bore a "substantial relation to interstate commerce." He concluded that possessing a gun within a single state could only be found to substantially affect interstate commerce if the Court were to "pile inference upon inference" (1634). In the end, "The possession of a gun in a local school zone is in no sense an economic activity that might, through repetition elsewhere, substantially affect any sort of interstate commerce" (1634).

The Court's departure from a seemingly well established practice of showing deference to Congress over the commerce power was a defining moment for the Rehnquist Court. *Lopez* is *the* key federalism case because it establishes for the first time in sixty years that the Court is willing to find limits to Congress's commerce power, thus reinforcing the concept of enumerated powers and the notion that even with a broad commerce clause doctrine, some powers are reserved to the states. *Lopez* does not stand alone for this proposition, however. The Rehnquist Court has handed down other important cases involving federalism, including *Printz*.

PRINTZ V. UNITED STATES

Other than the commerce power, one of the most important federalism provisions in the Constitution is the Tenth Amendment. Under the logic of the Constitution, the Tenth Amendment is always a backdrop for Commerce Clause decisions, as well as for the other enumerated powers, because if Congress has not been granted a power under Article I of the Constitution, the Tenth Amendment explicitly reserves that power to "the states, respectively, or to the people." While the Tenth Amendment may have existed in the background of *Lopez*, it was at the fore in *Printz v. United States* (1997).

In *Printz*, the Court struck down provisions of the Brady Handgun Violence Prevention Act of 1993, for violating state autonomy guaranteed by the Tenth Amendment and exceeding the powers enumerated in Article I.[26] The Brady Bill required state and local law enforcement officers to conduct background checks, as defined by the federal statute. Congress did not provide funding for its regulatory scheme, and law enforcement officers in Arizona brought a lawsuit to have the law declared unconstitutional. In a 5–4 opinion, the Supreme Court reaffirmed the Tenth Amendment principles that it had set forth in *New York v. United States* just five years earlier: "We held in *New York* that Congress cannot compel the States to enact or enforce a federal regulatory program. Today we hold that Congress cannot circumvent that prohibition by conscripting the State's officers directly. The federal government may neither issue directives requiring the States to address particular problems, nor command the States' officers, or those of their political subdivisions, to administer or enforce a federal regulatory program" (944). *Printz* thus invalidated those provisions of the Brady Bill that required states to conduct background checks on prospective gun owners.

Lopez and *Printz* indicate that the Rehnquist Court takes seriously the notions of limited federal powers and state sovereignty. That it does is made all the more clear by a wave of other Supreme Court cases that have struck down federal legislation for violating federalism principles under the commerce power, strengthened sovereign immunity doctrine derived from the Tenth and Eleventh Amendments, and more narrowly circumscribed Section 5 of the Fourteenth Amendment.[27] Until these cases were decided, there was little reason for Congress to fear judicial review based on federalism principles. In addition, before these decisions a number of scholars had provided theoretical justifications for the absence of judicial scrutiny over federalism (e.g., Ackerman 1991; Choper 1980; Wechsler 1954).

It is important to note that although the Rehnquist Court has shown a renewed willingness to invalidate federal legislation on federalism grounds, the Court has also refused federalism challenges to several pieces of federal legislation (see Clayton 1999, 174). For instance, only a few days after *Lopez* was handed down in 1995, the Court rejected a commerce clause challenge to the federal Racketeer Influenced and Corrupt Organizations Act (RICO) in *U.S. v. Robertson*. In a per curiam opinion, the Court restated the broad reach of Congress's commerce power: "The 'affecting commerce' test was developed in our jurisprudence to define the extent of Congress's power over purely intrastate commercial activities that nonetheless have substantial interstate effects . . ." and "a corporation is generally engaged 'in commerce'" when it is itself "directly engaged in the production, distribution, or acquisition of goods and services in interstate commerce" (671). And two years later, in *Terry v. Reno* (1997), the Court rejected without comment a commerce clause challenge to Freedom of Access to [Abortion] Clinics Entrances Act of 1994. With respect to state autonomy and the Tenth Amendment, the Court invalidated state term limits on federal elected officials in *U.S. Term Limits, Inc. v. Thornton* (1995), rejecting the state's argument that the Tenth Amendment principles of dual sovereignty allowed states to add qualifications for candidates for federal office. And in *Barclays Bank v. Franchise Tax Bd.* (1994), the Court upheld a California corporate tax scheme that had been challenged for unconstitutionally interfering with interstate commerce, but the Court explicitly allowed for federal preemption of the state tax under Congress's commerce power. Given the Court's willingness to uphold some federal legislation and exercises of federal power while rejecting others, the renewed scrutiny by the Court may indicate that we are in the midst of another period of judicial dualism (see McCloskey 1960). The question now is: What impact have the federalism cases and renewed judicial scrutiny and dualism had on lawmaking, and what impact are they likely to have in the future?

Legislating in the Light of Renewed Scrutiny and Dualism: VAWA and the Hate Crimes Bill

A search of the *Congressional Record* for the use of key federalism terms indicates an increase in the attention paid to the issue in Congress. Figure 4.2 shows the results of an electronic search for the number of records in the *Congressional Record* with the terms, "Enumerated Power," "Tenth Amendment," "Federalism," and "Article I Section 8." In the 101st Congress (1989–90), only four records contain the phrase "enumerated power." But the electronic search yielded over thirty records containing that phrase in each Congress from 1995 through 1999. As figure 4.2 illustrates, the same trend holds true for the other search terms. The results indicate that during the 1990s, members of Congress paid increasing attention to constitutional issues of federalism.

To connect the increased attention paid to federalism in Congress with the Court decisions, I now turn to two pieces of legislation considered in Congress immediately before and after *Lopez* and *Printz*. The Violence against Women Act (VAWA) was passed in 1994, just before *Lopez*, and the Hate Crimes Prevention Act of 1997–98 (Hate Crimes Bill) was considered in both houses in the wake of *Lopez*, *Printz*, and other federalism decisions. These statutes address similar public policy and federalism issues.

THE VIOLENCE AGAINST WOMEN ACT

The story of VAWA begins in 1990 and culminates when it was passed as part of the Violent Crime Control Act of 1994, a massive federal criminal law and justice statute.[28] Fortunately, the legislative history of VAWA has been developed in detail, particularly in a law journal article by Victoria Nourse (1996). Professor Nourse was counsel to the Senate Judiciary Committee and played

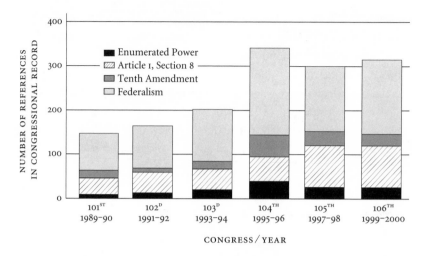

FIGURE 4.2 Federalism References in Congressional Record in Successive Congresses

an important role in drafting VAWA. Her article on the history of the civil rights provisions of VAWA also addresses the constitutional issues raised by the bill. In addition to Nourse's article, I draw upon other secondary sources and interviews that I conducted with those involved in drafting and debating VAWA.

According to an attorney who worked for the Senate Judiciary Committee at that time, Senator Joseph Biden (D-Del.), the chair of the Senate Judiciary Committee, instructed staff members that he wanted to introduce crime legislation dealing with rape, domestic violence, and other crimes against women (CS4 interview). There were two original purposes: politically, Senator Biden wanted Democrats to have the "crime issue" on their side and shore up the support of women's groups, an important Democratic constituency, going into the national elections in 1992; on the public policy side, he was interested in protecting women who were victims of violence in situations where state laws failed to do so (CS4 interview).

Most provisions of VAWA fell into one of two substantive categories: criminal law, and civil rights or remedial.[29] VAWA provided federal causes of action, both criminal and civil, for certain violent acts against women, such as domestic abuse and stalking. The civil rights provisions were controversial from the beginning (Nourse 1996, 3, 16). They were conceived under a theory that violence can be discrimination, and with the goal of providing women an alternative forum for redressing injuries (Nourse 1996, 3). Sponsors of the bill "acknowledged, early on, that the touchstone of a civil rights remedy is its ability to redress the failures of State law" (Nourse 1996, 3). Nourse summarizes the focus of the debate as follows:

> [T]he Committee reports and hearings focus on law as much as personal harm. . . . In many ways, the story told was one of law veiled by the idea of relationship, a law that perceived "marital disputes" where there were felonies; that refused to see force as force as long as it was tied to an acquaintance. . . . After decades of state law reform, "it [was] still easier to convict a car thief than a rapist [and] authorities [were] more likely to arrest a man for a parking ticket than for beating his wife. . . ."[30]

Despite this foundation, the analogy to existing civil rights protections would leave many unconvinced. Unlike the racially-motivated violence first outlawed by Congress in the Reconstruction era, violence perpetrated against women did not seem primarily conspiratorial, widely identified with organized political movements, or the product of publicly institutionalized slavery. Compared to America's shameful history of racial discrimination, the critics urged, violence against women seemed far less political and far more personal; the product of private relationships, not public discrimination (1996, 3–4).

This summary of the controversy around VAWA indicates that much of the debate involved the political and policy elements surrounding civil rights claims, and many opponents of VAWA opposed the civil rights provisions on the grounds that violence against women should not be considered a civil rights issue.[31] The Senate committee hearings, for instance, were dominated by testimony from female victims of violence and about the legal hurdles that women faced under state laws (see Nourse 1996, 9).

Although the focus of opposition to VAWA was on the expansion of civil rights, some members raised a potential commerce power problem, although constitutionality was "not very central" to the debate over VAWA (CS4 interview). There were several factors that apparently gave rise to a constitutional awareness. According to counsel for the Senate Judiciary Committee, "VAWA was controversial, so people were looking for things" (CS4 interview). A few opponents of the bill raised the constitutional arguments as one justification for opposition, and yet they did not have caselaw on their side. In the early 1990s, as VAWA was being considered, the Court's commerce power jurisprudence still appeared to be one of deference to Congress. Consequently, opponents of VAWA had to make broad states' rights arguments grounded more in philosophy than in any real threat posed by the Court. As one counsel to the House Judiciary Committee Counsel told me, some members were "adamant about a sort of philosophical federalism based opposition to sort of federalizing all these VAWA cases against women" (CS2 interview).

The constitutional problems could not be ignored by supporters of VAWA, and not only because the problems were raised by the opposition in Congress. There was also evidence that some judges were opposed to VAWA. The Conference of Chief Justices of State Supreme Courts voted to oppose the bill, and of particular note, Chief Justice William Rehnquist had made several public statements against the expansion of federal law that might increase levels of litigation in federal courts (see Maloney 1996; Nourse 1996). Rehnquist vocally opposed federalizing family law and domestic disputes.[32] However, the opposition posed by Rehnquist and other judges appeared to the committee staff to be focused on judicial caseloads, not constitutionality (see Nourse 1996, 16). And finally, some in Congress may have been aware that *Lopez* was coming down the pike; the Fifth Circuit had already declared the GFSZA unconstitutional, and oral arguments were scheduled to be heard on election day, 1994. Still, counsel for the Senate Judiciary Committee was "not aware of *Lopez* at the time," and had she been, "it would not have been [her] first priority" (CS4).

This all created some minor concern in Congress about the constitutional issue. The drafters of VAWA tried to make the bill conform to precedent, but as one of the key architects of the law told me, "Most staffers did not see a federalism problem. They knew that historically the Court had been deferential to Congress on these issues" (CS4 interview). The safe constitutional strategy, to the extent that there was a strategy, seemed to be to mirror other statutes that had been upheld by the Court. Specifically, the drafters looked to civil rights laws written since the Court upheld the Civil Rights Act of 1964, and therefore they included factual findings that indicated the extent of violence against women in the country. [33] One such finding was that almost "50 percent of rape victims lose their jobs or are forced to quit because of the crime's severity. . . ."[34] The drafters believed that if they showed evidence of a national problem and some connection to economic effects, it was "well settled" that the Court would uphold the Act (CS4 interview). The civil rights provisions of VAWA did not include a jurisdictional statement based on the commerce power, although the criminal provisions did. In the end, there was more attention paid to the constitutional issue in the debate over VAWA than in the debates over GFSZA and the Brady Bill, but only marginally so.

THE HATE CRIMES PREVENTION ACT

The Hate Crimes Bill raises concerns similar to those raised by VAWA. In response to the brutal murder of James Byrd by white supremacists in Texas, the House Judiciary Committee held hearings on H.R. 3081 on July 22, 1998, and the Senate Judiciary Committee held hearings on S. 1529 on July 8, 1998. The proposed Hate Crimes Bill would "enhance Federal enforcement of hate crimes." There is already a federal statute that punishes certain hate crimes, but only if the victim fits into one of six "federally protected areas."[35] The proposed Hate Crimes Bill would do away with the protected areas requirement and open up federal jurisdiction over hate crimes in other ways.

Like VAWA, the Hate Crimes Bill has been somewhat controversial on public policy grounds. Much of the opposition to the Hate Crimes Bill has come from conservative Republicans, who gained a majority in both Houses of Congress in 1994—making the composition of Congress different from when VAWA passed before the 1994 election. And by 1998 there existed a cluster of Supreme Court constitutional-federalism cases, including *Lopez* on the commerce power. I observed the House Judiciary Committee's hearings on the bill, July 22, 1998, and I interviewed several of the committee's counsel about the hearings that day and the day after. There is no doubt that the interstate commerce clause was on the minds of Republicans, Democrats, and witnesses alike.

The Hate Crimes Bill, whether it ultimately becomes law or not, has clearly been drafted to reflect the language of the majority opinion in *Lopez*—unlike VAWA, which was drafted and passed before *Lopez*. Judiciary Committee staff were well aware of the language of *Lopez* and of the federalism attitudes of the five-Justice majority on the Court. In Section 2 of H.R. 3081, Congress makes findings that hate crimes are a national problem and that they have an effect on interstate commerce, as it did in the 1994 amendment to the GFSZA and in the first section of VAWA. But in the Hate Crimes Bill, Congress has done even more to address the commerce power issue. Section 4(B) of H.R. 3081 required, among other things, the following: "(i) in connection with the offense, the defendant or victim travels in interstate or foreign commerce, uses a facility or instrumentality of interstate commerce of interstate or foreign commerce, or engages in any activity affecting interstate or foreign commerce; or (ii) the offense is in or affects interstate or foreign commerce." This language is strikingly reflective of the majority opinion in *Lopez*.

The hearing of the House Judiciary Committee on July 22 consisted of two panels that took most of the day. The first was composed of the testimony of

Bill Lann Lee, at the time the acting assistant attorney general for the Civil Rights Division of the Department of Justice. He testified as to his general desire for expanding federal hate crimes law, but he also specifically addressed the Commerce Clause. He argued that the "interstate commerce element contained in [H.R. 3081] would ensure that federal prosecutions for hate crimes . . . would be brought only in cases in which the federal interest is most clear."

The second panel was composed of six witnesses, including two law professors testifying on constitutionality. Professor Cass Sunstein, of the University of Chicago Law School, testified, "It is unlikely that *Lopez* would be used to strike down the [Hate Crimes] bill." He pointed to the close, 5–4 vote in the case, to the separate concurring opinion by Justice Kennedy, joined by Justice O'Connor (suggesting limits to the decision), and to his own legal analysis of *Lopez*. On the other hand, Professor John C. Harrison of the University of Virginia Law School testified, "Many, perhaps most, of the crimes covered by H.R. 3081 fall within the zone made very doubtful by *Lopez*. They are local. They have no real interstate nexus." In short, he argued that the bill does not fit into the *Lopez* categories, regardless of the language quoted above, and that the Court is therefore unlikely to uphold the Hate Crimes Bill if it is enacted.

The committee members also paid significant attention to the Commerce Clause, which took up much if not most of the remaining time after the witnesses made their statements. Both proponents and opponents of the bill hammered away at the witnesses regarding interstate commerce, states' rights, and *Lopez*, which most committee members referred to by name rather than to Article I, Section 8, of the Constitution or the Commerce Clause. For example, Representative Ed Bryant (R-Tenn.) began his questioning of Assistant Attorney General Lee by asking, "Is there a *Lopez* problem?" Republicans were not alone: even liberal Democrats addressed the constitutional issues. Representative Robert Scott (D-Va.), a proponent of the Hate Crimes Bill, said, "I understand there are constitutional constraints on what we can do about it, and I look forward to using the hearing to fashion a bill which can meet the technical requirements." Another liberal, Representative Maxine Waters (D- Calif.), took great pains in her questioning of Lee to establish that "there must be an interstate nexus."

After the House Judiciary Committee hearings, I interviewed several of the committee staff and asked why so much attention was paid to constitutionality that day. One counsel for the Judiciary Committee told me, "Well, you have a Supreme Court that has expressed concern over this issue—the Commerce Clause—and you have *Lopez*, and so those who are opposed to federal [hate crimes] legislation can use the issue against the bill" (cs3 interview). Another staff member told me, "You have some of these members who, you know, especially Republicans, are against civil rights legislation, and now, hey, the Court has handed them an argument" (cs11 interview). Another counsel to the House Judiciary Committee who opposed the legislation said, "Sure, it's helpful [for the opponents of the Hate Crimes Bill] to have the Court on board. *Lopez* helps the arguments against [the] Hate Crimes [Bill] . . ." (cs5 interview).

The Senate Judiciary Committee also held hearings, on the Senate version of the Hate Crimes Bill, S1529. On July 8, 1998, three panels and a total of nine witnesses testified before the full committee, including Eric Holder Jr., deputy attorney general, U.S. Senator Ron Wyden (D-Ore.), Judge Richard J. Arcara, representing the U.S. Judicial Conference, Edward Jagels, state's attorney from California, William C. Sowder, district attorney from Lubbock, Texas, Frances R. Mullens, the mother of a hate crimes victim, and the law professors Lawrence Alexander of the University of San Diego, Chai R. Feldblum of Georgetown University, and William J. Stuntz of the University of Virginia. Again, much of the testimony revolved around constitutionality and the federalization of criminal law, and much of the discussion was framed in terms of *Lopez* and the threat of judicial review.[36] And in the 106th Congress, on May 11, 1999, the Senate Judiciary Committee again held hearings on the Hate Crimes Bill, this time with the law professors Burt Neuborne of New York University and Akhil Amar of Yale offering different views on the constitutionality of the bill.[37]

The Hate Crimes Bill did not pass the 105th Congress, but it has been introduced in each Congress since. Whether or not the Hate Crimes Bill becomes law, and if it does whether or not it survives judicial scrutiny, the language of the bill and the debate over it have been framed in large part by the Commerce Clause and *Lopez*. The Judiciary Committee appears to be considering the legislation as it might not have done without the Court's recent federalism cases.

Assessing the Impact of Judicial Review on the Federalism Debate in Congress

It is important to be cautious in drawing conclusions about the effects of Court decisions and doctrines on constitutional deliberation in Congress based on the analyses in these two chapters. The statutes and bills analyzed

TABLE 4.2 Federal Legislation and Constitutional Deliberation in Congress

Legislation	Politics of the Legislation	Prospects for Judicial Review	Nature of Constitutional Deliberation
GFSZA (1990)	Low controversy, no opposition	Deference likely	Virtually none
Brady Bill (1994)	Highly controversial, well organized opposition, high level of opposition	Deference likely	Virtually none; one relevant Supreme Court case ignored
VAWA (1994)	Moderately to highly controversial, moderate level of opposition	Deference likely	Minor, no reliance on Court doctrine
Hate Crimes Bill (1997–98)	Moderately to highly controversial, moderate level of opposition	Uncertain or scrutiny and dualism likely	Serious; Court doctrine used

here are all moderately to highly salient, and the bills all reached advanced stages of the legislative process, unlike bills on which little or no action is taken (see Bachrach and Baratz 1962). With these caveats in mind, I believe that the evidence in this chapter demonstrates how the darkness of judicial deference as well as the uncertainty of judicial scrutiny can affect constitutional deliberation in Congress in different ways. Table 4.2 summarizes the relevant conditions under which the legislation examined in this chapter was considered, and the amount of constitutional deliberation that took place.

The GFSZA was uncontroversial and nonpartisan whereas the Brady Bill, VAWA, and Hate Crimes Bill were all controversial and ideologically divisive. Controversy and divisiveness bring out opposition, and opponents are the most likely parties to raise constitutional issues. Nonetheless, controversy and opposition were not enough to make the Tenth Amendment seriously debated when Congress considered the Brady Bill, although the controversy and opposition did help to bring the commerce power to the fore when it considered VAWA and the Hate Crimes Bill. Opposition to a bill may help to raise a constitutional issue, but by itself it may not be enough to give the constitutional issue traction and to assure that it will be deliberated in any detail.

During the sixty-year period of judicial deference that preceded *Lopez*, there was little incentive for members of Congress to consider judicial review or the constitutional issue rather than the more immediate incentives of being on the right side of the public policy issue—especially in the absence of significant controversy or opposition. The Brady Bill certainly raised some controversy, but mostly on substantive policy and Second Amendment grounds. Even with one recent Tenth Amendment case, *New York v. United States* (1992), Congress virtually ignored the federalism issue raised by the background check provisions. The main goals of supporters of the Brady Bill were political: to build a majority coalition with enough votes to pass the bill and to hold that coalition together. VAWA was also controversial, and there appears to have been some awareness of the federalism issues, but most of those involved in drafting it believed the Court would continue to be deferential to Congress in the area of federalism. VAWA presents an interesting situation. The opposition raised the constitutional issue but did not gain much momentum. The commerce power was certainly not ignored, but to the extent that it was considered, it was assumed that the Court would be deferential: the staff members who drafted the civil rights provisions of VAWA sought to make the language of the bill consistent with past statutes enacted under the auspices of the commerce power, assuming that the Court would continue to show deference to Congress.

In contrast, the Hate Crimes Bill has been considered in the context of recent caselaw involving the commerce power. Congress has not been able to avoid federalism and the Commerce Clause. The threat that the Court might strike the law down has been an active part of the committee debates over the bill, and the language of *Lopez* has worked its way into the language of the bill. The context of the *Lopez* decision made the debate over the Hate Crimes Bill different from that surrounding VAWA. The opponents of the Hate Crimes Bill could now invoke the possibility that the Court might strike down the Act. As a consequence, the constitutional issue had more traction and more momentum.

Lawmakers in Congress engaged in more substantial and serious constitutional deliberation when considering the Hate Crimes Bill than when considering VAWA. I believe that in large part, this is because with its federalism decisions in the 1990s, the Supreme Court illuminated federalism as a constitutional value and presented a real threat to the Hate Crimes Bill that was not present when VAWA was passed. However, some might attribute the rise in federalism references illustrated in figure 4.2, and the federalism debate during consideration of the Hate Crimes Bill, to the Republican Party's electoral victories in 1994, when they gained a majority of both the House of Representatives and the Senate. Republicans are usually associated with limited federal government and enhanced state autonomy. Undoubtedly, the shift in party control of Congress has influenced the agenda in Congress, and has probably likewise influenced substantive debates. However, the legislative history of the Hate Crimes Bill indicates that Democrats as well as Republicans paid significant attention to the Commerce Clause in an attempt to negate arguments that the legislation is unconstitutional. Additionally, as I described in chapter 2, it was a Republican Congress that passed an amendment to the GFSZA in 1996 to revive the statute after it had been struck down in *Lopez*, and the federalism angle on the legislation did not prevent Republicans from supporting it.

Moreover, there are numerous other examples of legislative debate in the late 1990s and early twenty-first century in which Democrats raised and debated federalism in opposition to Republican-sponsored bills. Prominent examples include the Religious Liberty Protection Act (RLPA) and tort reform legislation such as the Product Liability Reform Act, the Product Liability Fairness Act, the Small Business Liability Act, the Class Action Fairness Act, and other bills. It is not necessary to develop complete legislative histories here. Briefly, though, each of these bills was supported primarily by Republicans, with Democrats raising federalism in opposition.

For instance, RLPA was proposed after the Court invalidated the Religious Freedom Restoration Act in *City of Boerne v. Flores* (1997), for exceeding Congress's authority under Section 5 of the Fourteenth Amendment. RLPA's sponsors argued that religious discrimination affects interstate commerce and that they could resurrect the policy underlying RFRA under the commerce power. Some of the original RFRA supporters refused to go along with the commerce power rationale, and several interest groups withdrew their support for the bill for the same reason (see den Dulk and Pickerill 2003). Additionally, the constitutionality of RLPA was questioned during hearings before the Judiciary Committees of both houses, and the Court's federalism decisions were invoked. For example, in a Senate Judiciary Committee hearing on June 23, 1998, the constitutional law professors Douglas Laylock of the University of Texas, Marci Hamilton of Yeshiva University, Christopher Eisgruber of New York University, and Michael McConnell of the University of Utah all gave testimony and answered senators' questions regarding the constitutionality of the Act under the Court's recent caselaw.[38]

There are other examples as well. Throughout the second half of the 1990s, the Republicans proposed tort reform legislation to protect companies and others from what they regard as frivolous lawsuits and runaway juries. For example, the Republicans have repeatedly introduced versions of the Product Liability Reform Act, the Class Action Fairness Act, the Fairness in Punitive Damages Act, and the Small Business Liability Reform Act since 1995. While Republicans claim that such legislation is necessary for the national economy and to protect American businesses, Democrats and a few Republicans consistently point out that tort law is traditionally an area reserved for state regulation. Federalism has been at issue in several hearings over tort reform legislation, and Democrats on both Judiciary Committees, such as Senator Patrick Leahy (D-Vt.), Representative John Conyers (D-Mich.), Representative Barney Frank (D-Mass.), Representative Melvin Watt (D-N.C.), and Representative Bobby Scott (D-Va.), among others, are fond of raising federalism concerns, often reminding their Republican colleagues of the Court's federalism majority, all members of which are Republican appointees.[39]

These examples also came up in my interviews. A Republican member of the House Judiciary Committee told me he was "disappointed" with his Republican colleagues for being "inconsistent" and "not seriously considering" the federalism issues at stake with these types of statutes (MC4 interview). The legislative director for a Republican member of the House told me, "There's no consistency here, meaning Congress at large. . . . Barney Frank is the best at bringing up the point that Republicans are inconsistent [on these federalism issues]" (PS6 interview). And counsel for the House Judiciary Committee told me, "you still see that both parties will take the opportunity to violate federalism, the concept of federalism, if they think it serves their political advantage or serves a cause they believe in. . . . That's why Mel Watt out here likes to be very sarcastic and say, 'as the chairman of the states' rights cause' on this, I'm going to call you on this. And Barney Frank loves to do it too—point out when Republicans are violating these principles" (CS5 interview).

My point is simply to illustrate that we should resist the temptation to characterize federalism as a purely Republican issue. Rather, it can be an equal-opportunity constitutional issue raised by anyone who opposes legislation. Although Republicans may be traditionally associated with limited federal government, they have proposed and supported legislation that expands federal power and potentially intrudes on state sovereignty, and Democrats have not hesitated to call them on it. Hence, it is reasonable to conclude that the trend represented in figure 4.2 has been significantly influenced by the Court's recent federalism decisions, and is not simply a result of the 1994 elections.

Neal Devins (2001) has argued that Congress has paid little attention to the *Lopez* and *Printz* decisions. However, Devins considered only the instances in which Congress dealt explicitly with those decisions, and not with federalism more generally. Moreover, as Keith Whittington has argued, the Rehnquist Court's federalism decisions have not necessarily invited confrontation over federalism in the same manner as the *Lochner* and New Deal Courts did, and the Court "has moved carefully to avoid antagonizing the interests of power- ful actors who potentially could threaten the Court's legitimacy" (2001, 495, 509). Whittington notes that in *Lopez*, the Court remained within the doc- trinal parameters established by the New Deal Court rather than departing from it. He concludes that "the Lopez Court is more developmental than reactionary, feeling its way toward a distinctly post-New Deal decentralization of the federal system," and that "along with other political actors, the Rehn- quist Court is participating in a *political process* of constitutional change" (2001, 519–20) (emphasis added).

Whittington accurately accounts for the natural interaction between the Court and Congress over constitutional meaning. Those who expect a consti- tutional revolution, a constitutional moment, or other form of severe con- frontation between the Court and Congress simply do not appreciate the more routine and typical type of interaction between Court and Congress in the political process. The Rehnquist Court has certainly changed perceptions of the constitutional landscape with respect to federalism, but I believe it has challenged Congress more than choked it. The challenge presented to Con- gress is to provide constitutional, and not simply public policy or political, justifications for legislation involving federalism. As the debate over the Hate Crimes Bill suggests, this is now likely to occur by having Congress debate legislation in a manner that incorporates the Court's legal constitutional doc- trines, such as the substantial effects test.

Undoubtedly, this is not the type of deeper independent deliberation that some coordinate construction advocates would prefer, and it does not amount to challenges of the Court's interpretations. However, I again submit that deliberation motivated by the threat of judicial review is better than no deliberation, or deliberation motivated only by public policy or public opin- ion. For instance, the debate over the Hate Crimes Bill may have been oriented toward satisfying Court doctrine, but it forced members of Congress to pub- licly debate the constitutional dimension of the bill and articulate constitutional justifications in addition to public policy justifications. This sort of pressure is unlikely to prevent Congress from pursuing new areas of public policy altogether, but it will likely induce the Court and Congress to negotiate over different constitutional visions of federalism. Additionally, while lawmakers in Congress may be deliberating the constitutional dimension to legislation in legalistic and instrumental terms, such a debate does promote an awareness, and perhaps some post hoc musing, about the nature of federal power in a constitutional democracy. Moreover, this type of deliberation is likely to lead to legislation that includes and balances the preferences of both institutions. And this, it would seem, is again exactly what a separated system is designed to produce, and what a republic of reasons demands.

Although it is important to use caution in generalizing from the type of statutes analyzed here, the analysis is highly suggestive that judicial review has important effects on the likelihood and content of constitutional deliberation in Congress. When there has been a real prospect of judicial scrutiny, the Court's doctrine seems to have helped motivate and shape constitutional deliberation in Congress, whereas members of Congress appear less likely to seriously consider the commerce power and the Tenth Amendment in the darkness of judicial deference. It appears that as a check in a system of checks and balances, judicial review can help motivate members of Congress to consider the meaning of constitutional principles. This is a natural byproduct of a separated system, and an aspiration of a republic of reasons. Nonetheless, how generalizable the analysis is remains to be seen. The question has important implications for understanding constitutional interpretation and the role of judicial review in lawmaking—the subject of the next chapter.

FIVE

The Nature of Things:

Anticipation and

Negotiation,

Interaction and

Reaction

★

While preceding chapters illustrate specific instances where the Court's constitutional decisions have affected the legislative process in Congress, the question remains whether any generalizations can be made about the effect of judicial review on constitutional deliberation in Congress and on legislation. In this chapter, I try to make some general observations about constitutional deliberation in Congress and the impact of judicial review in the lawmaking process. I review responses from additional interviews that I conducted with a range of respondents involved in the legislative process. As I will explain, in these interviews I did not ask about specific legislation, but instead asked about the role of constitutional debate in Congress generally. I then conclude the chapter with some thoughts about the appropriate role of the Supreme Court and judicial review in constitutional interpretation.

Congress and Constitutional Deliberation

Evidence from preceding chapters supports the *general* proposition that constitutional issues are not influential in routine congressional decision making, but that in certain circumstances members of Congress do engage in constitutional deliberation. Another way I assess the importance (or unimportance) of constitutional issues in the legislative process is to analyze additional interview responses from the interviews that I conducted with members of Congress and other lawmaking participants. In key respects, my interview approach here was designed and intended to build on the work on congressional decision making and policy agendas by John Kingdon (1995; 1984; 1989) as well as surveys of congressional attitudes toward constitutional issues conducted by Donald Morgan (1966).

In my in-depth interviews with lawmakers, I questioned not only those directly involved in the "federalism legislation" analyzed in chapter 4 but also approximately thirty other former and current members of Congress, congressional staff, lobbyists, and others without direct involvement.[1] I asked this group a more general set of questions about the relevance of constitutional issues in Congress to determine any generalized effects that they might have on debate, deliberation, and the crafting of legislation in Congress. Among other questions, I asked interviewees to assess the most important factors in the drafting and consideration of bills. I also asked whether constitutional issues are routinely, or ever, considered. When an interviewee responded that they were, I followed up by asking why and by whom. The responses showed a strong consistency across the two chambers of Congress and across political parties, staff positions, and committee affiliations.

As a general rule, respondents did not believe that constitutionality was an important consideration in Congress when legislation was drafted and considered. For example, a former Democratic member of the Senate Judiciary Committee, who is regarded as a liberal, said that constitutionality was rarely very important in the debate over public policy and legislation, and he ranked the importance of issues during the consideration of bills in Congress this way: "Policy issues first, how do you get a consensus to pass the bill, six other things, then constitutionality" (MC1 interview). And a former Republican member of the House Judiciary Committee, regarded as a conservative, told me that while he cared about the Constitution, constitutionality and the Court's constitutional decisions were not usually an important part of the decision-making process for him because, "When I go home and talk to my constituents, they ask me to help solve problems in Congress. They don't ask if it's constitutional. They want common sense" (MC2 interview). A senator and a representative, Democrat and Republican, each of whom served on a Judiciary Committee, agreed that constitutionality was not generally a priority when legislation was considered. Rather, they readily acknowledged that public policy, the need to build a majority coalition, and concerns of constituents back home take precedence.

The congressional staff members whom I interviewed echoed the sentiments of the members of Congress quoted above. For example, when I told a legislative director for a Republican member of the House that I was looking for evidence of constitutional deliberation in Congress, he responded with a chuckle, "You give Congress way too much credit" (ps2 interview). He went on to tell me that because "Congress is very much a reactive body," members of Congress pursue legislation in reaction to the popular political issues of the day, regardless of any relevant constitutional issues. And the legislative director for a Republican senator told me that constitutionality was not important in formulating a position on legislation because, "We know that the Senator is not going to go home and not get re-elected because he voted for legislation which was later struck down as unconstitutional" (ps1 interview). The chief of staff and legislative director for a Democratic member of the House could not recall a legislative debate in which a constitutional issue was important for his representative; according to this staff member, his representative was first "concerned about the position of his constituency and second his own policy preferences" (ps7 interview). Generally speaking, this is how legislators (and their staffs) believe they are elected to act.

Another legislative director for a Republican member of the House of Representatives who had worked on Capitol Hill for over eight years agreed: "I think the most important issues from our point of view are identifying a public policy concern and doing so in a way that is ideologically in tune with the Congressman's position. And that's the framework within which we draft legislation" (ps4 interview). While acknowledging that constitutionality takes a back seat to policy and ideological concerns, this legislative director offered another reason why constitutional issues might be ignored: "For the most part, we're dealing within the bounds of stuff that Congress has already done that is already public law, or has been public law, and it has not occurred to us that it may be struck down as unconstitutional" (ps4 interview). This observation suggests that because so much of the legislative agenda builds on existing law, as I noted in chapter 2, participants in the legislative process assume the previous legislation to be constitutional, and thus new proposals that amend or are closely related to existing legislation must also be constitutional.

It might be argued that the personal staff members for a member of Congress are more likely to miss the intricacies of the legislative process, especially work done in congressional committees, where constitutional issues may be more likely to arise. However, the legal counsel and other professional staff of various committees reinforced their observations. For instance, a counsel for the House Judiciary Committee responded, "Now, for most legislation that comes up, there's little debate about the constitutional authority for it. . . . I think basically, some members will just say, this is what I want done, let's do it. And they don't think a lot about whether it violates the Constitution" (cs5 interview). A professional staff member for the House Judiciary Committee said, "When it comes to constitutional issues, most members say, 'that's not my job—that's the Supreme Court's job' " (cs9 interview). And a long-time staff member and attorney for the House Agriculture Committee who worked on energy and natural resources replied, "We think about [constitutional issues] less than we should. I think it would be worthwhile to have a basic course for Hill staff on some of these key issues—there's almost a total lack of understanding here" (cs6 interview).

It is not only members of Congress and their staffs who view constitutionality as peripheral in legislative debates. An attorney and lobbyist for a public interest group that has lobbied members of Congress for regulatory legislation observed, "Because legislators want to enact a bill first, they'll worry about constitutionality later. What they want is to be able to tell their constituents that they got a bill passed. . . . When legislation is struck down by the courts, it does not hurt the politician politically. [The politician can say] the *courts* did that. It's too bad, but that's the way it goes" (IG1 interview). A former U.S. attorney general agreed, "I just think very few Congressmen even think about constitutional issues generally. You know, Congress, unfortunately, is very political, and constitutional safeguards are rarely considered" (AG1 interview). And in an informal discussion after a lecture, a sitting Supreme Court Justice said of members of Congress, "They don't care about the Court. They don't care about the Constitution. They don't care about whether these things ever get applied or enforced. They just pass the stuff."

These observations, by a fairly wide range of lawmakers inside and outside Congress, fit well with conventional models of congressional decision making and indicate why we might not expect to find much constitutional deliberation in Congress. What matters most to voters is that a law enacting the policy gets passed, and members of Congress are astutely aware of that fact in daily political life; as Mayhew found in his classic study, members of Congress are concerned with claiming credit for legislation and voting on the "right side" of the issue (1974). Consequently, neither potential constitutional problems nor the threat of judicial review is a primary consideration during the formation of policy and legislation. Moreover, members themselves must speculate over the policy impact of a statute, and supporters of legislation must work to build and maintain a majority inside Congress. In addition much of the legislative agenda builds on existing policies and statutes. As the one legislative director indicated, when a legislative matter is "within the bounds of what

Congress has already done that is already public law," the inclination is to assume constitutionality, even though it is possible that constitutional problems were never considered originally or that amendments to existing law might create new constitutional problems.

While some of those quoted above believed that lawmakers in Congress never think about constitutionality at all, most stressed that under certain conditions constitutional issues are likely to get raised and are occasionally debated. For instance, although the former attorney general whom I interviewed told me that in his experience with Congress, constitutional issues were "rarely considered," he thought that some members did occasionally raise them, and that "once somebody starts raising them, then other people [in Congress] start thinking about them" (AG1 interview).

As for the circumstances in which constitutionality is likely to be raised, three factors emerged from the interviews as the most important: (1) the interests of committees or individual members, (2) the "notoriety" of a Court decision or its caselaw, and (3) the "politics" of the legislation and the underlying constitutional issue.[2]

INTERESTS OF COMMITTEES OR INDIVIDUAL MEMBERS

First, according to many of those interviewed, the nature of certain committees or the "idiosyncratic" interests of individual members of Congress can make it more likely that constitutionality will get raised (PS5, CS7 interviews). It is more likely to be raised in some committees than others because of the subject matter of the committee's jurisdiction and the "fastidiousness of the staff" (CS7 interview). Most respondents identified the Judiciary Committees as the most likely places for constitutional issues to be considered. Both the House and the Senate Judiciary Committees have subcommittees on the Constitution and are staffed with numerous attorneys. Of course, even on the Judiciary Committees a majority of the attorneys on the staff are assigned to specific areas of public policy and statutory law such as crime, antitrust, and intellectual property. Many members of the Judiciary Committees as well as the attorneys who work for them "specialize in issues of choice and count on others to address constitutional issues" (CS8 interview).

Of all those I interviewed, twelve had served on or worked for one of the two Judiciary Committees. According to all twelve, there is no systematic method of identifying constitutional questions in those committees. A former counsel for the Senate Judiciary Committee told me, "It is unpredictable when members will raise constitutional issues" (CS4 interview). On the other hand, a professional staff member with the House Judiciary Committee for nearly two decades said, "Once a bill gains momentum, preparation for hearings begin. The staff puts together a 'hearing scenario,' and staffers decide who will testify," and it is at this point that constitutional issues will first be identified and "taken seriously" if they are going to be taken seriously at all (cs9 interview). Even at this point, however, most of the Judiciary Committee personnel told me that there was no systematic way to identify or address constitutional problems. Generally, the focus for hearings is on presenting facts about the specific policy that a piece of legislation is intended to address. For example, in considering federal legislation relating to juvenile justice, the primary concern in the Judiciary Committees would be the frequency and types of juvenile crime, which areas of the country experienced the most serious problems, effective means of curbing juvenile crime and dealing with juvenile offenders, and funding for federal programs (cs5 interview).

Nonetheless, the subcommittees on the Constitution and the full Judiciary Committees sometimes hold hearings that address the constitutionality of legislation, and as shown by the legislative histories of the Child Labor Act, the Civil Rights Act of 1964, and the proposed Hate Crimes Prevention Act of 1998 examined in previous chapters, members can seriously debate constitutional issues. Interview responses indicate that while constitutionality is more likely to be addressed in the Judiciary Committees than elsewhere, the reasons are much the same as elsewhere: notoriety of a Court decision or of caselaw generally, and the politics of the bill. I will address these two as separate factors a bit later. What is important about the Judiciary Committees is that they are the places where many others in Congress *expect* constitutional issues to be addressed, and in fact they often are.

In interviewing members of the Judiciary Committees and their staffs, I was concerned that I might be overestimating the amount of constitutional deliberation that occurs in Congress by selecting the most likely place for such deliberation to occur. As a control, I also interviewed four staff members of the House and Senate Agriculture and Natural Resources Committees who worked mainly on energy and natural resources. Each was an attorney with at least six years of committee experience. One staff member with the Senate Energy and Natural Resources Committee, who had worked for four congressional committees over a fifteen-year period, explained why counsel on committees do not often address constitutionality: "On most committees, as you well know, there are a few lawyers, relatively small number of lawyers, and most of them are professional staff with law degrees. I mean they're not really practicing law, and chief counsels on committees are often times preoccupied with other kinds of issues. After being around for awhile, they're not paying attention to everything the Supreme Court's doing usually, as much as a regular practitioner would do" (CS7 interview).

There is an exception that each of the respondents mentioned as important. I found that some specific issues were on the minds of the staff and counsel I interviewed on the committees concerned with energy and natural resources. Two of the four respondents referred in vague terms to the Commerce Clause and *Lopez* as potential obstacles, but all four mentioned the Takings Clause of the Fifth Amendment, which prohibits the federal government from taking private property without "just compensation," and they noted which members on the committees were most likely to be concerned about it. One respondent reported concern that the Takings Clause might be implicated by the Endangered Species Act, which can prevent property owners from engaging in certain kinds of activity on their land if doing so would adversely affect endangered animals (CS10 interview). Another mentioned the Takings Clause in connection with government regulation of water use and water rights (CS6 interview).

While all four respondents recognized that the Takings Clause was discussed, they emphasized that as policy and legislation were being considered, what took place was not "debates" but "discussions" (CS6, CS11 interviews). The respondents did not recall that the constitutional issues had become important in public hearings or floor debates, but rather at the policy-formation stage. When asked if Supreme Court caselaw motivated these "discussions," all four respondents admitted to not knowing the caselaw on the topic, and they noted that constitutional arguments against the taking of private property seemed to be more philosophical in orientation and not rooted in Supreme Court cases. They did identify who was raising the issues, though. One respondent observed how the issue "has become political, and private property rights has become, well, it's a political watch group trend here" (CS11 interview). In addition to noting interest group politics, these committee staff members identified members from certain regions of the country who were more likely to raise the Takings Clause. "Western Members—property, property rights is sacred" (CS11 interview).

This last observation indicates that some constitutional issues are tied not only to certain committees, because of their jurisdiction, but also to certain individual members. The Takings Clause is apparently important to specific members of Congress, as well as in committees and subcommittees that address land use and natural resources. In particular, certain conservative Republicans like Representative Helen Chenoweth-Hage (R-Idaho), and Senators Slade Gorton (R-Wash.) and Frank Murkowski (R-Alaska) were mentioned as members who showed concern about takings issues. For these members, the public policy issue is embodied in the Takings Clause. All these members self-selected to committees that deal with natural resources, and all represent constituencies perceived to be concerned with private property rights. Thus, the public policy issue of private property rights is a "pet issue" for some of these members, and it is a public policy issue that is inherently related to the Takings Clause. These members use the Takings Clause to support ideological and public policy positions that favor protection of private property rights.

In addition to members who have pet issues with constitutional implications, respondents referred to members who seem to raise constitutional issues in almost an idiosyncratic fashion. A number of respondents mentioned Senator Robert Byrd (D-W. Va.), and staff members on the House and Senate Judiciary Committees in particular cited as an example his crusade against the statutory line item veto that Congress passed and the Supreme Court subsequently struck down as unconstitutional. Other staff members mentioned Representative Ron Paul (R-Texas), a Republican with strong libertarian views (and a former presidential nominee of the Libertarian party), who uses constitutional arguments to support his positions for limited federal government and against expansive government programs. Lastly, Senator Mitch McConnell (R-Ky.) was cited for using the First Amendment's free speech guarantee to support his arguments against campaign finance reform. Senator McConnell's use of constitutional issues is somewhat different, however. Whereas the western members who raise the Takings Clause, Senator Byrd, and Representative Paul all ground their constitutional arguments primarily in philosophical or policy preferences, Senator McConnell also relies on a well-known body of Supreme Court caselaw that began with the landmark case *Buckley v. Valeo* (1976). This leads me to the next factor that influences constitutional arguments in Congress.

NOTORIETY OF SUPREME COURT DECISION OR CASELAW

According to an attorney who has worked on four congressional committees in fifteen years, "If you get something that has been in the papers, a lot of people have thought about it. I'm trying to think of a case like that, well, *Chevron*, or one of those kinds of cases. If it's fairly well known and it has some sort of broad holding that people are aware of, it kind of sinks into their cortexes" (CS7 interview). This statement was seconded by other lawmaking participants with whom I spoke. In some instances, the Supreme Court decision or doctrine is so well known that the constitutional issue *must* be addressed. When asked which constitutional issues get raised and debated in Congress, those relating to the First Amendment were cited most often.

The First Amendment was often mentioned in connection with campaign finance reform. Many respondents were familiar with the arguments of opponents of campaign finance legislation throughout the late 1990s that the legislation was unconstitutional, and that Supreme Court decisions supported their position. Many staff members knew the landmark decision, *Buckley v. Valeo*, by name. A number of respondents also identified the First Amendment implications of regulation of the internet and telecommunications, and were aware that the Supreme Court had recently struck down some laws for violating free speech. They were not always aware of the name of the case, but they identified the Court doctrine and believed that members and staff "definitely took it into consideration" and "were trying to comply with" the caselaw when they worked on legislation such as the Child On-line Protection Act (CS5 interview).

Respondents also recognized Supreme Court caselaw involving religion. Several mentioned the Religious Freedom Restoration Act, struck down in *City of Boerne v. Flores* (1997), as well as the subsequent attempt to pass the Religious Liberty Protection Act in response to that decision. At least two staff members mentioned school vouchers for private schools, telling me that there had been discussion in Congress about federally funded vouchers for private schools, and that "the First Amendment issue is discussed" because of "Supreme Court requirements" involving the Establishment Clause of the First Amendment (PS7, PS5 interviews).

Several of the counsel to the Judiciary Committees and other staff talked about *Lopez* and the commerce power without being prompted. One respondent, who had been both a personal staff member for a Republican senator and a clerk for a Supreme Court Justice, said, "I was working in Congress when *Lopez* came down, and I remember that day. That created a big buzz in Congress that day. And I think it definitely changed the intellectual landscape over there—because it made people start to think about enumerated powers" (PS8 interview). He and others told me that the commerce power had been raised in discussions about tort reform in Congress, including legislative proposals concerning product liability and class-action reforms.

Others told me that they had heard various discussions over the constitutionality of federal criminal laws after *Lopez* was handed down (cs8, ps5, ps8, AG1 interviews).

Whenever respondents were able to identify constitutional issues that had been discussed and debated, they often identified them in terms of Supreme Court decisions and efforts of Congress to write legislation that would satisfy the Court. While they could not always be specific about a decision, the lawmaking participants often knew when there was established Supreme Court doctrine. Sometimes they knew the names of specific cases, like *Buckley v. Valeo* and *United States v. Lopez*, and at other times they simply knew that court doctrine somehow limited what Congress could do. In their discussions of how these issues were debated and why it was important to satisfy the Court, it became evident that much of the constitutional deliberation in Congress takes place, or is perceived to take place, in the context of well-known Supreme Court caselaw. Some of the time, a Court decision must be addressed because it is very recent or otherwise famous. At the same time, however, it also became evident that the perceived need to address the Court's caselaw was part of the politics of the bill, especially the political opposition to a policy or proposed legislation, which leads me to the third general factor that influences constitutional deliberation in Congress.

THE POLITICS OF THINGS

What one respondent called "the politics of things" (cs7 interview) includes the salience of a public policy issue and the level of consensus or opposition to proposed legislation. A former counsel to the Senate Judiciary Committee explained, "In Congress and on the Judiciary Committee, time is very limited, so we don't have hearings on things unless there's salience" (cs4 interview). A former legislative assistant to a Democratic member of the Senate Judiciary Committee told me that "legislation is an adversarial process in a way. In court, a judge will not raise all the issues, defenses etc. for each lawyer, and opposing lawyers don't raise issues for one another. In the Senate, there is no mechanism for constitutional issues to be incorporated into the debate. That's what the opposition is for—on the floor, in committee, the administration, interest groups, etc." (ps2 interview). He continued, "The opposition is key. They will raise, or have the incentives to raise, constitutional issues if they support their arguments and policy positions. It would be hard to imagine someone who supports a policy that has some reasonable chance of being constitutional raising the constitutional issue. They would leave it to the opposition to raise" (PS2 interview). When I asked a former member of Congress who had served on the Judiciary Committee how constitutional issues get raised in Congress, he responded, "Lobbyists who are affected [by constitutional issues or Court decisions] will raise the issue with Congress . . ." (MC5 interview).

A common example raised by respondents involved gun control and the Second Amendment. As we saw in some detail in chapter 4, gun control is a high-visibility issue that stirs passions on both sides. Opponents of gun control are well organized, and whenever a Judiciary Committee is going to consider a bill on the issue, the forces opposed to gun control, particularly interest groups like the National Rifle Association (NRA), raise the "right to bear arms" language from the Second Amendment. Usually, the issue will then be aired by the committee. Gun control has salience and the NRA is a well-organized and politically influential interest group whose leaders and members regularly argue against gun control legislation, in part because they believe it infringes individuals' right to bear arms under the Second Amendment. As the history of the Brady Bill in chapter 4 illustrated, the NRA has been successful in influencing the debate over firearms regulation. Although the NRA and gun-rights supporters in Congress routinely advance constitutional arguments against gun control, they do not rely much on caselaw because there is little Second Amendment jurisprudence.

Opponents of other legislative efforts use Supreme Court doctrine more frequently. Two of the highly salient areas where this occurs, both mentioned in interviews, are abortion regulation—especially those relating to funding and the procedure that opponents call partial birth abortion—and campaign finance reform (where *Buckley v. Valeo* casts a long shadow). Abortion regulations are always highly divisive, and when legislation is proposed regarding abortion procedures and federal funding of abortions, opponents raise the constitutional issue in the context of the landmark Supreme Court decision, *Roe v. Wade* (1973), and its progeny (CS5 interview). As for campaign finance reform, several interview respondents commented that while the opponents of campaign finance reform voice their objections primarily on policy grounds, they use the Supreme Court doctrine as support (PS4, PS3 interviews).

Many of those interviewed believed that constitutional issues were most likely to be pursued by the opponents of legislation, and that constitutional arguments would have more teeth if supported by Supreme Court decisions. The consensus was that members first take their position on legislation based on their policy preferences, and then use all arguments possible to support that position. In discussing the proposed legislation against hate crimes, the legislative director for a Republican member of the House told me, "I mean my boss was already against hate crimes legislation on public policy grounds. . . . I would suspect that as a public policy matter, if it came in front of us, and we debated it on the floor of the House, and there were bolstering arguments from constitutional scholars that it was unconstitutional, it would be another reason to oppose it" (PS4 interview).

The consistency between responses to general interviews analyzed here and the analyses in previous chapters is suggestive of a few general patterns. To begin with, constitutional issues are not priorities in Congress. Politics and policy dominate congressional decision making, and members of Congress do not systematically consider the constitutional authority for their actions. Much of the time, there is no need to consider constitutional issues, but there is always a need to consider the policy and political implications of proposed legislation. However, the responses to my general interview questions support findings from earlier chapters that constitutional issues do occasionally affect behavior and legislation. While the conditions under which constitutional issues are raised vary with the legislation involved, there appear to be two main ones.

First, certain issues are germane to the jurisdiction of a committee or are "pet issues" of a particular member of Congress. Often, a member who cares deeply about a constitutional issue will also serve on a committee likely to deal with it. This was the case with the Takings Clause and conservative members from the Northwest who served on committees that dealt with natural resources.

Second, the politics of a particular piece of legislation may help to create conditions under which constitutional issues are raised, particularly the politics of opposition. Generally speaking, opponents of legislation oppose the public policy embodied in the legislation, and they use constitutional arguments to justify their opposition, although this does not have to be the case. As a former counsel to the Senate Judiciary Committee observed, "Constitutional issues are raised in Congress opportunistically" (CS4 interview). For instance, many opponents of campaign finance reform disagree entirely with the policy of regulating campaign finance, and they also use the constitutional problem created under the First Amendment when the government regulates political speech. For some members, the constitutional argument is probably sincere—that is, they believe regulation of campaign contributions to be a serious violation of First Amendment principles—while others simply use the First Amendment to combat legislation that they would oppose even without a constitutional argument at their disposal. In any event, opponents of legislation, particularly if represented by interest groups or otherwise organized and mobilized, are often the most likely participants in Congress to raise constitutional issues and force debate over them.

The constitutional deliberation that does take place can do so on two dimensions: a more philosophical one over specific constitutional values or principles, or a more instrumental one over satisfying the Supreme Court's doctrine in a given area. As we have seen, some members and organized groups are particularly passionate about certain issues, and they will make arguments without the support of Supreme Court caselaw. For example, members interested in private property rights may use the principles underlying the Fifth Amendment Takings Clause as a justification for protecting private property rights. Similarly, guns-rights advocates will argue passionately over the importance of protecting individuals' right to bear arms under the Second Amendment.

However, when it comes to constitutional issues, Congress is often a reactive body. Congress is reactive not only to the policy and political pressures that it faces, but also to court decisions. As we saw in chapter 2, Congress often reacts to the Court by modifying legislation to address constitutional problems after the Court has declared the legislation unconstitutional. And even when Congress deliberates constitutionality in *anticipation* of constitutional problems, it is frequently *reacting* to existing Supreme Court caselaw and doctrine. Not only does caselaw make it more likely that constitutionality will get raised in Congress, but apparently it provides momentum in Congress, as well as a context for the substance of the debate. While supporters of legislation may be able to ignore philosophical arguments from a few pesky opponents, it is more difficult to avoid arguments that the Supreme Court is likely to invalidate the legislation.

The Impact of Judicial Review on Constitutional Deliberation in a Separated System

In discussing the role of presidents in lawmaking, Charles O. Jones argues, "Misinterpreting or oversimplifying the president's role in lawmaking may be a consequence of a failure to account fully for the complex features of the lawmaking process and the legislature . . ." (1994, 183). The same might be said of the role of the Supreme Court and judicial review in lawmaking. To slightly alter Jones's observation: "Misinterpreting or oversimplifying [judicial review's] role in lawmaking may be a consequence of a failure to account fully for the complex features of the lawmaking process and the legislature. Lawmaking in a democratic system of separated institutions will be substantially more intricate and variable than [theories of judicial review assume]. The many arenas of decisionmaking provide multiple points of access and foster a permeability that makes it difficult to predict either participation or outcomes" (1994, 183).

Like presidents, the Supreme Court is involved in a system of producing laws, and as Jones argues, "understanding the production of laws requires analysis of lawmaking" (1994, 207). Scholars, journalists, and others often judge presidents by the amount of agreement between, on the one hand, the president's positions on legislation and, on the other, roll call votes in Congress or other similarly limited indicators. Critiquing this view, Jones notes that these judgments oversimplify lawmaking by judging presidents according to one decision-point at one moment in time, when in fact presidents have other opportunities to influence the production of laws.

Jones's observations about the role of presidents in lawmaking are applicable to the role of the Supreme Court and judicial review, because, mirroring common misperceptions about presidents in lawmaking, constitutional scholars and others often evaluate how the Court should and does exercise judicial review from an improper vantage point. Interaction between the Court and Congress does not usually occur in extraordinary periods that lead to constitutional moments, revolutions, or showdowns. The "normal" or "routine" role of judicial review in the lawmaking process is more subtle, complex, and variable than commonly perceived, because judicial review is usually exercised in the context of a continuous process in which political actors and institutions anticipate, negotiate, interact, and react. After Congress has passed legislation and it has been signed into law, the lawmaking sequence has barely begun, much less been completed. Collectively, the statute as passed by Congress, the implementation of the statute by executive agencies, and the interpretation of the statute by courts, make up the law—neither the statute nor a judicial decision stands alone as a definitive item. By the time a statute gets to the Supreme Court for review, the Court's contribution to the law is a reaction to what many other institutions have done already.

When the Court exercises judicial review, it creates, illuminates, or elevates a constitutional issue and declares that the statute, or more likely a portion of a statute, cannot be applied. The Court does not, however, eliminate the statute from the law books, so to speak; only Congress and the President can do so by passing new legislation to repeal the old. As Supreme Court Justice Antonin Scalia observed about the Court's exercise of judicial review in a public speech, "We don't strike laws down. We just ignore them" (Scalia 2000). Justice Scalia's comment recognizes that the Court's exercise of judicial review in effect sets the statute aside, or suspends it, and adds a constitutional dimension to the law, of which the statute is a central part. Policies are constantly revisited and revised in Congress. Law is revealed and revised through these different parts of the process. Judicial action is one point at which the law is further revealed and refined, often encouraging Congress to bargain with the Court. Given the incremental nature of the lawmaking process, it should not be surprising that judicial review can play this incremental and alternative role, similarly to the role of presidents in lawmaking (see Jones 1994).

Recall the earlier quotation from a former senator when asked what the most important considerations were in the legislative process: "[P]olicy issues first, how do you get a consensus to pass the bill, six other things, then constitutionality" (MC1 interview). In other words, the primary goals for lawmakers in Congress are to design a statute that will achieve the desired policy and to get the legislation passed. With information about the Court's preferences, Congress can speculate what the Court might do, and it might, in a process that resembles bargaining, make concessions to or otherwise satisfy the Court. It appears that constitutional deliberation in Congress frequently takes place in this context: the Court establishes the parameters for the debate, and creates some reason for members of Congress to speculate over the constitutionality of a statute. This does not mean that Congress cannot challenge the Court, only that the Court creates the context in which such a challenge might take place. Congress can ignore the Court and sometimes does. But when the Court has helped define or create a constitutional context, the likelihood that Congress will address constitutionality is increased. At best, judicial review forces Congress to craft constitutional statutes, and at a minimum, the Court reminds Congress that it operates within a constitutional framework.

I will conclude here with a brief look at two implications of the research in this book. The first is related to the role of the Court in federalism issues specifically, the second to the role of the Court in constitutional interpretation more generally. My goal is to sketch out possible ways to understand the role of the Court in constitutional interpretation given the role that judicial review seems to play in our separated system, while leaving a more fully developed theoretical exposition for another day.

With respect to federalism matters, I believe that my investigation of constitutional deliberation over federalism may shed some light on recent debates regarding the appropriate role of the Court in policing federalism. As I outlined in chapter 3, there are two primary arguments made by legal scholars regarding judicial review and federalism. The political safeguards camp argues that the judiciary should not decide federalism cases, but should instead leave the boundaries between state and federal power to be resolved in the political process; thus adherents to the political safeguards approach oppose the Rehnquist Court's recent decisions (see, e.g., Choper 1980; Colker and Brudney 2001; Kramer 2000; Nagel 2001; Tushnet 1999; Wechsler 1959). Conversely, the judicial safeguards camp argues that Congress cannot be trusted to limit its own powers and that the Court must exercise judicial review over federalism to preserve constitutional limits on federal power; accordingly, these scholars favor the Rehnquist Court's decisions (see, e.g., Calabresi 1995, 2001; Greve 1999; Hamilton 2001; Yoo 1997). While these two camps differ on whether the Court should be involved in federalism disputes, they agree on one thing: the Court's federalism decisions have denied Congress its will by killing pertinent legislation. The political safeguards proponents view this as problematic, while the judicial safeguards proponents view it as desirable.

I disagree with the premise with which each of these theories begins. The evidence in this book suggests that the Court is often, if not usually, a participant in an intergovernmental debate over the distribution of power. The Court does not usually prohibit Congress from exercising power. Rather, the exercise of judicial review over federalism can increase attention to the issue in Congress. Accordingly, I agree with the judicial safeguards advocates that the Court should decide federalism issues, but I differ on the reasons why. At the same time, I agree with the political safeguards scholars that federalism boundaries will and should be determined by the political process, but I believe that the Court is an essential part of that process. The Court is not saving the country from Congress by obstructing the legislative process, nor does it exist entirely separate from the lawmaking process. Instead I agree with arguments put forward by Ann Althouse and Keith Whittington (Althouse 2001; Whittington 2001). Althouse argues that at the core of many of the Rehnquist Court's decisions is a message to Congress in which at least some in the Court's "federalism five" majority are challenging Congress to consider the federalism dimension of legislation more carefully and to make serious attempts to justify new federal legislation. And as I mentioned in chapter 4, Whittington argues that "the Rehnquist Court is *participating* in a *political process* of constitutional change," in which Congress is also participating (emphasis added; 2001, 520).

Regardless of the true motivations of the justices, the notion of the court as an institutional participant in the political process is consistent with the interaction between Couth and Congress in past instances. The new threat presented by the Court over federalism does not in theory, and almost certainly will not in practice, prevent Congress from passing new legislation that pushes traditional notions of federal power. It does, however, create conditions under which members of Congress may be more likely to articulate reasons why the federal government ought to have the power to act in a new area. If the Court's position on the issue presents political problems for a majority in Congress, Congress can present an alternative constitutional vision or engage in negotiations and bargaining with the Court—which is almost certainly inevitable anyway. Thus, I believe that the Rehnquist Court's decisions should be viewed as a reinitiation of dialogues and negotiations with Congress that remained dormant for decades, and that this is an appropriate role for the Court and judicial review. The Court is neither an insurmountable obstacle for the legislative majority nor a savior of the people from unwanted government. And to eliminate the Court from the debate would disrupt inter-institutional lawmaking, in which each unique institution of government makes unique contributions to ever-changing laws. Most importantly, the justices bring unique perspectives on—and methods for—constitutional interpretation.

One might counter my argument by pointing to the battle between Congress and the Court over the Religious Freedom Restoration Act and *Boerne*. The Court's majority opinion seemed to shut off any possibility of a congressional response to the Court's constitutional law doctrine. But just because the *Boerne* Court claims that Congress cannot challenge it does not mean that Congress cannot or will not actually do so. As I discussed in chapter 2, the Court in *Chadha* declared that Congress could not use legislative vetoes, but Congress appears to have ignored the Court's holding in a number of statutes. And as I have also discussed earlier in this chapter, some members of Congress have in fact attempted to respond to *Boerne* by introducing the Religious Liberty Protection Act and justifying it with an alternative constitutional theory. Finally, there may actually be times when the Court is the last word on a federalism matter, just as presidential vetoes are sometimes the last word on legislation. That the Court *occasionally* takes a strong stand on an issue and Congress is unable to muster support for responding to the Court does not mean that the Court always or even usually presents an absolute barrier to Congress. Given the analyses in this book, it should be clear that the example of RFRA and *Boerne* is most certainly the exception and not the rule when considering the nature of interactions between Court and Congress over constitutional issues.

The Gun Free School Zones Act and *Lopez* are a better example of the important role that judicial review plays in the federalism debate—and they represent what I believe is a much more typical and likely scenario. Congress passed a statute regulating the *possession* of an item on school grounds. While I tend to agree with those who believe that it is a stretch of the imagination to argue that mere possession of anything is interstate or commercial, especially when it is tied specifically to *local* schools, some supporters of the constitutionality of the GFSZA, including four justices on the Court, believed the contrary. What is of significance for my argument is that members of Congress did not even pretend to have thought about the issue, much less to have deliberated over their authority to pass the original statute. This was not an instance where Congress publicly debated the underlying constitutional basis for exercising power, as it did when it passed the Child Labor Act or the Civil Rights Act of 1965. Instead, it was an instance where Congress abdicated any responsibility for considering the limits of its own powers.

The Court's decision in *Lopez* has not served to reduce the scope of federal power to that which prevailed before the New Deal, nor has it resulted in a sweeping attack on the political process or a "constitutional impasse" (Whittington 2001; see also Althouse 2001). Rather, *Lopez* has given the commerce power some traction in Congress. Congress responded to the ruling by amending the GFSZA and providing a more complete justification for the legislation, and participants in the lawmaking process have been motivated to consider the scope of federalism issues such as the commerce power in the context of newly proposed legislation such as the Hate Crimes Bill. Now, when members of Congress want to legislate in an area involving its interstate commerce power, they are at least somewhat more likely to engage the constitutional issue, and to collect evidence and build a record establishing their power to legislate.

This is a healthy occurrence for a constitutional democracy and a republic of reasons. Federal power should not evolve in an expansive manner without *public deliberation* over the direction of that power. Even if the expansion of the federal government's power over a particular area has strong public policy or other justifications, and even if it is inevitable, that expansion should not occur without serious attention to its consequences for constitutional democracy. The boundaries of federalism are indeed a result of the political process, as the political safeguards scholars advocate, but the Court is an essential part of that process. Judicial review is simply one device in the political process that forces members of Congress to negotiate and bargain over those boundaries.

It is appropriate to conclude by briefly considering the role of the Court and constitutional interpretation from a broader theoretical perspective. In general, I agree with scholars who take a pluralistic view of constitutional interpretation, in which multiple institutions all have some legitimate claim to independently interpreting the Constitution. For example, Susan Burgess (1992) and Keith Whittington (1999) both acknowledge that some constitutional deliberation in Congress takes place in the legalistic context of the Court's doctrine; Robert Burt (1992) argues that government institutions share an equal responsibility for interpreting the Constitution; and Terri Peretti (1999) argues that the Court is a redundant institution and an equal participant in a political process in which institutions seek to influence the direction of policy. And there have been times, "constitutional moments" according to Bruce Ackerman (1991), when major shifts in America's constitutional values have been the result of pressure from outside the Court, to which the Court ultimately accedes. Clearly then, the Court has not been a "supreme" interpreter of the Constitution in American history in the manner advocated by judicial supremacists. On the other hand, it is not at all clear that Congress is usually an "equal" partner with the Court, or that Congress routinely engages in serious coordinate construction of the Constitution.

When considering the roles of the Court and Congress, it is imperative that we appreciate the unique nature and design of different governmental institutions. As advocates of judicial supremacy and other constitutional theorists have explained, on the whole the judiciary is much better equipped to consider constitutional questions (e.g., Alexander and Schauer 1997; Bickel 1962), and similarly, Congress is better equipped and designed to efficiently resolve different types of political and public policy disputes than to initiate and engage in serious constitutional deliberation (see, e.g., Garrett and Vermeule 2001). And as I argued earlier, Ackerman's constitutional moments are, by his own admission, rare. During routine times of lawmaking, members of Congress are not likely to engage in serious constitutional "construction" or "creation." As a routine matter, judicial review is a constitutional check that encourages bargaining, negotiation and compromise—not unlike the presidential veto (Cameron 2000).

Thus, I would describe the role of the Court and judicial review as one of "judicial primacy." I do not propose that this term amounts to a radical rethinking or grand theory of judicial review or constitutional construction, but rather that it captures what some coordinate construction and "Constitution outside the Courts" advocates have described when they identify a role for Congress and other institutions in constitutional construction while acknowledging a special role for the Court (for related arguments, see Agresto, 1980; Jacobsohn 1986; Macedo 1988). Judicial primacy means that the Court has the *primary* institutional responsibility for interpreting the Constitution, and that Congress's motivations and its likelihood of engaging in constitutional construction are limited by the majoritarian and representative nature of the institution (see, e.g., Devins 2001). It also recognizes, however, that the Court is not "supreme" in the sense that it always has the final say and is unaccountable to Congress, or that every constitutional issue is a legal, or justiciable, issue. A theory of judicial primacy appreciates representative policymaking and statute making to be the *primary* (as opposed to the only) responsibilities of Congress, and independent constitutional evaluation to be the *primary* (as opposed to the only) responsibility of the Court. Given the interactive, sequential, and alterative nature of lawmaking, neither institution can be *solely* responsible for either activity.

This is not to say that each institution cannot be effective at other activities, only that they are secondary. For example, the Court may be able to affect the implementation of public policy, but institutionally it is not as well equipped as the other branches of government to do so (Rosenberg 1991). And similarly, Congress can sometimes be effective at constitutional interpretation, but members of Congress are not generally motivated to deliberate over the ultimate meaning of the Constitution. There may be instances where the Court, bound by *stare decisis*, is not open to innovative or unconventional constitutional claims. If a particular claim has political salience, it may be that Congress or other political venues will, and should, be open to it when the Court is not. Thus, it would be inappropriate to cut Congress loose from any responsibility whatsoever over constitutional deliberation. Moreover, if the Court should create some sort of constitutional impasse, which is at the core of Ackerman's theory of constitutional moments, and a majority in Congress and "the people" disagree with the Court, the Court will likely be forced to ultimately retreat and acquiesce. But as I have argued, this is not the normal course, and as Whittington (2001) has argued, the Court can push Congress without creating a "constitutional impasse."

If we take the notion of constitutionalism seriously, it is desirable to have an institution empowered to make the primary determinations about constitutional meaning, for many of the reasons put forth by Larry Alexander and Frederick Schauer in defense of judicial supremacy (1997). Likewise, if we take the notion of democratic and representative lawmaking seriously, it is desirable to entrust that power to democratic and republican institutions. On the other hand, it would be dangerous to exonerate Congress from any responsibility over constitutional interpretation. While constitutional interpretation may be a secondary responsibility for Congress, the Court's constitutional interpretations should not go unchecked, and there may be times when alternative political venues are needed for airing constitutional claims. We should expect the Court's exercise of judicial review to naturally result in a relationship with Congress characterized by interaction and reaction, by negotiation and anticipation. In a sense, then, the true role of judicial review in our system is something in between judicial supremacy and an egalitarian view of coordinate construction.

Judicial Review Decisions

and Relevant Legislation

(Chapter 2 Dataset)

Case Name and Citation	Statute and U.S. Code Citation	Congressional Response
Babbitt v. Youpee, 519 U.S. 234 (1997)	Indian Land Consolidation Act, 25 U.S.C. § 2206 (1983, as amended 1984)	none
Printz v. United States, 521 U.S. 898 (1997)	Brady Handgun Violence Prevention Act, 18 U.S.C. § 922(s) (1993)	none
City of Boerne v. Flores, 521 U.S. 507 (1997)	Religious Freedom Restoration Act of 1993 (RFRA), 42 U.S.C. §§ 2000bb et seq. (1993)	none
Reno v. ACLU, 521 U.S. 844 (1997)	Communications Decency Act, 47 U.S.C. §§ 223(a)(1) (B)(ii), 223(d) (1996)	none
Seminole Tribe of Fla. v. Florida, 517 U.S. 44 (1996)	Indian Gaming Regulatory Act, 25 U.S.C.S. § 2701 (1988)	none
United States v. IBM, 517 U.S. 843 (1996)	Internal Revenue Code provisions, 26 U.S.C.S. § 4371 (1954)	none
Denver Area Educ. Telecommunications Consortium v. FCC, 518 U.S. 727 (1996)	Cable Television Consumer Protection & Competition Act of 1992, 47 U.S.C.S. §§ 532(h) (1)(10)(b)–(c) (1992)	none
Colorado Republican Fed. Campaign Comm. v. FEC, 518 U.S. 604 (1996)	Federal Election Campaign Act of 1971, 2 U.S.C.S. § 441a(d) (3) (1971, as amended 1974, 1976)	none
United States v. Nat'l Treasury Employees Union, 513 U.S. 454 (1995)	Ethics Reform Act of 1989, 5 U.S.C. App., § 501(b) (1989)	none

Case Name and Citation	Statute and U.S. Code Citation	Congressional Response
Plaut v. Spendthrift Farms, 514 U.S. 211 (1995)	§ 27A(b) of Securities and Exchange Act of 1934, 15 U.S.C.S. § 78aa-1(b) (1934, as amended 1991)	none
United States v. Lopez, 514 U.S. 549 (1995)	Gun Free School Zones Act, 18 U.S.C.S. § 922(q)(1)(A) (1990)	amended statute (1996)
Rubin v. Coors Brewing Co., 514 U.S. 476 (1995)	Federal Alcohol Administrative Act of 1935, 27 U.S.C.S. 205 (e)(2) (1935)	none
New York v. United States, 505 U.S. 144 (1992)	Low-Level Radioactive Waste Policy Amendments, 42 U.S.C. § 2021e(d)(2)(C) (1985)	none
Metro. Washington Airports Auth. v. Citizens for the Abatement of Aircraft Noise, 501 U.S. 252 (1991)	Metropolitan Washington Airports Act of 1986 ("Transfer Act"), 49 U.S.C. App., § 2451–61 (1986)	amended statute (1991)
U.S. v. Eichman, 496 U.S. 310 (1990)	Flag Protection Act of 1989, 18 U.S.C. § 700 (1989)	none
Sable Communications of California v. FCC, 492 U.S. 115 (1989)	Commercial Telephone Communications provisions of Federal Communications Act, 47 U.S.C. § 223(b) (1934, as amended 1988)	amended statute (1989)
Hodel v. Irving, 481 U.S. 704 (1987)	Indian Land Consolidation Act of 1983, 25 U.S.C. § 2206 (1983)	amended statute (1990)
FEC v. Massachusetts Citizens for Life, 479 U.S. 238 (1986)	Federal Election Campaign Act, 2 U.S.C. § 441b (1971, as amended 1976)	none
Bowsher v. Synar, 478 U.S. 714 (1986)	Balanced Budget and Emergency Deficit Control Act, 2 U.S.C. § 901 (1985)	amended statute (1987)
FEC v. Nat'l Conservative PAC, 470 U.S. 480 (1985)	Presidential Election Campaign Fund Act, 26 U.S.C. § 9012(f) (1971)	none
Regan v. Time, Inc., 468 U.S. 641 (1984)	Restrictions on reproduction of U.S. currency, 18 U.S.C. §§ 474, 504(1) (1948, 1958)	amended statute (1992)

Case Name and Citation	Statute and U.S. Code Citation	Congressional Response
FCC v. League of Women Voters, 468 U.S. 364 (1984)	Public Broadcasting Act of 1967; Public Broadcasting Amendments Act of 1981, 47 U.S.C. § 399 (1967, as amended 1981)	amended statute (1988)
U.S. Senate v. FTC, 463 U.S. 1216 (1983)	Federal Trade Commission Improvements Act of 1980 (two-house legislative veto provisions), 15 U.S.C. § 57a-1 (1980)	repealed (1984)
Process Gas Consumers Group v. Consumer Energy Council, 463 U.S. 1216 (1983)	Natural Gas Policy Act of 1978 (one-house legislative veto provision), 15 USC § 3342(c) (1978)	repealed (1987)
INS v. Chadha, 462 U.S. 919 (1983)	Immigration and Nationality Act (one-house legislative veto provision), 8 U.S.C. § 1254(c)(2) (1952)	repealed, passed new statute (1990)
United States v. Grace, 461 U.S. 171 (1983)	Supreme Court Grounds, 40 U.S.C. § 13k (1949)	none
Bolger v. Youngs Drug Prods. Corp., 463 U.S. 60 (1983)	Comstock Act ("mail matter" provisions), 39 U.S.C. § 3001(e)(2) (1970)	none
Northern Pipeline Const. Co. v. Marathon Pipeline, 458 U.S. 50 (1982)	Bankruptcy Act of 1978 provision, 28 U.S.C. § 1471(b) (1978)	repealed, passed new statute (1984)
Railway Labor Executives' Ass'n. v. Gibbons, 455 U.S. 457 (1982)	Rock Island Railroad Transition & Employment Act; Staggers Rail Act of 1980, 45 U.S.C. §§ 1001 et seq. (1980)	amended (1983)
United States v. Will, 449 U.S. 200 (1980)	Postal Revenue & Federal Salary Act of 1967, 2 U.S.C. §§ 351–361 (1967); Federal Pay Comparability Act of 1970, 5 U.S.C. §§ 5305–06 (1971)	repealed, passed new statute (1990)
Califano v. Westcott, 443 U.S. 76 (1979)	Social Security Act provision, 42 U.S.C. § 607(a) (1968)	amended statute (1981)
Marshall v. Barlow's, 436 U.S. 307 (1978)	Occupational Safety & Health Act provision, 29 U.S.C. § 657(a) (1970)	none

Case Name and Citation	Statute and U.S. Code Citation	Congressional Response
Califano v. Sibowitz, 430 U.S. 924 (1977)	Social Security Act provisions, 42 U.S.C. § 402(c)(1)(C) (1950)	amended statute (1977)
Railroad Retirement Bd. v. Kalina, 431 U.S. 909 (1977)	Railroad Retirement Act, 45 U.S.C. § 231a(c)(3)(ii) (1937, as amended 1974)	amended statute (1983)
Califano v. Goldfarb, 430 U.S. 199 (1977)	Social Security Act provisions, 42 U.S.C. § 402(f)(1)(D) (1939, as amended 1950)	amended statute (1977)
Nat'l League of Cities v. Usery, 426 U.S. 833 (1976)	Fair Labor Standards Act, 29 U.S.C. § 102(b) (1966. as amended 1974)	amended statute (1977)
Buckley v. Valeo, 424 U.S. 1 (1976)	Federal Election Campaign Act of 1971, 18 U.S.C. §§ 608(a), 608(e) (1972, as amended 1974)	repealed, passed new statute (1976)
Buckley v. Valeo, 424 U.S. 1 (1976)	Federal Election Campaign Act of 1971, 2 U.S.C. § 437(c) (1972, as amended 1974)	amended statute (1976)
Weinberger v. Weisenfeld, 420 U.S. 636 (1975)	Social Security Act provisions, 42 U.S.C. § 402(g) (1939)	amended statute (1977)
Jimenez v. Weinberger, 417 U.S. 628 (1974)	Social Security Act provisions, 42 U.S.C. § 416(h)(3)(B) (1939, as amended 1965)	none
Department of Agric. v. Murry, 413 U.S. 508 (1973)	Food Stamp Act of 1964, 7 U.S. § 2014(b) (1964, as amended 1971)	amended statute (1977)
Department of Agric. v. Moreno, 413 U.S. 528 (1973)	Food Stamp Act of 1964, 7 U.S.C. § 2012 (1964, as amended 1971)	amended statute (1977)
Frontiero v. Richardson, 411 U.S. 677 (1973)	Career Compensation Act of 1949, 37 U.S.C. §§ 401, 403 (1949, as amended 1962)	amended statute (1973)
Frontiero v. Richardson, 411 U.S. 677 (1973)	Dependents' Medical Care Act of 1956, 10 U.S.C. §§ 1072, 1076 (1956, as amended 1958)	amended statute (1980)
Richardson v. Davis, 409 U.S. 1069 (1972)	Social Security Act provisions, 42 U.S.C. §§ 403(a), 416(h)(3) (1968)	amended statute (1977)
Chief of Capitol Police v. Jeannette Rankin Brigade, 409 U.S. 972 (1972)	U.S. Capitol Grounds provisions, 40 U.S.C. § 193g (1946)	none
Tilton v. Richardson, 403 U.S. 672 (1971)	Higher Education Facilities Act of 1963, 20 U.S.C. § 711–21 (1963)	amended statute (1972)

Case Name and Citation	Statute and U.S. Code Citation	Congressional Response
United States v. United States Coin & Currency, 401 U.S. 715 (1971)	Internal Revenue Code provisions, 26 U.S.C. §§ 4411, 4412, 4901, 7302 (1954)	none
Blount v. Rizzi (d/b/a The Mailbox), 400 U.S. 410 (1971)	Postal Reorganization Act of 1970, 39 U.S.C. § 4006, moved to 39 U.S.C. §§ 3006–7 (1960, 1970)	none
Oregon v. Mitchell, 400 U.S. 112 (1970)	Voting Rights Act Amendments of 1970, 42 U.S.C. § 1973bb (1970)	constitutional amendment (1971)
Turner v. United States, 396 U.S. 398 (1970)	Narcotic Drugs Import & Export Act, 21 U.S.C. § 174, 26 U.S.C. § 4704 (1909)	repealed, passed new statute (1970)
Schacht v. United States, 398 U.S. 58 (1970)	Uniform Code of Military Justice, Articles 80, 130, 134, 18 U.S.C. § 702 (1956)	none
Leary v. United States, 395 U.S. 6 (1969)	Narcotic Drugs Import & Export Act of 1956, 21 U.S.C. § 176a (1956)	repealed, passed new statute (1970)
Leary v. United States, 395 U.S. 6 (1969)	Marijuana Tax Act of 1954, 26 U.S.C. § 4744(a)(2) (1954)	repealed (1970)
O'Callahan v. Parker, 395 U.S. 258 (1969)	Uniform Code of Military Justice, Arts. 80, 130, 134, 10 U.S.C. §§ 880, 993, 934 (1956)	none
Marchetti v. U.S., 390 U.S. 39 (1968)	Internal Revenue Code provisions, 26 U.S.C. §§ 4411, 4412 (1954)	amended statute (1974)
United States v. Jackson, 390 U.S. 570 (1968)	Lindbergh Kidnapping Act, 18 U.S.C. § 1201(a) (1948)	amended statute (1972)
Haynes v. Johnson 390 U.S. 85 (1968)	National Firearms Act (Internal Revenue Code provisions), 26 U.S.C. §§ 5841, 5851 (1954)	amended statute (1968)
Grosso v. United States, 390 U.S. 62 (1968)	Internal Revenue Code provisions, 26 U.S.C. §§ 4401, 4411 (1954)	amended statute (1974)
United States v. Robel, 389 U.S. 258 (1967)	Subversive Activities Control Act of 1950, 50 U.S.C. 784 (1950)	repealed (1993)

Case Name and Citation	Statute and U.S. Code Citation	Congressional Response
Afroyim v. Rusk, 387 U.S. 253 (1967)	Immigration & Nationality Act of 1952, 8 U.S.C. § 801, moved to 8 U.S.C. § 1481 (1952)	repealed (1978)
United States v. Romano, 382 U.S. 136 (1965)	Excise Tax Technical Changes Act (Internal Revenue Code), 26 U.S.C. § 5601(b)(1) (1958)	amended statute (1976)
Albertson v. Subversive Activities Control Bd., 382 U.S. 70 (1965)	Subversive Activities Control Act of 1950, 50 U.S.C. § 786(d)(4) (1950)	repealed (1968)
Lamont v. Postmaster Gen., 381 U.S. 301 (1965)	Postal Services & Federal Employees Act of 1962, 39 U.S.C. § 4008 (1962)	repealed, passed new statute (1970)
United States v. Brown, 381 U.S. 437 (1965)	Labor Management Reporting & Disclosure Act, 29 U.S.C. § 504 (1959)	amended statute (1984)
Schneider v. Rusk, 377 U.S. 163 (1964)	Immigration & Nationality Act of 1952, 8 U.S.C. § 1484 (1952)	repealed (1978)
Aptheker v. Secretary of State, 378 U.S. 500 (1964)	Subversive Activities Control Act of 1950, 50 U.S.C. § 785 (1950)	repealed (1993)
Kennedy v. Mendoza-Martinez, 373 U.S. 144 (1963)	Immigration & Nationality Act provisions, 8 U.S.C. § 1481(a)(10) (1952)	repealed (1976)
McElroy v. United States, 361 U.S. 281 (1960)	Uniform Code of Military Justice, Article 2(11), 10 U.S.C. § 802 (1950)	none
Kinsella v. Singleton, 361 U.S. 234 (1960)	Uniform Code of Military Justice, Article 2(11), 10 U.S.C. 802 (1950)	none
Grisham v. Hagan, 361 U.S. 278 (1960)	Uniform Code of Military Justice, Article 2(11), 10 U.S.C. 802 (1950)	none
Trop v. Dulles, 356 U.S. 86 (1958)	Aliens & Nationality Code, 8 U.S.C. § 1481(a)(8) (1940, as amended 1944)	repealed (1978)
Reid v. Covert, 354 U.S. 1 (1957)	Uniform Code of Military Justice, Art. 2(11), 50 U.S.C. § 552(11) (1950)	none
Toth v. Quarles, 350 U.S. 11 (1955)	Uniform Code of Military Justice, Article 3(a), 50 U.S.C. § 53 (1950)	amended statute (1992)

There were two purposes behind the forty-four interviews that I conducted for this project. First, I interviewed current and former members of Congress, staff (personal and committee staff), and lobbyists and attorneys for interest groups who were in some way involved in drafting and negotiating the specific statutes analyzed in chapter 4 (the Gun Free School Zones Act, Brady Bill, and Hate Crimes Act). Fifteen of the respondents answered questions in this first category.

These interviews were designed to develop an accurate and reliable description of how the statutes were conceived, drafted, altered, debated, and passed. The specific questions I asked are included at the end of this appendix. I wanted to give those involved with the legislation an opportunity to describe the important issues that influenced the language of the legislation and support for the legislation, in the respondents' own words. If they did not discuss whether constitutionality was raised or how it was discussed or debated, I prompted respondents with specific references to and questions about the constitutional issues relevant to the legislation (the commerce power, the Tenth Amendment, or both). I tried to interview participants on both sides of each issue, but most of the respondents in this category were Democrats. To some extent, interviewing more Democrats was necessary for unearthing the details behind these specific statutes because they were Democratic legislation, drafted and passed by Democrats who were in the majority in Congress at the time.

Second, I interviewed a wide range of respondents with more general experience of lawmaking in Congress, as either participants or observers, including current and former members of Congress, personal and committee staff, an attorney general and other officials from the U.S. Department of Justice, federal judges, a judicial clerk, lobbyists, and journalists. Some of the respondents from the first category, who had experience with the specific legislation analyzed in this book, also answered questions about constitutional issues in the legislative process more generally. Over thirty-five respondents responded to some or all of the general questions. The general interview questions I asked are included at the end of this appendix.

Overall Nature of the Interviews

These interviews were semi-structured. That is, while I worked with an established structure of interview questions, I left open many opportunities for follow-up questions that might stray from my predetermined questions. In fact, the questions from both categories—specific and general—were designed to begin with open-ended questions that allowed the respondents to make unprompted observations. If respondents made observations or comments relevant to constitutional issues in the legislative process, I asked follow-up questions. If they failed to make unprompted observations or comments about constitutional issues, I asked questions designed to refresh their memories or otherwise prompt them to recall debates.

Interviews were designed to last thirty to forty-five minutes. Most lasted at least thirty, and a few lasted well over an hour, allowing me to probe for many details regarding the debates over the legislation I was interested in and constitutional deliberation in Congress more generally. Some interviews lasted less than thirty minutes, a few to only ten or fifteen. Shortened interviews are inevitable with some subjects because of constraints on their time. In particular, opportunities to speak with current members of Congress or other government officials in high positions are difficult to come by, and in a few cases I had to take what I could get. In two instances, interviews on Capitol Hill were interrupted for roll-call votes after ten or fifteen minutes without the chance to resume the interview later.

All respondents were promised anonymity to assure truthful responses to the interview questions. It was apparent in several cases that the condition of anonymity was absolutely necessary for the interview to even take place. I asked each interviewee if I could record the interview on audiotape. Many respondents were hesitant or resistant, and in order not to make them uncomfortable, I usually did not press the issue. When I could not tape an interview, I took written notes during the interview, and immediately afterward drafted a summary of the interview, recording as many quotations and observations in writing as I could recall with confidence. Twenty-one of the interviews were recorded on audiotape and transcribed.

Interview Subjects

In selecting interview subjects, I sought to interview members of Congress, personal staff, committee staff, and other professional staff, and lobbyists who had been directly involved in drafting and debating over legislation. I also wanted to interview at least a few others outside Congress who had been participants in the legislative process or at least close observers, such as members of the executive and judicial branches, journalists, and researchers with think tanks. Many of those whom I interviewed had held more than one position. For example, one respondent had been a personal staff member for a senator and a clerk to a U.S. Supreme Court Justice. Another had been a federal prosecutor, counsel for the House Judiciary Committee, head of the Justice Department's legislative program, and a lobbyist for a private law firm. Often these respondents gave answers reflecting their changing perspectives.

The following is a list of the number of respondents in each category. Because some respondents served in multiple positions, the total number of positions (49) exceeds the total number of respondents (44):

  6 members of Congress (2 senators, 4 representatives)
 17 personal staff members (chief of staff, legislative director, legislative assistant)
 14 members of committee and other professional staff
  4 lobbyists, attorneys for interest groups
  4 journalists, researchers for think tanks
  1 attorney general
  1 federal judge
  2 counsel in Justice Department

In citing the interviews, I used the following codes:

  (MC#) Member of Congress
  (PS#) Personal staff for a member of Congress
  (CS#) Committee or other professional staff
  (IG#) Lobbyist or attorney for interest group
  (AG#) U.S. attorney general
  (MS#) Miscellaneous others

If a respondent could be classified in more than one category, I cited that respondent with the code most relevant to the substantive information he or she spoke to, and I noted in the text of the book that the respondent served in more than one capacity.

Interview Questions for Specific Legislation

1. Tell me about the [name the statute]. Give me a guided tour of the process for that bill.
   a. How did the idea for the bill originate?
   b. What were the key developments while the legislation was being considered?
2. What were the most important factors that led to its passage?
   a. Can you pinpoint why that was so important?
   b. Who made it important?
3. Were there specific mark-up sessions that in your mind were the most important in leading to compromises or passage?
   a. Give me a guided tour of that session. OR
   b. Why not?
4. Were there specific committee hearings that in your mind significantly influenced the final version of the bill?
   a. Give me a guided tour of those hearings. OR
   b. Why not?
5. Were there specific informal or closed-door meetings or negotiations you were aware of that may have influenced the bill?
   a. What more can you tell me about those meetings or negotiations?
6. Who were the most important participants in drafting this legislation?
   a. In Congress?
      —Specific members? Committee?
   b. Outside Congress?
      —Interest groups or lobbyists?
      —President, members of administration?
   c. Others?
7. (If respondent has not mentioned constitutional issues yet:) Do you recall constitutional issues being raised at any point?
   a. Did constitutional issues even occur to you or others?
   b. Did you have any concerns regarding constitutional issues or the Supreme Court?
8. If time, ask general questions—other examples of constitutional issues in legislation?

General Interview Questions

1. From your experience, what do you think are the most important issues during the legislative process?
   a. Why?
   b. Examples?
2. Generally, do you think people in Congress consider the Constitution or the Supreme Court's constitutional doctrine?
   a. Who raises issues? (Staff? Members? Interest groups? Legislative counsel? Committees?)
   b. Where in Congress are constitutional issues raised?
   c. Which constitutional issues are most likely to be raised? Why?
   d. When in the legislative process are constitutional issues raised?
   e. How are they debated (philosophical, court doctrine, or other)?
   f. What is the usual impact of constitutional decisions on legislation and votes? Do constitutional issues ever win over other issues (policy, political)?
   g. What tools or mechanisms exist in Congress to help address constitutional issues?
3. Do you think the Court communicates with Congress?
   a. Why or why not?
   b. How? Through opinions? Are members of Congress aware of Court opinions?
   c. What do people in Congress think about the Supreme Court? Do they think they must follow the Court's decisions?
4. If time, ask about knowledge of specific statutes.

INTRODUCTION

1 Other examples of federalism decisions handed down by the Supreme Court include: *New York v. United States* (1992); *Seminole Tribe of Florida v. Florida* (1996); *Printz v. United States* (1997); *Alden v. Maine* (1999); *Florida Prepaid Postsecondary Ed. Expense Bd. v. College Savings Bank* (1999); *Morrison v. United States* (2000); *Kimel v. Florida Board of Regents* (2000); *Board of Trustees of the University of Alabama v. Garrett* (2001).

2 I elaborate on the usefulness and value of examining federalism issues in chapter 3.

3 For a more detailed description of the interview design and interview respondents, see appendix B.

ONE *Constitutional Deliberation in a Separated System*

1 Shipan uses the term "judicial review" to mean *any* review by the judiciary of administrative action by the administrative agency, not only constitutional review or interpretation.

2 The staff members and others who originally drafted the GFSZA were disappointed by the *Lopez* decision but determined to revive it. While there were no hearings, committee consideration, or floor debate on the subject, "findings" were added at the beginning of the GFSZA stating that guns transported across state lines in commerce are a national problem and have adverse effects on education. Additionally, the drafters revised the language of the GFSZA to limit the crime of possessing a gun in a "school zone" to possession of a gun that had traveled in interstate commerce.

TWO *Roadblock, Speed Bump, or Detour?*

1 This does not mean that members of Congress did not try to override *Roe* by constitutional amendment or other legislative means, but only that successful congressional enactments did not ultimately rise to the level of an override.

2 A two-dimensional model of policy preferences does not assume an explanation for Supreme Court decision making. Justices may vote their true policy preferences as argued by proponents of the Attitudinal Model (see Segal and Spaeth 1993), they may strategically vote to maximize their policy preferences in light of institutional and other constraints as proponents of rational choice models argue (see Epstein and Knight 1998; Eskridge 1993, 1991), or they may even be influenced

by legal reasoning. The importance of the constitutional policy dimension is that the primary issues for the Court—ideologically as well as legally—involve constitutional issues, while the primary issue of concern for Congress is the public policy embodied in the statute. (For a more detailed discussion of trade-offs along multiple policy dimensions and spatial models see Schwartz 1992; and Enelow and Hinich 1984).

3   I did not include *Boos v. Barry*, 485 U.S. 312 (1988), which involved provisions of the District of Columbia Code.

4   For a complete list of Supreme Court decisions and statutes included in the dataset, see appendix A.

5   I looked at pieces of legislative history available in *CQ Weekly* reports, *Congressional and Administrative News,* and the *Congressional Record*.

6   Of course, the modification to unconstitutional legislation may not actually solve the constitutional problem identified by the Court and may be subject to further judicial review in the future. In simply coding for a congressional response to the Court, I was only interested in whether Congress actually changed the statute in a manner that addressed the Court's decision.

7   For a complete list of the statutes, Supreme Court decisions, and citations, see appendix A.

8   29 U.S.C. 657(a), P.L. 91-596, S 8(a).

9   28 U.S.C. 1471(b), P.L. 95-598, Title IV, Sect. 405(a)–(c), 92 Stat. 2686.

10   The Senate voted 57–10 and the House 286–48 to override Truman's veto.

11   P.L. 90-237, 5 Stat. 766 (1968).

12   See, e.g., House Report No. 733 (HR 12601) (90th Cong., 1967); Conference Report no. 103 (90th Cong., December 12, 1967).

13   P.L. 101-649, Title III, Sect. 302(h), 104 Stat. 5053, Nov. 29, 1990. In this statute and in others, Congress has claimed authority to use legislative vetoes as part of its rulemaking powers found in Article I, Section 5, of the U.S. Constitution: "Each House may determine the Rules for its Proceedings."

14   While Congress has challenged the Court by continuing the practice of legislative vetoes, it has in at least one instance deferred to the Court on the matter. In *Process Gas Consumers Group v. Consumer Energy Council* (1983), the Court summarily affirmed a lower court ruling that struck down legislative veto provisions of the Natural Gas Policy Act of 1978 (15 U.S.C. 3342(c), P.L. 95-621, 92 Stat. 3372). Congress formally repealed those legislative veto provisions in 1987 (P.L. 100-42, 101 Stat. 314) without replacing them.

15   P.L. 103-322, 108 Stat. 1996 et seq. (Sept. 13, 1994).

16   The interview responses are used primarily for my analyses in chapters 4 and 5, and the structure of the interviews is described in more detail in those chapters and in appendix B.

17   P.L. 104-208, Div. A, Title I, 101 (f), Title IV, 657, 658(b). 110 Stat. 3009-362, 3009-372.

18   The old provisions were repealed in P.L. 94-283, Title II, Section 201(a), 90 Stat. 496, and the new regulations in P.L. 94-283, Title I, Section 112(a), 90 Stat. 487 (May 11, 1976).

19 P.L. 98-76, Title I, Sections 104(a),(b), 106 (a)–(g), Title IV 409 (a), 413 (a), 414 (a), 415; 97 Stat. 415, 417, 418, 435, 436 (1983).

20 P.L. 95-113, Title XIII, Sect. 1301, 91 Stat. 962

21 See House Report 95-464, pp. 102–3.

22 As with *Lopez* and the GFSZA, the interview responses are used primarily in my analyses in chapters 4 and 5. For a more detailed description of the interviews, see those chapters and appendix B.

THREE *The Shadows of Uncertain Scrutiny*

1 Here, I use "policy" to mean the public policy that is being pursued. The "bill," "legislation," or "statute" is the legislative proposal that would, if enacted, be the legal vehicle through which the policy is implemented and applied. For example, a bill regulating firearms has as its public policy the goal of gun control, while the legislation provides the legal means of pursuing and implementing that policy. I conceive of "lawmaking" as a broad activity that includes policy making and statute making, as well as executive actions and adjudication (see, e.g., Jones 1995; Morgan 1966).

2 The statistics in chapter 3 indicate that the Court struck down seventy-four federal statutes in forty-four years, a rate of less than two unconstitutional federal statutes per year.

3 Of course, those who use constitutional arguments to oppose legislation may do so sincerely or opportunistically. The key points I am exploring in this chapter and the following one are whether constitutional issues get raised, when and why they get raised, and how they get debated. Thus, the important issue here is not so much what motivates opponents of legislation but that we should expect them to be more likely to raise relevant constitutional issues during consideration of a bill.

4 The Court had also upheld other federal regulation of interstate commerce during this period. For example, under the authority of the Interstate Commerce Act, the Interstate Commerce Commission ("ICC") set new rates and established other regulations for railroads that applied to some railroads engaged in *intrastate* activities. Nonetheless, the Court upheld the regulations because the rates for intrastate railway travel had a "close and substantial relation to interstate commerce." *Houston, E. & W.T.R. Co. v. United States* ("*Shreveport*"), 342 U.S. 342 (1914). See also *Southern Railway Co. v. United States*, 222 U.S. 20 (1911), and *Railroad Commission of Wisconsin v. Chicago, Burlington & Quincy Railroad*, 257 U.S. 563 (1922).

5 45 Stat. 159, Ch. 64 (1921).

6 See House Report 77 (61st Cong., 1921).

7 For detailed accounts of the history of the child labor legislation during this period see Braeman 1964; Faulkner 1931; Fuller 1923; Link 1955; and Wood 1968.

8 S. 6562, 59th Cong., 2d Sess.

9 *Congressional Record*, 59th Cong., 2d Sess., pp. 1552–57, 1792–1826, 1867–83 (January 23, 28, and 29, 1907).

10 *Congressional Record*, 59th Cong., 2d. Sess., at 2136, 2393 (see also Braeman 1964, 25).

11 36 Stat. at L. 825, chap. 395, U. S. Comp. Stat. Supp. 1911, p. 1343.

12 H.R. Rep. No 46 (Part 1), 64th Cong., 1st Sess. 13–14 (1916).

13 Wilson's shift occurred immediately after he had changed his position on important trade and antitrust policies, in what one author has called "The Turning Point in Wilsonian Progressivism" (Link 1955, 130–35).

14 *Congressional Record*, 64th Cong., 1st Sess., p. 12301 (also quoted in Wood 1968, 71).

15 Here the Court was referring to *Hipolite Egg Co. v. United States* (1911), in which it upheld the constitutionality of the Pure Food and Drugs Act.

16 It should be noted that Congress did not give up on child labor legislation after *Dagenhart*. Congress turned to a different constitutional provision, the taxing power under Article I, Section 8, and passed the Child Labor Tax Act of 1919. The Act taxed 10 percent of the annual profits of employers who employed children. Again, members of Congress engaged in significant constitutional deliberation over the taxing power, but the Supreme Court invalidated the Act in *Bailey v. Drexel Furniture Co.*, 259 U.S. 20 (1922) (*"Child Labor Tax Case"*) (see Fuller 1923, 241–42; Wood 1968, 175–219). Eventually, Congress would be able to regulate child labor after the New Deal cases.

17 The Court also based its decision on separation of powers grounds, declaring that the Act unconstitutionally delegated legislative power to the executive branch by granting the National Recovery Administration power to promulgate the codes.

18 Senate Report 872, reprinted in *United States Code Congressional & Administrative News*, 1964, 88th Cong., 2255–2524.

19 House Report no. 914, 88th Cong., Nov. 20, 1963; see also *The Civil Rights Act of 1964: Text Analysis, Legislative History* (Washington: Bureau of National Affairs, 1964).

20 Those testifying included Robert F. Kennedy (U.S. attorney general), Dean Rusk (secretary of state), Willard Wirtz (secretary of labor), Erwin N. Griswold (dean of Harvard Law School and former member of the U.S. Civil Rights Commission), Paul Freund (constitutional law scholar, Harvard Law School), Peter Rozelle (commissioner of the National Football League), and Roy Wilkins (executive director of the National Association for the Advancement of Colored People).

21 See *Congressional Record*, 88th Cong., 1st Sess., 1963, Hearings before Senate Commerce Committee on S. 1732.

22 Senate Commerce Committee Hearings on S. 1732, 88th Cong., 1st Sess., Parts 1 and 2 (also quoted in part in Gunther 1985, 159–62).

23 P.L. 88-352, 78 Stat. 241.

24 18 U.S.C. 891, Pub. Law 90-321, sec. 201, 1968.

25 See also *Russell v. United States*, 471 U.S. 858 (1985), in which the Court upheld federal anti-arson legislation as a legitimate exercise of the commerce power.

FOUR *The Missing Constitution*

1 In the interest of time and space, I do not discuss all of the Rehnquist Court's federalism decisions in full. However, the seriousness of the current judicial re-

view threat is reinforced by other federalism decisions involving the commerce power, sovereign immunity and Section 5 of the Fourteenth Amendment (*New York v. United States* [1992]; *Seminole Tribe of Florida v. Florida* [1996]; *Alden v. Maine* [1999]; *Florida Prepaid Postsecondary Ed. Expense Bd. v. College Savings Bank* [1999]; *Morrison v. United States* [2000]; *Kimel v. Florida Board of Regents* [2000]; *Board of Trustees of the University of Alabama v. Garrett* [2001]).

2 At the time of the initial research for this book, the hate crimes bill was still under consideration in Congress. In addition, portions of VAWA were struck down by the Court in *United States v. Morrison* (2000), after research for the project was completed.

3 Several of the interviews were conducted by telephone and in locations outside Washington.

4 A more detailed description of the interview design, respondents, and questions is included in appendix B.

5 S. 3266.

6 *Congressional Record*, October 27, 1990, p. S17595. The sponsor of the GFSZA in the House, Representative Edward Feighan, made similar arguments in favor of the GFSZA (See *Congressional Record*, November 20, 1989, p. E3988).

7 See, *New York Times*, April 23, 1990, A23.

8 Law enforcement officials in cities and states also urged local support for the Brady Bill (see, e.g., "Police Chiefs Back Pistol Purchase Bill," *St. Louis Dispatch*, August 30, 1990, Illinois Five Star Edition, 11I).

9 "Reagan Backs 7-Day Wait for Pistol Buyers," *Los Angeles Times*, March 29, 1991, A1.

10 "Reagan Expected to Endorse 'Brady Bill' Waiting Period for Buying Handguns," *Washington Post*, March 28, 1991, A9.

11 During this time period, for example, the *Los Angeles Times* (March 29, 1991, A1) reported that U.S. Representatives Les AuCoin (D-Oreg.) and Susan Molinari (D-N.Y.) were "key defections from the NRA's position," and the *Washington Post* (April 24, 1991, A7) reported that "Reps. Michael A. Andrews (D-Texas) and Butler Derrick (D-S.C.), longtime supporters of the National Rifle Association (NRA), which opposes the Brady Bill, have announced they were switching their positions and would vote for the measure because of their concerns about gun-related violence."

12 "Brady Bill Sent to House Floor for Vote," *Washington Post*, April 24, 1991, A7.

13 "Brady Bill, Senate Version," *Washington Post*, June 18, 1991, A20.

14 "5-Day Wait on Handgun Sales Ok'd by Senate," *Washington Post*, June 29, 1991.

15 "Guns Lose in Latest Poll," *Los Angeles Times*, June 7, 1993, B6.

16 For newspaper accounts of the subcommittee action, see "Legislation to Delay Handgun Purchases Advances in House," *New York Times*, October 30, 1993, 1–7; "House Subcommittee Backs Latest Gun Control Effort," *Los Angeles Times*, October 30, 1993, A-27.

17 "Senate Passes Crime Package, Shelves Brady Bill," *Washington Post*, November 20, 1993, A1.

18 See "Senate Approves Brady Bill, 63-36," *Washington Post*, November 21, 1993, A1;

"In Surprise Shift, Senate Ends GOP Filibuster, Ok's Brady Bill," *Los Angeles Times*, November 21, 1993; also Interviews CS2 and IG2.

19 "Brady Bill Changes Bring Deadlock; GOP Senators Block Final Approval," *Washington Post*, November 23, 1993, A1.

20 "Gun-Control Act Wins Final Battle as G.O.P. Retreats," *New York Times*, November 24, 1993, A1.

21 *Congressional Record*, November 19, 1993, S16413.

22 *Congressional Record*, November 11, 1993, H9100.

23 *Congressional Record*, November 10, 1993, H9104.

24 For a discussion of interpretations of the Second Amendment, see Levinson 1989. See also *Lewis v. United States*, 445 U.S. 55 (1980), in which the Supreme Court upheld a federal statute making it a federal crime to ship sawed-off shotguns in interstate commerce, explicitly holding that the law did not violate the Second Amendment.

25 According to some of the lawyers I spoke with, the NRA did make a small but ineffective lobbying effort to bring the *New York* decision to the attention of members of Congress, apparently by circulating a memo to alert them that the Court had decided a case recently that might affect the Brady Bill. Two interviewees made reference to some sort of NRA correspondence raising the issue, but I have been unable to obtain a copy of that correspondence after repeated requests through various offices. According to at least one supporter of the Brady Bill whom I spoke with, the memo made reference to a recent Supreme Court case but incorrectly cited a decision other than *New York v. United States*. I interviewed an official from the NRA by telephone who did not confirm the existence of this memo. What is important for the analysis here is that the NRA may have attempted to make federalism an issue, but was unsuccessful because it was asking its supporters to now vote against a provision that it had urged them to support in recent years.

26 18 U.S.C. 921 et seq.

27 *New York v. United States* (1992); *Seminole Tribe of Florida v. Florida* (1996); *Alden v. Maine* (1999); *Florida Prepaid Postsecondary Ed. Expense Bd. v. College Savings Bank* (1999); *Morrison v. United States* (2000); *Kimel v. Florida Board of Regents* (2000); *Board of Trustee of the University of Alabama v. Garrett* (2001).

28 Pub. L. 103-322, Title IV, 108 Stat. 1902; 42 U.S.C. 13701 et seq.

29 There are also some provisions of VAWA addressing evidentiary issues, judicial administration, and appropriations, which are not relevant here.

30 Citing 137 *Congressional Record* S. 597 (statement of Senator Joseph Biden, D-Del.).

31 See also Senate Report no. 197, 102d Cong., 1st Sess. (1991).

32 See, e.g., speeches reprinted at 138 *Congressional Record* S443–44 (January 27, 1992) and 138 *Congressional Record* E746 (March 19, 1992).

33 This "strategy" was validated by some of the limited testimony that addressed the constitutional issue. See, e.g., the statement of Professor Cass Sunstein, in *Violence against Women: Victims of the System: Hearing Before the Committee on the Judiciary*, 102d Cong., 1st. Sess., 369, 116–17.

34 S. Rep. No. 102-197, 53 (citing Elizabeth M. Ellis, Beverly M. Atkeson, and Karen S. Calhoun, "An Assessment of Long-Term Reaction to Rape," *Journal of Abnormal Psychology* 90 [1981]: 264).

35 18 U.S.C. 245.

36 Senate Hearing 105-904.

37 Senate Hearing 106-517 (May 11, 1999).

38 Senate Hearing 105-997 (June 23, 1998).

39 E.g., House Judiciary Committee Hearing (September 29, 1999) (see also House Report 106-494); Senate Hearing 106-496 (May 5, 1999) (see also Senate Report 106-420); Senate Hearing 105-882 (March 4, 1997); House Judiciary Committee Hearing (March 5, 1998); House Judiciary Committee Hearing (April 10, 1997) (see also House Report 106-494, dissenting views).

FIVE *The Nature of Things*

1 As I have described in earlier chapters and in more detail in appendix B, I divide my interview respondents into two categories: those with direct involvement in the drafting and consideration of the statutes involving federalism issues that I examined in chapter 4, and those involved in the lawmaking process more generally with no direct involvement in the federalism statutes.

2 Another place where constitutional issues might get raised is with legislative counsel. Frequently, the staffs in Congress ask legislative counsel to draft legislation that would address a particular policy idea. According to most of those I interviewed from both chambers, the legislative counsel in the House are more heavily relied upon for drafting and identifying potential problems with proposed legislation than their Senate counterparts. I do not include legislative counsel in the categories here, however, because nearly every respondent, including two attorneys in the Office of Legislative Counsel in the House, stressed that even if legislative counsel were to identify a potential constitutional issue, the likelihood that the constitutional issue will actually be raised and addressed by others in Congress is still determined by the three factors listed here.

Ackerman, Bruce. 1991. *We the People: Foundations*. Cambridge: Harvard University Press.

Agresto, John. 1980. The Limits of Judicial Supremacy: A Proposal for "Checked Activism." *Georgia Law Review* 14:471–95.

———. 1984. *The Supreme Court and Constitutional Democracy*. Ithaca: Cornell University Press.

Alexander, Larry, and Frederick Schauer. 1997. On Extrajudicial Constitutional Interpretation. *Harvard Law Review* 110:1359–87.

Althouse, Ann. 2001. Inside the Federalism Cases: Concern about the Federal Courts. *Annals of the American Academy of Political and Social Science* 547:132–44.

Arnold, Douglass. 1990. *The Logic of Congressional Action*. New Haven: Yale University Press.

Bachrach, Peter, and Morton S. Baratz. 1962. Two Faces of Power. *American Political Science Review* 56:947–52.

Bamberger, Michael A. 2000. *Reckless Legislation: How Lawmakers Ignore the Constitution*. New Brunswick, N.J.: Rutgers University Press.

Bates, Robert H., ed. 1998. *Analytic Narratives*. Princeton: Princeton University Press.

Berger, Raoul. 1969. *Congress v. the Supreme Court*. Cambridge: Harvard University Press.

Bickel, Alexander. 1962. *The Least Dangerous Branch: The Supreme Court at the Bar of Politics*. 2d ed. New Haven: Yale University Press.

Bork, Robert H. 1990. *The Tempting of America: The Political Seduction of the Law*. New York: Free Press.

Bowers, Claude G. 1932. *Beveridge and the Progressive Era*. Cambridge: Houghton Mifflin.

Braeman, John. 1964. Albert J. Beveridge and the First National Child Labor Bill. *Indiana Magazine of History* 1:1–36.

Burgess, Susan R. 1992. *Contest for Constitutional Authority: The Abortion and War Powers Debates*. Lawrence: University Press of Kansas.

Burt, Robert A. 1992. *The Constitution in Conflict*. Cambridge: Belknap.

Calabresi, Steven. 1995. A Government of Limited and Enumerated Powers: In Defense of United States v. Lopez. *Michigan Law Review* 94:752–831.

———. 2001. Federalism and the Rehnquist Court: A Normative Defense. *Annals of the American Academy of Political and Social Science* 574:24–36.

Cameron, Charles M. 2000. *Veto Bargaining: Presidents and the Politics of Negative Power*. Cambridge: Cambridge University Press.

Canon, Bradley C., and Charles A. Johnson. 1999. *Judicial Policies: Implementation and Impact*. 2d ed. Washington: CQ Press.

Choper, Jesse H. 1980. *Judicial Review and the National Political Process: A Functional Reconsideration of the Role of the Supreme Court*. Chicago: University of Chicago Press.

Clayton, Cornell. 1999. Law, Politics, and the Rehnquist Court: Structural Influences on Supreme Court Decision Making. In *The Supreme Court and Political Jurisprudence: New and Old Institutionalisms*, ed. H. Gillman and C. Clayton. Lawrence: University Press of Kansas.

Colker, Ruth, and James J. Brudney. 2001. Dissing Congress. *Michigan Law Review* 100:80–144.

Cooter, Robert D. 2000. *The Strategic Constitution*. Princeton: Princeton University Press.

Corwin, Edward S. 1938. *Court over Constitution: A Study of Judicial Review as an Instrument of Popular Government*. Princeton: Princeton University Press.

Curtis, Michael K., ed. 1993. *The Constitution and the Flag*. Ed. P. Finkelman. Vol. 2. *Collections of Documents and Articles on Major Questions of American Law: The Constitution and the Flag*. New York: Garland.

Cushman, Barry. 1992. A Stream of Legal Consciousness: The Current of Commerce Doctrine from Swift to Jones & Laughlin. *Fordham Law Review* 61:105.

———. 1998. *Rethinking the New Deal Court: The Structure of a Constitutional Revolution*. New York: Oxford University Press.

Dahl, Robert. 1957. Decision-Making in a Democracy: The Supreme Courts as a National Policy Maker. *Journal of Public Law* 6:279.

den Dulk, Kevin R., and J. Mitchell Pickerill. 2003. Bridging the Lawmaking Process: The Effects of Organized Groups on Court-Congress Interaction. *Polity* 25: 419–440.

Devins, Neal. 1996. *Shaping Constitutional Values: Elected Government, the Supreme Court, and the Abortion Debate*. Baltimore: Johns Hopkins University Press.

———. 2001. Congress as Culprit: How Lawmakers Spurred on the Court's Anti-Congress Crusade. *Duke Law Journal* 51:435–64.

Dimond, Paul R. 1989. *The Supreme Court and Judicial Choice: The Role of Provisional Review in a Democracy*. Ann Arbor: University of Michigan Press.

Dworkin, Ronald. 1981. The Forum of Principle. *New York University Law Review* 56:469–518.

Ely, John Hart. 1980. *Democracy and Distrust: A Theory of Judicial Review*. Cambridge: Harvard University Press.

Enelow, James M., and Melvin J. Hinich. 1984. *The Spatial Theory of Voting: An Introduction*. Cambridge: Cambridge University Press.

Epp, Charles R. 1999. *The Rights Revolution: Lawyers, Activists, and Supreme Courts in Comparative Perspective*. Chicago: University of Chicago Press.

Epstein, Lee, and Jack Knight. 1998. *The Choices Justices Make*. Washington: CQ Press.

Epstein, Lee, and Thomas G. Walker. 1995. The Role of the Supreme Court in American Society: Playing the Reconstruction Game. In *Contemplating Courts*, ed. Epstein. Washington: CQ Press.

Epstein, Richard. 1987. The Proper Scope of the Commerce Power. *Virginia Law Review* 73:1387.

Eskridge, William N., Jr. 1991. Overriding Supreme Court Statutory Interpretation Decisions. *Yale Law Review* 101:331.

——. 1993. The Judicial Review Game. *Northwestern University Law Review* 88:382–95.

Eskridge, William N., Jr., and John Ferejohn. 1992. The Article I, Section 7 Game. *Georgetown Law Journal* 80:523–64.

Faulkner, Harold U. 1931. *The Quest for Social Justice, 1898–1914.* Ed. A. M. Schlesinger and D. R. Fox. Vol. 11, *The History of American Life.* New York: Macmillan.

Fenno, Richard. 1973. *Congressmen in Committees.* Boston: Little, Brown.

——. 1977. U.S. House Members in Their Constituencies: An Exploration. *American Political Science Review* 71:883–917.

——. 1978. *Home Style: House Members in Their Districts.* Boston: Little, Brown.

Fisher, Louis. 1978. *The Constitution among Friends: Congress, the President and the Law.* New York: St. Martin's.

——. 1985. Constitutional Interpretation by Members of Congress. *North Carolina Law Review* 63:707–47.

——. 1988. *Constitutional Dialogues: Interpretation as a Political Process.* Princeton: Princeton University Press.

——. 1990. Separation of Powers: Interpretation Outside the Courts. *Pepperdine Law Review* 18:57–93.

——. 1993. The Legislative Veto: Invalidated, It Survives. *Law and Contemporary Problems* 56:273–304.

——. 1997. *Constitutional Conflicts between Congress and the President.* 4th ed. Lawrence: University Press of Kansas.

Fisher, Louis, and Neal Devins. 2001. *The Political Dynamics of Constitutional Law.* 3d ed. St. Paul: West.

Fuller, Raymond G. 1923. *Child Labor and the Constitution.* New York: Thomas Y. Crowell.

Garrett, Elizabeth, and Adrian Vermeule. 2001. Institutional Design of a Thayerian Congress. *Duke Law Journal* 50:1277–1333.

Gely, Rafael, and Pablo T. Spiller. 1990. A Rational Choice Theory of Supreme Court Statutory Decisions with Applications to the State Farm and Grove City Cases. *Journal of Law and Economics, and Organization* 6:263–300.

——. 1992. The Political Economy of Supreme Court Constitutional Decisions: The Case of Roosevelt's Court-Packing Plan. *International Review of Law and Economics* 12:45–67.

Goldstein, Robert J. 2000. *Flag Burning and Free Speech: The Case of Texas v. Johnson.* Ed. P. C. Hoffer and N. E. H. Hull, *Landmark Law Cases and American Society.* Lawrence: University Press of Kansas.

Graber, Mark A. 1998. Establishing Judicial Review? *Political Research Quarterly* 51:221–39.

——. 1999. The Problematic Establishment of Judicial Review. In *The Supreme Court in American Politics: New Institutionalist Interpretations.* Ed. H. Gillman and C. Clayton. Lawrence: University Press of Kansas.

Greve, Michael S. 1999. *Real Federalism: Why It Matters, How It Could Happen*. Washington: AEI Press.

Griffin, Stephen. 1996. *American Constitutionalism: From Theory to Politics*. Princeton: Princeton University Press.

Groseclose, Tim, and Nolan McCarty. 2001. The Politics of Blame: Bargaining before an Audience. *American Journal of Political Science* 45:100–119.

Gunther, Gerald. 1985. *Constitutional Law*. 11th ed. Mineola: Foundation.

Hamilton, Marci. 2001. The Elusive Safeguards of Federalism. *Annals of the American Academy of Political and Social Science* 574:93–131.

Hand, Learned. 1958. *The Bill of Rights*. New York: Atheneum.

Hausegger, Lori, and Lawrence Baum. 1999. Inviting Congressional Action: A Study of Supreme Court Motivations in Statutory Interpretation. *American Journal of Political Science* 43:162–85.

Hettinger, Virginia, and Christopher Zorn. 1999. Signals, Models, and Congressional Overrides of the Supreme Court. Paper read at Annual Meeting of the Midwest Political Science Association, April 13–15, 1999, at Chicago.

Ingberman, Daniel E., and Dennis A. Yao. 1991. Presidential Commitment and the Veto. *American Journal of Political Science* 35:357–89.

Jackson, John E., and John Kingdon. 1992. Ideology, Interest Group Scores, and Legislative Votes. *American Journal of Political Science* 36:805–23.

Jacobsohn, Gary J. 1986. *The Supreme Court and the Decline of Constitutional Aspiration*. Totowa, N.J.: Rowman and Littlefield.

Jones, Charles O. 1994. *The Presidency in a Separated System*. Washington: Brookings Institution.

———. 1995. A Way of Life and Law: Presidential Address, American Political Science Association, 1994. *American Political Science Review* 89:1–9.

———. 1998. *The Speculative Imagination in Democratic Lawmaking*. Oxford: Oxford University Press.

Katzmann, Robert A. 1997. *Courts and Congress*. Washington: Brookings Institution Press / Governance Institute.

———, ed. 1988. *Judges and Legislators: Toward Institutional Comity*. Washington: Brookings Institution.

King, Gary, Robert O. Keohane, and Sydney Verba. 1994. *Designing Social Inquiry: Scientific Inference in Qualitative Research*. Princeton: Princeton University Press.

Kingdon, John. 1984. *Agendas, Alternative and Public Policies*. Boston: Little, Brown.

———. 1989. *Congressmen's Voting Decisions*. Ann Arbor: University of Michigan Press.

———. 1995. *Agendas, Alternatives and Public Policies*. 2d ed. New York: Longman.

Kramer, Larry D. 2000. Putting the Politics Back into the Political Safeguards of Federalism. *Columbia Law Review* 100:215–93.

Krehbiel, Keith. 1991. *Information and Legislative Organization*. Ann Arbor: University of Michigan Press.

———. 1998. *Pivotal Politics: A Theory of U.S. Lawmaking*. Chicago: University of Chicago Press.

Levinson, Sanford. 1988. *Constitutional Faith*. Princeton: Princeton University Press.

——. 1989. The Embarrassing Second Amendment. *Yale Law Journal* 99:637–59.

Link, Arthur S. 1955. *A History of the United States Since the 1890's*. New York: Alfred A. Knopf.

Macedo, Stephen. 1988. Liberal Virtues, Constitutional Community. *Review of Politics* 50:215–40.

Maloney, Kerrie E. 1996. Gender Motivated Violence and the Commerce Clause: The Civil Rights Provision of the Violence against Women Act after Lopez. *Columbia Law Review* 84:1886–1941.

Martin, Andrew D. 2001. Congressional Decision Making and the Separation of Powers. *American Political Science Review* 95:361–78.

Mayhew, David R. 1974. *Congress: The Electoral Connection*. New Haven: Yale University Press.

McCloskey, Robert G. 1960. *The American Supreme Court*. Chicago: University of Chicago Press.

Meernik, James, and Joseph Ignagni. 1997. Judicial Review and Coordinate Construction of the Constitution. *American Journal of Political Science* 41:447–67.

Mikva, Abner J. 1983. How Well Does Congress Support and Defend the Constitution? *North Carolina Law Review* 61:587–611.

Moore, Wayne D. 1996. *Constitutional Rights and Powers of the People*. Princeton: Princeton University Press.

Morgan, Donald G. 1966. *Congress and the Constitution: A Study of Responsibility*. Cambridge: Belknap.

Murphy, Walter F. 1986. Who Shall Interpret? The Quest for the Ultimate Constitutional Interpreter. *Review of Politics* 48:401–23.

Nagel, Robert F. 1989. *Constitutional Cultures: The Mentality and Consequences of Judicial Review*. Berkeley: University of California Press.

——. 2001. *The Implosion of American Federalism*. New York: Oxford University Press.

Nourse, Victoria F. 1996. Where Violence, Relationship, and Equality Meet: The Violence against Women Act's Civil Rights Remedy. *Wisconsin Women's Law Journal* 11:1–36.

Peretti, Terri Jennings. 1999. *In Defense of a Political Court*. Princeton: Princeton University Press.

Peterson, Mark A. 1990. *Legislating Together: The White House and Capitol Hill from Eisenhower to Reagan*. Cambridge: Harvard University Press.

Rauch, Basil. 1944. *The History of the New Deal, 1933–1938*. New York: Creative Age.

Rogers, James R. 2001. Information and Judicial Review: A Signaling Game of Legislative-Judicial Interaction. *American Journal of Political Science* 45:84–99.

Rosenberg, Gerald N. 1991. *The Hollow Hope: Can Courts Bring About Social Change?* Chicago: University of Chicago Press.

Scalia, Antonin. 2000. Constitutional Interpretation. In *Sherman L. Bellwood Lecture at the University of Idaho College of Law*. Moscow, Idaho.

Schwartz, Edward P. 1992. Policy, Precedent, and Power: A Positive Theory of Supreme Court Decision Making. *Journal of Law, Economics and Organization* 8:219–52.

Segal, Jeffrey A. 1997. Separation-of-Powers Games in the Positive Theory of Congress and the Court. *American Political Science Review* 91:28–44.

Segal, Jeffrey A., and Harold Spaeth. 1993. *The Supreme Court and the Attitudinal Model*. Cambridge: Cambridge University Press.

Shepsle, Kenneth. 1979. Institutional Arrangements and Equilibrium in Multidimensional Voting Models. *American Journal of Political Science* 23:27–59.

Shepsle, Kenneth A., and Barry R. Weingast, eds. 1995. *Positive Theories of Congressional Institutions*. Ann Arbor: University of Michigan Press.

Shipan, Charles R. 1997. *Designing Judicial Review: Interest Groups, Congress and Communications Policy*. Ann Arbor: University of Michigan Press.

Spaeth, Harold. *United States Supreme Court Database*. 1997.

Sullivan, Terry. 1990. Bargaining with the President. *American Political Science Review* 84:1167–95.

Sunstein, Cass R. 1993. *The Partial Constitution*. Cambridge: Harvard University Press.

Task Force on Federalization of Criminal Law, American Bar Association, and Criminal Justice Section. 1998. The Federalization of Criminal Law: Defending Liberty Pursuing Justice. Washington: American Bar Association.

Tushnet, Mark. 1999. *Taking the Constitution Away from the Courts*. Princeton: Princeton University Press.

Walker, Samuel. 1994. *Hate Speech: The History of an American Controversy*. Lincoln: University of Nebraska Press.

Wechsler, Herbert. 1954. The Political Safeguards of Federalism: The Role of the States in the Composition and Selection of the National Government. *Columbia Law Review* 54:543.

———. 1959. Toward Neutral Principles of Law. *Harvard Law Review* 73:1–35.

Weingast, Barry. 1979. A Rational Choice Perspective on Congressional Norms. *American Journal of Political Science* 23:245–62.

Whittington, Keith. 1999. *Constitutional Construction: Divided Powers and Constitutional Meaning*. Cambridge: Harvard University Press.

———. 2001. Taking What They Give Us: Explaining the Court's Federalism Offensive. *Duke Law Journal* 51:477–520.

Willis, E. E., W. M. Forrester, Robert Ashmore Tuck, John Dowdy, and Basil L. Whitener. 1963. *Unmasking the Civil Rights Bill: The Dissenting Views*. Washington: Fundamental American Freedoms.

Wood, Stephen B. 1968. *Constitutional Politics in the Progressive Era: Child Labor and the Law*. Chicago: University of Chicago Press.

Woolley, John T. 1991. Institutions, the Election Cycle, and the Presidential Veto. *American Journal of Political Science* 35:279–304.

Yoo, John C. 1997. The Judicial Safeguards of Federalism. *Southern California Law Review* 70:1311–1405.

J. Mitchell Pickerill is an assistant
professor of political science at
Washington State University.

Library of Congress Cataloging-in-
Publication Data
Pickerill, J. Mitchell.
Constitutional deliberation in Congress :
the impact of judicial review in a
separated system / J. Mitchell Pickerill.
p. cm. — (Constitutional conflicts)
Includes bibliographical references.
ISBN 0-8223-3235-3 (cloth : alk. paper)
ISBN 0-8223-3262-0 (pbk. : alk. paper)
1. Legislation—United States.   2. Judicial
review—United States.   I. Title.
II. Series.
KF4945.P53 2004
347.73'12—dc21   2003012570